INSTRUCTOR'S MANUAL

for

MACHINE TOOLS AND MACHINING PRACTICES

by

Richard R. Kibbe

Machine Technology/Lane Community College

Roland O. Meyer
John E. Neely

Warren T. White

JOHN WILEY & SONS

NEW YORK . LONDON . SYDNEY . TORONTO

ISBN 0 471 02081 8
Printed in the United States of America

10 9 8 7 6 5 4 3 2 1

CONTENTS

INTRODUCTION 1

APPLICATION TO TEACHING PROGRAMS 9

ADDITIONAL PROJECTS 17

Rotary Valve 19

Wheel Puller 31

Tap Wrench 39

Screw Jack 45

T-Handle Tap Wrench 50

MEASURING KITS FOR POST TESTS 53

POST TEST QUESTIONS

Volume I 61

Volume II 191

POST TEST ANSWERS

Volume I 295

Volume II 300

AUDIOVISUAL RESOURCES 307

INTRODUCTION

Machine Tools and Machining Practices is an instructional system for machinist training for use in apprenticeship programs, vocational-technical schools, and community colleges with machine tool programs. The authors have had prior experience in the development of the Vocational Instructional Package (VIP) program sponsored by the Oregon Board of Education, and in the Individualized Machinists' Curriculum (IMC) sponsored by the California Community Colleges. These earlier materials have been implemented in several schools in the western United States and a validity study was made by one of the IMC contributors, Richard Dixon, as part of his Masters Degree work[1].

The general plan of this system was derived in a variety of ways. Feedback from the users of the VIP and IMC materials was obtained and analyzed. State sponsored task analyses were compared from different parts of the country. The State of California Machinist-Apprentice materials and the Air Force Machinists programs were analyzed relative to these two volumes and the National Association of Machinists topic and hour distribution was also considered. A published study of workpiece size and percentages of machining time in each machining category was also an integral part of the planning.

In addition, the editor traveled the United States from California to Connecticut, visiting machine tool training programs in schools and industries to examine laboratories, study programs, and to obtain ideas from other teachers of machine shop practices. Some notable facilities included the machine shops at Utah Technical College in Salt Lake City (Figures 1 to 4); Larimer County Vocational-Technical Center in Colorado (Figures 5 to 8); North Technical School, Special School District of St. Louis County, Missouri, with three extraordinary machine shops; and the Muskingum Area Joint Vocational School, Zanesville, Ohio, as an example of a standardized state program. Course outlines, lab manuals, and other detailed information were obtained from these and numerous other schools and industrial training programs to aid in determining the content and depth of treatment for these volumes.

We have also taken the position that these materials should be visually intensive and from the point of view of the operator whenever possible. The writing is directed to the student to give him a maximum of identification with the materials.

We have noted over many years of teaching machine shop practices that most of our students have high visual acuity and high spatial comprehension, but typically depressed reading ability. In light of these observations, we have had reading analyses performed on these and other materials and have been careful to approximate ninth grade reading level.

Considering that most of the programs that we have analyzed are conventially structured into fixed time lecture and laboratory classes, we have taken care to make

---

[1] Dixon, Richard, "Determining Content Validity of the Individualized Learning System--Individualized Machinist's Curriculum Post Tests," unpublished master's thesis, California Polytechnical State University, San Luis Obispo, 1974.

Figure 1. An example of a well designed, well lighted machine tool teaching lab. The mezzanine in the upper background permits interested visitors to conveniently observe lab activities without safety problems (Utah Technical College, Salt Lake City, Utah).

Figure 2. Toolbox storage and access is one of the classic problems in machine tool teaching programs. This is an excellent solution to the problem (Utah Technical College, Salt Lake City, Utah).

Figure 3. Numerically controlled machine tools have been a part of manufacturing for a full generation. Too few schools have adequate coverage of these machine tools. This is an excellent example of a lab area dedicated to this use (Utah Technical College, Salt Lake City, Utah).

Figure 4. The present day die shop could not survive economically without the EDM machine. Too few of these machines are to be found in school programs (Utah Technical College, Salt Lake City, Utah).

Figure 5. The Larimer County Vocational-Technical Center is a prime example of regional vocational schools that are appearing on the United States scene.

Figure 6. Vocational technical centers are typically a model of the industry they serve, as illustrated by this section of geared head lathes (Larimer County Voc-Tech Center).

Figure 7. Numerically controlled machine tools are also appearing more often as part of regional programs nationally (Larimer County Voc-Tech Center).

Figure 8. A well lighted classroom-study area with a view of the shop area is an excellent design. The program at this Voc-Tech Center is part conventional, part individualized (Larimer County Voc-Tech Center).

these materials suitable for conventional usage. We have also designed these materials to be a vehicle to either "hybrid" conventional—partially individualized (Figures 9 and 10), or for completely individualized open-entry, open-exit variable credit possibilities. However, in some cases, state and local laws or methods of reimbursement of funds, such as "census weeks" have more to do with the pattern of presentation than the desires of the teacher, the student, or the institution.

Figure 9. An excellent arrangement for supervision of the shop area. The instructor's shop desk is right in the middle of the operation (Linn-Benton Community College).

Figure 10. Individual study carrels are useful in conventional, hybrid and individualized programs for using nonprint media (Linn-Benton Community College).

Some programs have been able to present combinations of conventional time block and open-entry, open-exit variable credit individualized instruction even with the restrictions imposed by "census week" rules, by working closely with their own registrars and developing admisitrative computer programs to handle the special requirements[2].

On the basis of our experiences in working with the VIP-IMC system, we have devised a variety of presentation formats. Each section begins with introductory materials that generally define the class of machine or operation including historical development, ranges of sizes and capabilities and other materials that serve to orient the student to the topic generally. For the instructor in conventional lecture courses, the introductory materials offer assistance in lecture preparation.

The unit formats are of three types, according to the complexity of the subject matter. Common to all of these unit formats is a statement of purpose as to why the unit is important, followed by objectives in behavioral terms. After the objectives, the information is presented, followed by self-evaluation components in the form of self-tests and worksheets. It is this arrangement that makes a workbook unnecessary. The self-test is designed to be answered in the book, and the answers are given in the appendix of the same volume. Answering a self-test in this fashion calls upon a higher order of capability on the part of the student than selecting between alternatives. Whether the material is used in a conventional or individualized setting, the self-test is an effective learning reinforcement tool for the student. Most units are also provided with post tests, located in this <u>Instructor's Manual</u>. These are typically

---

[2] Allan Hancock College, Santa Maria, California

multiple choice format, which provides follow-up reinforcement and gives the instructor a simple, convenient scoring method for keeping a record of the textbook part of the student's progress. Where post tests are not supplied, the operations required in the unit in the way of performance, such as operating a calculator or sharpening an end mill, are essentially self-checking.

One of the perennial problems that metals and machine technology instructors face is working with students that have been "turned off" by traditional academic programs. Many of these students feel quite alienated from the academic mainstream and have acquired a self-image of being inadequate with disasterous results to their motivation for school work in any form. Organization of students into clubs with common objectives is a good way to establish a sense of community and overcome some of these problems.

The Vocational Industrial Clubs of America (VICA) is a national organization for trade, industrial, and health occupations students that has objectives for developing pride in craftsmanship and reaffirming the dignity of work. At the present time, they have nearly a quarter of a million members in some 7000 clubs in both secondary and post-secondary divisions. These clubs offer the students the opportunity to associate with other students and with adults in the field of work for which the student is preparing. The student also benefits in the process of club activity in the development of interpersonal and leadership skills. VICA is student financed, and supported additionally by a large cross-section of major manufacturing firms, trade and professional organizations, and labor unions.

Participation in VICA helps to build the student self-image through recognition. Just as athletes gain recognition through sports, VICA students have an opportunity to compare their developing skill against one another by competing in local, regional, and state contests (Figures 11 to 14) to qualify for participation in the VICA-U.S. Skills Olympics (VICA-USSO). This is an annual event in more than twenty skill categories, including Machine Shop. In addition, there are leadership skill contests in Club Business Procedure, Display, Extemporaneious Public Speaking, Job Interview, Safety, and other categories that call on the development of interpersonal skills. Since 1973,

Figure 11. Competitors for the machine shop category of VICA competing for the Oregon State Championship at Oregon State University.

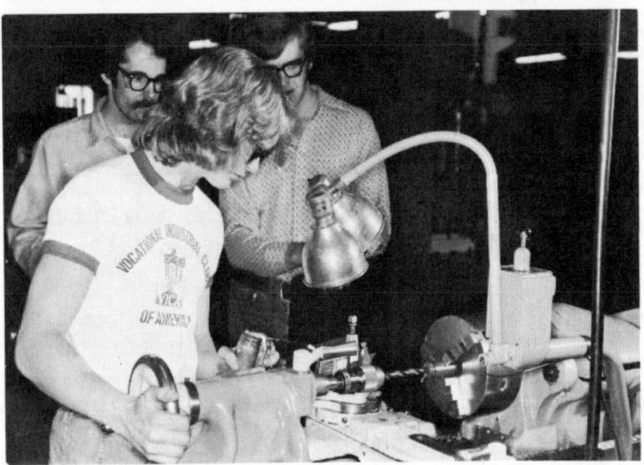

Figure 12. This VICA student is being observed by judges who take into account several factors of student performance (Oregon State University).

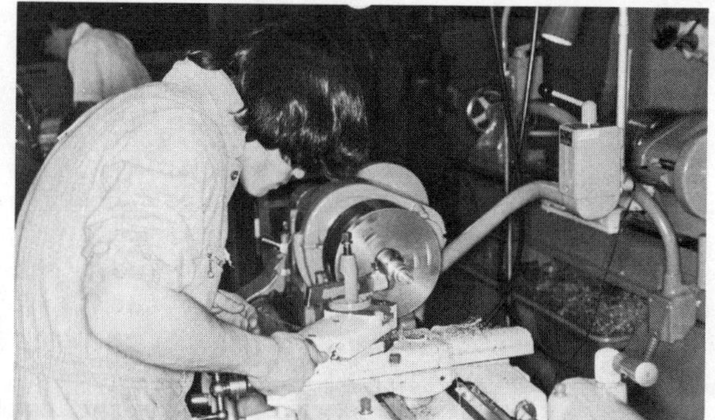

Figure 13. The State of Oregon machine shop championship went to this intense student, Charles Little (Oregon State University).

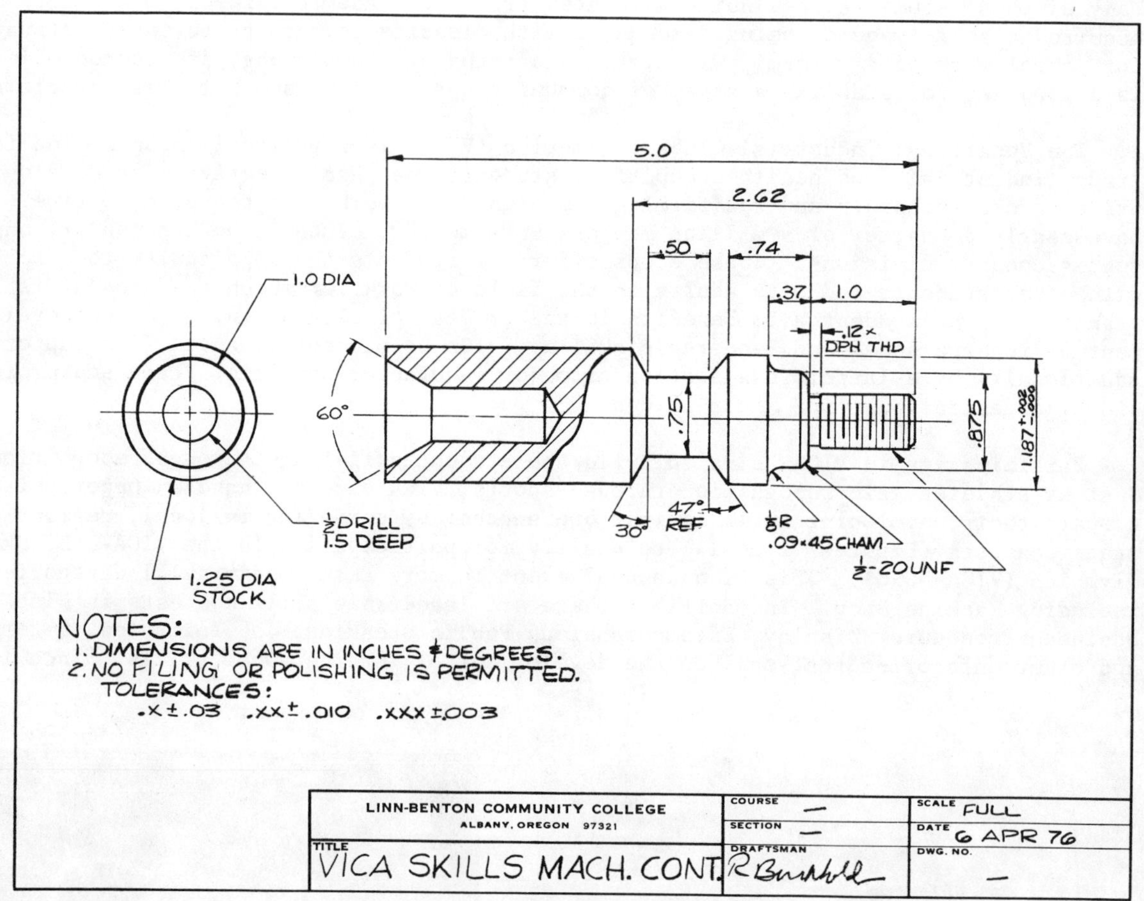

Figure 14. A typical workpieces designed specifically for skill competition (Linn-Benton Community College).

VICA has been the organization to represent the United States in International Skills Olympics competition. This international competition, which originated in Spain in 1947, now includes some nineteen countries world-wide. Machine Shop was included as a category for the U. S. team for the first time in 1975.

Teachers interested in establishing a club should contact:

Vocational Industrial Clubs of America, Inc.
105 North Virginia Avenue
Falls Church, Virginia 22046

This Instructor's Manual has been prepared for the purpose of assisting the teacher in the use of Machine Tools and Machining Practices. Suggestions are given on ways to adapt the texts to various programs that the instructor is now using or wishes to use. Every school shop has differences in arrangement, types of equipment, instructional funding, and school management requirements. Emphasis in instruction is also usually made in areas of machine technology that reflect the needs of the surrounding community. These differences make it virtually impossible to make a planned instructional system covering every detail for all school shops. Thus, the responsibility for the final arrangement is on the individual instructor.

All of the post tests and answers for Volumes I and II are included for the purpose of reproduction. Each test is on a separate page for ease of reproduction and use. Some extra projects with illustrations, process sheets, and drawings are provided. These may be useful to add to existing projects in any program. The suggested kits found in this manual are intended only for examples. The instructor may wish to devise kits that fit his program and shop area.

This Instructor's Manual may be reproduced in any way for use with Machine Tools and Machining Practices textbooks.

APPLICATION TO TEACHING PROGRAMS

CONVENTIONALLY STRUCTURED PROGRAMS

These machining texts can be used to a great advantage in the fixed time lecture-laboratory since specific objectives are given for each unit and the lesson plan is, in effect, already prepared for the instructor. The introduction to each section contains a broader range of information than the units and is excellent material for a lecture base. A typical lecture can begin by setting forth the objective for the unit, and then continuing with an explanation of the information given in the unit. The lecture provides a forum for questions and answers on those difficult concepts that are to be found in these units. Two or more units may be covered in a single session if the units are short.

While lecture-laboratory type programs are in themselves individualized to some extent in the instructor-student relationship, many are in a transitional mode and, to some degree, have the individualized type of instruction. Machine Tools and Machining Practices was written to fill this need as it is adaptable to any program ranging from conventional to individualized.

The possibility of a hybrid program exists for those classes that have some fast learners who must either be moved ahead of the class or given additional tasks on the same level as the rest of the class in order to keep them busy. While the lecture-lab program is in operation for the bulk of the class, these adept students could be allowed to continue ahead on their own in an individualized fashion. This, of course, is only made possible by the comprehensive format of these texts.

It would be helpful to have some student operated media, either film strips, film loops, or cassette tapes. However, in the classroom longer films may be useful and can be shown in a class situation where the same films might not work out quite as well if they were student operated unless something like a TV monitor with a dial retrieval system is used.

Testing and Exercises

The self-test may be used as a testing procedure in the class session so that the instructor and the student will be aware if all the information has been understood clearly. The units and their question sequence help to prepare examinations and lectures for the busy instructor. A continuous feedback to the instructor of student progress is made possible with the post tests. Selected test questions from self-tests and post tests may be used for final examinations.

The post test should be considered as a final test of the student for each unit when he has completed the worksheets or other exercises, so that, when he completes the post test and it is graded, it will be a check on his progress along with the project or exercise. A few kits will be needed where appropriate for some post tests. The parts for the kits can be easily made in the shop.

Small group sessions in the shop may also be used to further clarify and explain some of those difficult areas that the student will find. Along with this, a demonstration could be used to give the students involved added understanding of the procedure for a machining operation.

The instructor should go through the book and plan the order of presentation that he wishes to use. He should also make the decision on which exercises or projects that he wants to use and perhaps substitute some of his own or some of those included in this Instructor's Manual where they might be needed. It would be advisable to write process sheets for extra projects or exercises used for Volume I. After the student has gained a sufficient understanding of the sequence of operations on machine tools, he should then begin preparing his own process sheets and organizing his own projects. For the most part, the texts make this break off point between Volumes I and II; however, it is up to the individual instructor to determine at what point his students would begin to have sufficient self-confidence to be taken off this setp-by-step guidance.

Sequence of Units

The text as written may be in a suitable sequence for some instructors, but in some programs it might be desirable to make some changes in the presented sequence, perhaps skipping over some units, going on to others, and picking up the units that were missed at a later time when they are more relevant. For some programs, it may be practical to omit some units altogether if they are not needed. The sequence of exercises and projects may be used as presented in the texts or substitutes may be given to the class with instructions to ignore those in the text.

Grading

Grading becomes a simplified matter in that the finished post test can constitute a certain percentage of the student's grade. Again, this is up to the instructor's own preference. Also, the exercise or project is graded according to student proficiency on the machine, his ability to hold critical dimensions, to obtain finishes, and to some extent, the time he needs to complete projects. Since the project is performance based and established on certain criteria, the project must then be done over or that part repeated that does not come up to specifications.

Post test keys may be made for quick grading rather than referring to the answer sheet in the Instructor's Manual each time. A copy of each post test is used as an overlay with the location of the correct answers punched out. When positioned over the student's test, the hole locations are quickly marked with a red pencil. The student's marks are then readily compared to the correct answers.

Motivation

Students remain motivated only when they have a reasonable amount of success in what they are doing. It might be advantageous to have a selection of exercises or projects so that a student may choose an alternate to the original required project that would not be as difficult for his particular level of aptitude or ability. He will always have a reasonable amount of success in this way. However, the instructor should have some control over this selection by helping his students make an appropriate decision. Other instructor responsibilities such as record keeping, setting up a management system, and duplication of materials are discussed later.

INDIVIDUALIZED SYSTEMS

Machine Tools and Machining Practices may be used in individualized instructional systems since these texts not only provide an excellent basic instructional system for the conventional or lecture-lab type of instruction, but they are also designed for use in individualized programs. Since the instructional format of the texts is ideal for the individualized approach and its objectives are based on student performance, the text is highly adaptable to use with open-entry, open-exit, variable credit programs. The advantage in using the individualized method of instruction is largely in favor of the student and it is adaptable to human differences such as different learning rates and abilities which can vary in each person from one area of instruction to another.

A recent Wisconsin study in post-secondary schools revealed that individualized systems work best with students whose motivation is average or better, and conventional lecture-lab systems work best for low motivated students. The instructor is not encouraged to use individualized instruction where low student motivation is a factor.

Role of the Student

Students learn in different ways such as by hearing an instructor, observing visual materials, reading, or by simply doing the operation and this visually intensive text provides those kinds of learning that students tend to retain. This system of instruction gives the student more self-reliance since he must practice a certain amount of self-organization and individual study.

A different form of motivation for the student is found in individualized instruction. For example, instead of motivation by competition which to a great extent requires that all students do the same thing at about the same time, the student should be motivated instead with a desire to excel in that work which he is doing, and also by the fact that he is experiencing a new self-reliance and success where perhaps he has never achieved much success before. A student is also motivated through having the one-to-one relationship with his instructor who gives him help and encouragement from time to time.

The student is given definite stated performance objectives and he is paced in a logical sequence throughout his total program so at any given time he knows exactly what he should be doing and at what point he will move into the next unit or project. He knows he must achieve the required performance level in the exercise on which he is working before he can move on to the next. This requirement tends to motivate him to do the best job he can possibly do.

With the individualized approach, the student will never miss any assignments for being late or absent, since he simply resumes again where he left off. In the lecture-lab approach, if the student has missed a lecture, he is set back in some respect since he has missed that part of the theory and perhaps can never recover it. In the lecture he may not understand the principles being set forth and may be reluctant to ask questions, but with individualized learning he will not need to miss out on needed instruction since he simply continues in the text. Because he has this one-to-one relationship with his instructor, he can always ask for help on points he fails to understand.

Role of the Instructor

In this relationship, the instructor is a learning supervisor who deals with each student individually and points out their problems, directing them into solutions that are useful and helpful. In the totally individualized system, the instructor has more time to deal with each student individually since he is relieved of the responsibility of preparing lesson plans and spends little or no time in the classroom. The mundane task of repeating over and over those very basic concepts of machine shop study are no longer the instructor's responsibility, but they are learned by the student through self-study in the textbook units, audio-visuals, and references. His major responsibilities are guiding and helping students in the shop, answering more complex questions not covered in the text such as those related to difficulties with a particular machine, evaluate and grade their progress, keep records, and maintain the learning system and materials involved.

Machine Usage

Another advantage of the individualized approach is in the use of shop machinery. The individualized system provides a much more efficient approach to using the existing machines in the shop. For example, a class of 20 students would normally require 20 machines of the same kind for that particular day of instruction while all other equipment remains idle. With the individualized approach, the usage of machinery is distributed throughout the shop, and all machines may be used at the same time. Since beginning students may be using one kind of equipment, second or third term students will be using different machines, and students that have been enrolled for five or six terms will be using other more complex machinery.

After the individualized system has been in use for a given length of time, this distribution will develop into a complete dispersion of students to various levels of instruction and machine usage. Of course, this will not happen in the first few terms that this system is in use.

Management Systems

A new student or group of new students, when beginning this or any system of instruction, must have a very clear and comprehensive orientation in which an explanation is given to them outlining exactly what is expected of them and how the program works, giving them long range and short range goals. Since there will probably be no other class session after this first orientation session, the students should also be given a handout of instructions detailing the important aspects of the orientation session. The instructions should contain the projects required to complete the course and the name and number of units that must be studied with each project for the purpose of integrating both the projects and the units of instruction. Another way of integrating the projects and units would be to put the numbers of the units to be studied at the top of the first process or operation sheet of supplemental or other projects. This would remind the students to study those units prior to doing the project. The use of projects is recommended, limiting the number of exercises so that the individualized system would be mostly project oriented, preferably with projects that become useful tools or mechanisms when finished for the student to use or put in his tool box.

It must be emphasized that the student needs to have instructor directed pacing in the materials for a completely individualized system to eliminate the need to come to the instructor for every detail of learning or to find out what his next move will be since that could cause a good learning system to become chaotic, especially with large classes. When properly organized and controlled, this system can provide a quiet and pleasant atmosphere for both student and instructor.

The "hands on" approach is emphasized not only in the units of instruction and the machines, but also in media, whether it be cassette tape players, slide projectors, film strips, or video monitors. Any of these used in the program should be made freely available to the student when needed. Again, in the orientation session, the student should be told where and how to select and use properly that media that is needed for study with each unit.

Grading Systems

Any system of grading is adaptable to individualized instruction, but pass-no pass is probably the best grading system to use. For instance, letter grades may be used, but since the performance objectives are set to a certain level of competence, there should be no possibility of the student having a D grade, just as there should never be such a thing as a D machinist. Therefore, A and B grades probably are all that would be acceptable for this system when letter grades are the only option.

If variable credit, open-entry, open-exit procedures are used, then even the incomplete grade would not be needed, since the student simply continues on from one term to another on the same project or unit where he left off in the previous term. Each instructor should check with the registrar of his own college or school to determine the possibility of a variable credit, open-entry grading system.

Two options for assigning credits for the course would be either to assign credit by clock hours or by objectives. In the case of clock hours, the following formula could be used to determine the credit the student would get for a given number of hours.

$$\frac{CH \times W}{CR}$$

Where: CH = Clock hours per week
W = Number of weeks in a term
CR = Number of credits per term allotted for a given number of clock hours per week

Example: Assuming a term is 10 weeks and 12 credits are given for 24 clock hours per week, the number of clock hours for one credit is

$$\frac{24 \times 10}{12} = 20 \text{ clock hours per credit}$$

For credit by objectives, the student should have in his student instructions sheet an assignment of credit for each project; for example, a C-clamp might have an assignment of two credits or the V-blocks four credits, all of the projects totaling the entire number of credits required in the program. These projects could all be broken down for assigning credits on a basis of time for average students to do a given project. One of the advantages for giving credits by objectives is that all the students are required to spend their time actually working on something rather than "killing time" or just simply recording time and not producing anything.

Another advantage of this individualized system is the option available to students to have a minicourse; that is, a selected number of units and projects provided for learning the things in one area of instruction that the student needs to know to fill in or strengthen that which he has already learned. For example, a machinist who has already been working in the trade for a number of years, but finds that he is weak in precision grinding or perhaps milling machine work, would not need to take the whole course simply to learn the area of instruction that he needs to complete his knowledge of machine tools.

Record Keeping

Whichever system of instruction to be used, a record keeping device such as a progress chart is needed so that the instructor and students alike will know where the student is in the program at any given time. A large board on an accessible wall should provide this information to the students and should be maintained by the instructor daily. One system that is used with Machine Tools and Machining Practices is shown at the end of this section.

Two complete record systems can be placed on one sheet of 8½ x 11 inch paper for the records of the post tests for all units in Volumes I and II of Machine Tools and Machining Practices. Also on this sheet is a place provided for the name of the student and a second system of record keeping for the projects that are completed. The number of the project is on one side and across the grid the number of credits are assigned by filling in the blocks. These blocks could be filled in using colored markers. One color for each term so that the record would show which particular term the student completed the credit for a given project. Likewise in the unit record blocks, the same color of marker could be used to fill in the block showing completion of that particular unit.

This system of student scheduling is extremely flexible since he could come in at any particular time of the day if the shop were open, for instance, from 8 a.m. to 4 p.m. The instructor may prefer, however, to assign him a given time, in which case the assignment could be arranged around his other classes. In either case, the student would have great flexibility in setting up his schedule of classes.

Duplication of Materials

Post tests, projects, and the record sheet may be duplicated by offset press, ditto, or copiers such as Xerox or IBM. If the method you use for copying (such as ditto) does not produce acceptable resolution of photographic figures, then they may be replaced with a sketch or paste-up line drawing of your own choosing.

The materials in this Instructor's Manual may be freely duplicated for use with Machine Tools and Machining Practices.

Name________________________________

Units Completed:

	1	2	3	4	5	6	7	8	9	10
I-A										
B										
C										
D										
E										
F										
G										
H										
I										
II-A										
B										
C										
D										
E										
F										
G										
H										
I										

Each square represents one completed credit:

PROJECT NUMBER	1	2	3	4	5	6
1						
2						
3						
4						
5						
6						
7						
8						
9						
10						
11						
12						
13						
14						
15						
16						
17						
18						
19						
20						
21						
22						
23						
24						
25						
26						

RECORD SHEET

ADDITIONAL PROJECTS

Student projects may be obtained from many sources. They are often shared between instructors of various schools and may also be found in school shop magazines and circulars. One particularly abundant source is found in the students themselves. Student designed projects(Figures 1 to 5) are almost always something the student wants or needs. When a student builds the device that he has planned and drawn to scale, he is much more motivated than when he does a required project. Of course, the instructor should evaluate the student's plans to make sure the project is suitable for his level of training, and continue to provide assistance in its construction.

a. Assembled pump

b. Partially assembled pump

c. Parts of the pump

Figure 1. This gear-type hydraulic pump was designed and made by a student. It features hardened and ground shafts and needle bearings.

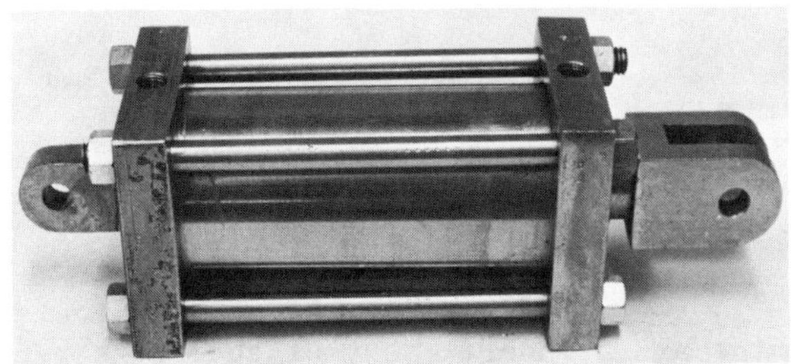

Figure 2. Hydraulic cylinder built by students.

Figure 3. This well-built heavy duty drill press was entirely designed and built by a student

Figure 4. Small winches such as this one make ideal projects for machine shop students.

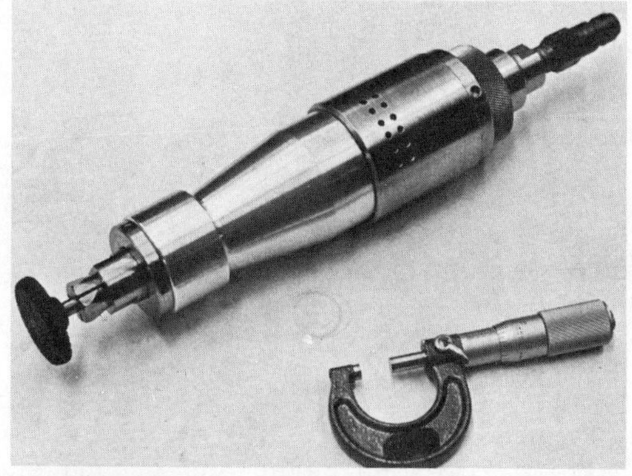

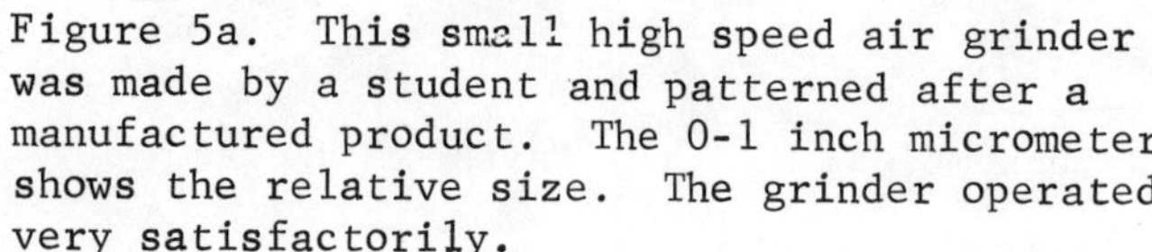

Figure 5a. This small high speed air grinder was made by a student and patterned after a manufactured product. The 0-1 inch micrometer shows the relative size. The grinder operated very satisfactorily.

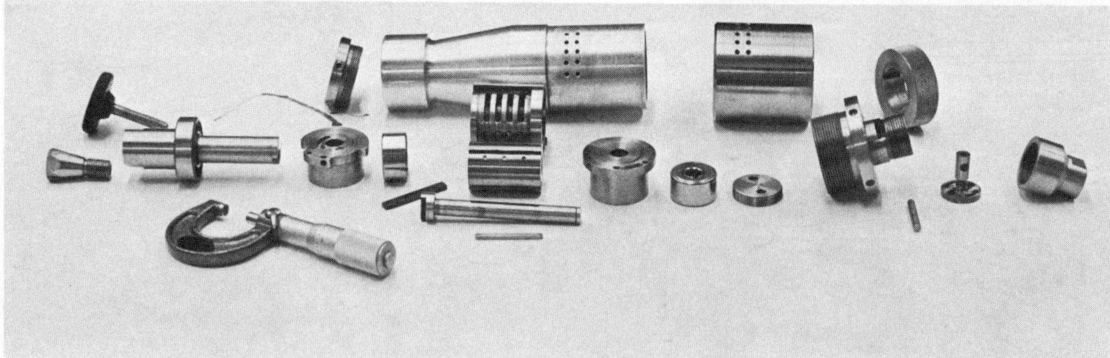

Figure 5b. The parts required to make the air grinder. Many of the parts were hardened and precision ground. Some redesign was necessary.

Projects with drawings are also provided in this section. Some of these projects include process sheets.

PROCESS SHEETS FOR MAKING THE ROTARY VALVE

The rotary valve is a project designed to involve a great many lathe and milling operations while using a relatively small amount of material (Figures 1a and b).

a. Assembled valve

b. Parts of the valve

Figure 1. Rotary valve. This valve may be used as a four way, three position tandem center hydraulic valve or, with slight modification of the rotor, as a closed center valve for air or oil.

The rotary valve project drawings show tolerances for all of the important fits. For this reason, the major parts could be made in any order. The valve body is either cut with an oxy-acetylene torch from plate or sawed from MS round stock. The rotor OD is brazed. This welding equipment may be in use when you need it; if so, simply work on a different part. When the valves are finished, they should all be interchangable parts. For example, any rotor should fit any valve body.

Note: Complete drawings may be found at the end of the process sheets.

Steps in Making Valve Body

1. Burn out a $3\frac{3}{4}$ in. diameter circle from 4 x $1\frac{1}{4}$ in. MS bar stock, using a slightly oxidizing preheat flame to avoid hardening the cut surface. Chip off any slag. Cool slowly. An alternate procedure would be to cut $1\frac{1}{4}$ in. from a $3\frac{1}{2}$ or 4 in. diameter MS round bar.

2. Set up the piece in a four-jaw chuck and center with chalk or the toolholder.

3. Drill through the center and bore to $1\frac{7}{8}$ in. diameter; this will leave $\frac{1}{16}$ in. for finish cuts.

4. Chuck the piece inside and rough machine the outside. Turn to size with an approximate 60 microinch finish. Face one side with the same finish.

5. Put the external jaws on the three-jaw chuck and place the previously finished face of the valve body in the jaws with a $\frac{1}{16}$ in. keystock spacer behind the work. This provides clearance for the boring tool when it comes through the work inside the chuck.

6. Bore to .025 in. undersize with a finish tool. Take several trial cuts to obtain the best finish, then try to machine to within the tolerance given on the drawing. Check the finish with comparison standards.

7. Face the body width to a size within the tolerance given on the drawing.

8. At this point, it is necessary to lay out reference lines and points to establish correct positions for the ports. This may be done by placing a scriber in the toolholder and clamping it so the point is at the exact center of the lathe; turn the #1 jaw to the horizontal position so you can set on a square head to level it. Apply layout dye. When you have done this, scribe a light line across the body of the valve with the scriber, making the "X" centerline. Turn the valve 90 degrees, and by using the other edge of the square head, level the same jaw again. Scribe a line across the body, making the "Y" centerline (Figure 2).

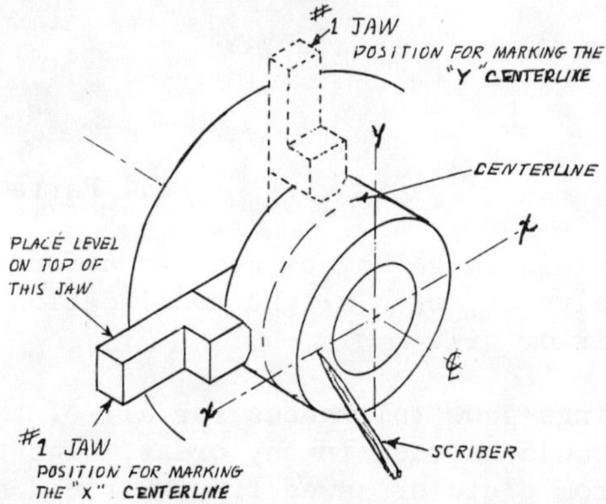

Figure 2. Laying out the "X" and "Y" centerlines in the lathe

9. Now mark a centerline on the periphery of the valve body and lay out positions of the ports in relation to the X and Y centerlines, using a protractor with a level. Always level on the <u>same jaw</u> with the protractor or square head.

10. The work may now be removed from the lathe and deburred where necessary.

11. The positions for the four ports may be center punched and drilled, first with a $\frac{1}{4}$ in. and then with the tap drill for a $\frac{1}{4}$ in. N.P.T. Leave at least $\frac{1}{16}$ in. of the $\frac{1}{4}$ in. diameter. This hole must be carefully deburred inside the body.

12. At this time, do not lay out to drill the $\frac{1}{4}$ in. assembly bolt holes since one of the flanges will be used later as a drill jig. Tap drill holes will then be made for $\frac{1}{4}$-20 socket head cap screws.

13. Set up the valve body in a vise on a small horizontal or vertical mill with the X centerline in a vertical position and with the base side up. Mill a flat $1\frac{3}{8}$ in. wide. Set up a $\frac{1}{4}$ in. cutter on the center of the flat and make a groove .065 in. deep. Remove the workpiece and deburr.

14. Lay out the center for the $\frac{5}{16}$-24 tapped hole. Drill and tap as shown on the drawing.

Steps in Making Valve Rotor

1. Since this part must be all machined without any eccentricity (which would be unavoidable if you had to take it out of a chuck and rechuck it), it should be turned between centers and finish machined in one setting. For this reason, the material should be cut about an inch longer than finish length or about 4 in. long. This will allow room for the dog. The material is 2 in. HR round.

2. The rotor should be rough machined all over, but the large OD should be turned to 1.875 in. to allow $\frac{1}{16}$ in. on a side for brazing. The rough width of the rotor should be left at about $1\frac{1}{8}$ in. so rounded edges of brazing can be machined square. Leave the $\frac{3}{4}$ in. diameter stem .030 in. oversize.

3. Braze on a little over $\frac{1}{16}$ in. as evenly as possible. (An alternate procedure would be to make the rotor of tool steel, harden and grind it to size.)

4. Rough machine to .050 in. oversize. Fill in any places missed with more brazing rod. Remachine.

5. Machine rotor to size and finish. Apply layout dye.

6. Hold rotor stem in a three-jaw chuck and lay out the X and Y centerlines as explained in making the valve body (Figures 3a and b). Use one jaw as a point of reference and a protractor with level to set the angles (Figures 4a and b). Scribe a very light centerline around the periphery of the rotor and two adjacent lines $\frac{1}{4}$ in. from the center (Figure 5). Lay out the various positions of the holes on the periphery and with a scriber, roughly draw the channels on the surface. Center punch where you will drill. Spot drill with a No. 2 center drill and drill the $\frac{1}{4}$ in. holes to the center of the rotor. All others should be drilled just to the margin of the $\frac{1}{4}$ in. drill to outline the ends of the channels (Figure 6). This layout procedure may also be done with a dividing head and scribe by using angular indexing. The drilling may be done, if desired, on the vertical mill with the setup in the next step.

Figure 3a. Position for layout of the X centerline

Figure 3b. Position for layout of the Y centerline

a

b

Figures 4a and b. The method of using a protractor and level for laying out angular locations. The same jaw is always used.

Figure 5. Centerlines are scribed on the periphery of the rotor.

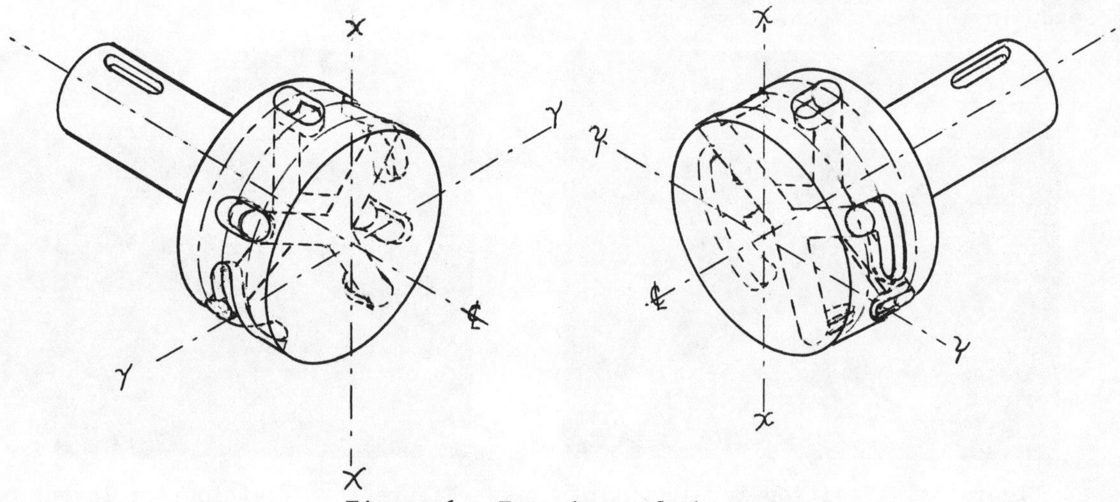

Figure 6. Two views of the rotor

7. Set up a small dividing head with a three-jaw chuck in a horizontal or vertical mill. Set up for end milling with a $\frac{1}{4}$ in. cutter. Center the cutter to the work and align one of the holes that you have drilled with the cutter; feed in $\frac{3}{16}$ in. deep. Make sure that you have selected the correct RPM and table feed. Begin milling a channel toward the center of the rotor. The dividing head should be locked in position for this operation. When you are ready to mill a channel around the periphery of the rotor, unlock the dividing head and lock the table. Feed the work into the cutter by turning the handle slowly on the dividing head (Figure 7).

   Change to a $\frac{3}{16}$ in. cutter and carefully mill the keyway.

Figure 7. A channel in the periphery of the rotor being milled.

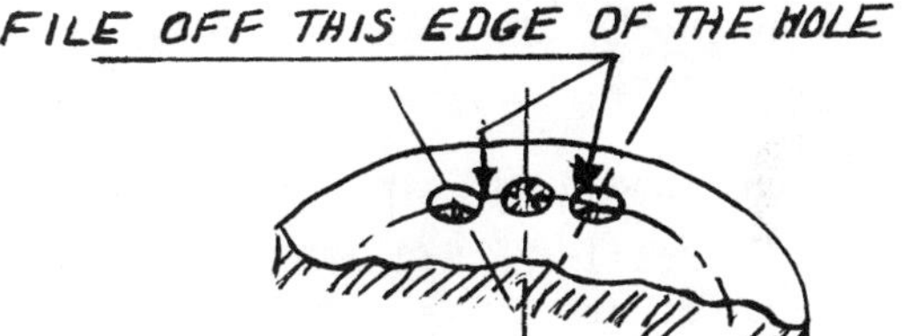

Figure 8. Drilling the detent sockets.

8. Lay out the arc and centers for drilling the detent sockets. The center one is on the X centerline and is drilled only to the depth of the drill margins. The two outer sockets are drilled $\frac{1}{16}$ in. deeper than the margins; this will prevent the detent from going past these positions. The inside edges of the two outer sockets must be filed so that the detent can "ride up" over these edges to come back to the center position (Figure 8).

9. A $\frac{1}{16}$ in. drilled hole through the rotor at the drain or return channel is necessary to balance the rotor. This helps to keep the valve from binding when under pressure.

Steps in Making Flanges and Bushing

1. The material used for the 1 in. thick flange is the same as that used for the valve body, 4 x $1\frac{1}{4}$ in. MS. Burn out a $3\frac{3}{4}$ in. circle from that bar and another circle the same diameter from a $\frac{5}{8}$ x 4 in. MS flat bar for the thinner flange. They may instead be cut off a $3\frac{1}{2}$ or 4 in. round MS bar.

2. Grasp the $1\frac{1}{4}$ in. thick material in a four-jaw chuck externally and rough drill to $\frac{5}{8}$ in. diameter. Machine the 2 in. diameter jub and face the end of the flange of that side. Try for a 60 microinch finish.

3. Remove work, change to a three-jaw chuck and grasp the flange by the hub.

4. Rough machine OD. Finish machine OD.

5. Bore to $\frac{25}{32}$ in. and counterbore to O-ring bore dimension given on the drawing, leaving $\frac{1}{8}$ in. to keep the bushing from extruding from the bore.

6. Machine the face of the flange and the alignment boss to the tolerances given. The bore, boss, and face must be machined in one setting.

7. Using a scriber clamped in a toolholder, mark a line where the bolt circle should be.

8. Remove work from chuck and deburr where needed.

9. At the X centerline, prick punch for the detent hole and the No. 1 hole of the bolt circle layout. Set your divider to the chord given in tables in the Machinery's Handbook. Lay out the seven holes by stepping off around the bolt circle with the dividers.

10. Spot and drill these seven holes with a $\frac{1}{4}$-20 tap drill. Use this flange to position and drill the holes in the valve body, and in turn, the valve body is used to drill the other flange. The valve body may now be tapped. Tap to the center from each side. An alternate procedure is to set up on a jig borer or vertical mill and drill to coordinates found in the Machinery's Handbook.

11. Drill the detent hole $\frac{1}{4}$ in. diameter and redrill the bolt holes in the flange with a $\frac{9}{32}$ in. drill. Chamfer.

12. Make a bronze bushing to press in having a class 2 interference fit, allowing inside clearance according to the amount of press, and leaving a class 2 sliding fit. Reference: "Fits and Tolerances" in the Machinery's Handbook.

13. Press in the bushing with a mechanical arbor press using high pressure lubricant.

14. Make the thinner flange by gripping $\frac{1}{8}$ in. of the material in a four-jaw chuck and reversing the finished side of the flange in a three-jaw chuck. Finish machine.

15. The detent spring is made by turning music wire on a $\frac{5}{32}$ in. mandrel in the vise. The detent is made by rounding the end of $\frac{1}{4}$ in. drill rod and cutting it to $\frac{5}{16}$ in. length. Harden and temper to RC 55.

Steps in Making Valve Handle

1. Several methods may be used to make the ball and taper part of the handle. A suggested method is to extend a piece of $\frac{15}{16}$ in. CF round from a three-jaw chuck and turn the $\frac{7}{8}$ in. diameter ball with a ball turning attachment. Then extend the piece further out from the chuck and turn the taper with a taper attachment. The ball could also be free handed and checked with a radius gage. The taper can either be

made with the compound or a taper attachment. The threaded end is machined by supporting it with a steady rest and gripping the ball end in a chuck. Protect the ball with copper or aluminum.

2. The hub for the handle should be finish machined and bored to size.

3. Set up the hub in an angle vise and tap drill and counterbore. Tap $\frac{1}{4}$-28.

4. Screw the hangle in the hub.

5. Using the keyway broach set, make a $\frac{1}{8}$ in. keyseat $\frac{1}{16}$ in. deep in the hub.

6. Cut off a $\frac{3}{16}$ in. square keystock $\frac{3}{4}$ in. long and round the ends to fit in the keyway in the rotor shaft.

7. Drill and tap -20 for a set screw in the hub 90 degrees off the keyway.

Show the finished parts to your instructor before assembly as he may want to check them.

Assembling the Valve

1. Make two paper gaskets and place one on each flange.

2. Place O-ring on the rotor shaft.

3. Lubricate all moving parts with light oil, including the bolts.

4. Bolt on the thick flange with rotor in place and with detent and spring in place.

5. Make sure the rotor turns freely.

6. Bolt on the thin flange.

7. Mount the handle with key in place, tighten the set screw.

8. Turn the valve handle. If it is too tight, take off the thin flange and put an extra paper gasket in place. Tighten the bolts and turn the valve. Repeat if necessary.

9. The valve is now ready for the hydraulic test if a test stand is available. It should operate a cylinder either direction and be able to stop and hold it in any position when in the center position if it is correctly made. There should be no leaks.

DRAWING I

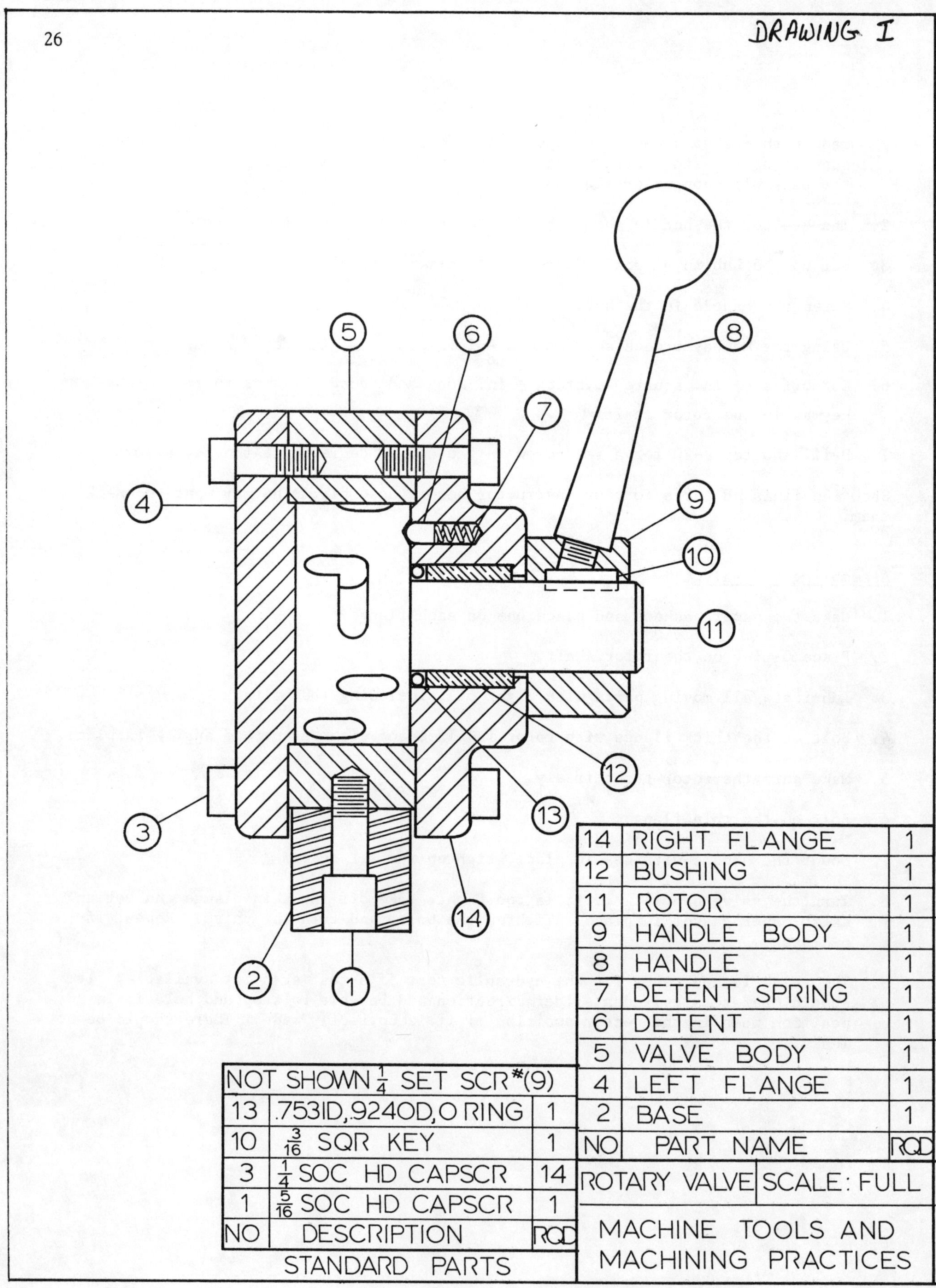

NO	PART NAME	RQD
14	RIGHT FLANGE	1
12	BUSHING	1
11	ROTOR	1
9	HANDLE BODY	1
8	HANDLE	1
7	DETENT SPRING	1
6	DETENT	1
5	VALVE BODY	1
4	LEFT FLANGE	1
2	BASE	1

NOT SHOWN $\frac{1}{4}$ SET SCR*(9)

NO	DESCRIPTION	RQD
13	.753ID,.924OD,O RING	1
10	$\frac{3}{16}$ SQR KEY	1
3	$\frac{1}{4}$ SOC HD CAPSCR	14
1	$\frac{5}{16}$ SOC HD CAPSCR	1

STANDARD PARTS

ROTARY VALVE | SCALE: FULL

MACHINE TOOLS AND MACHINING PRACTICES

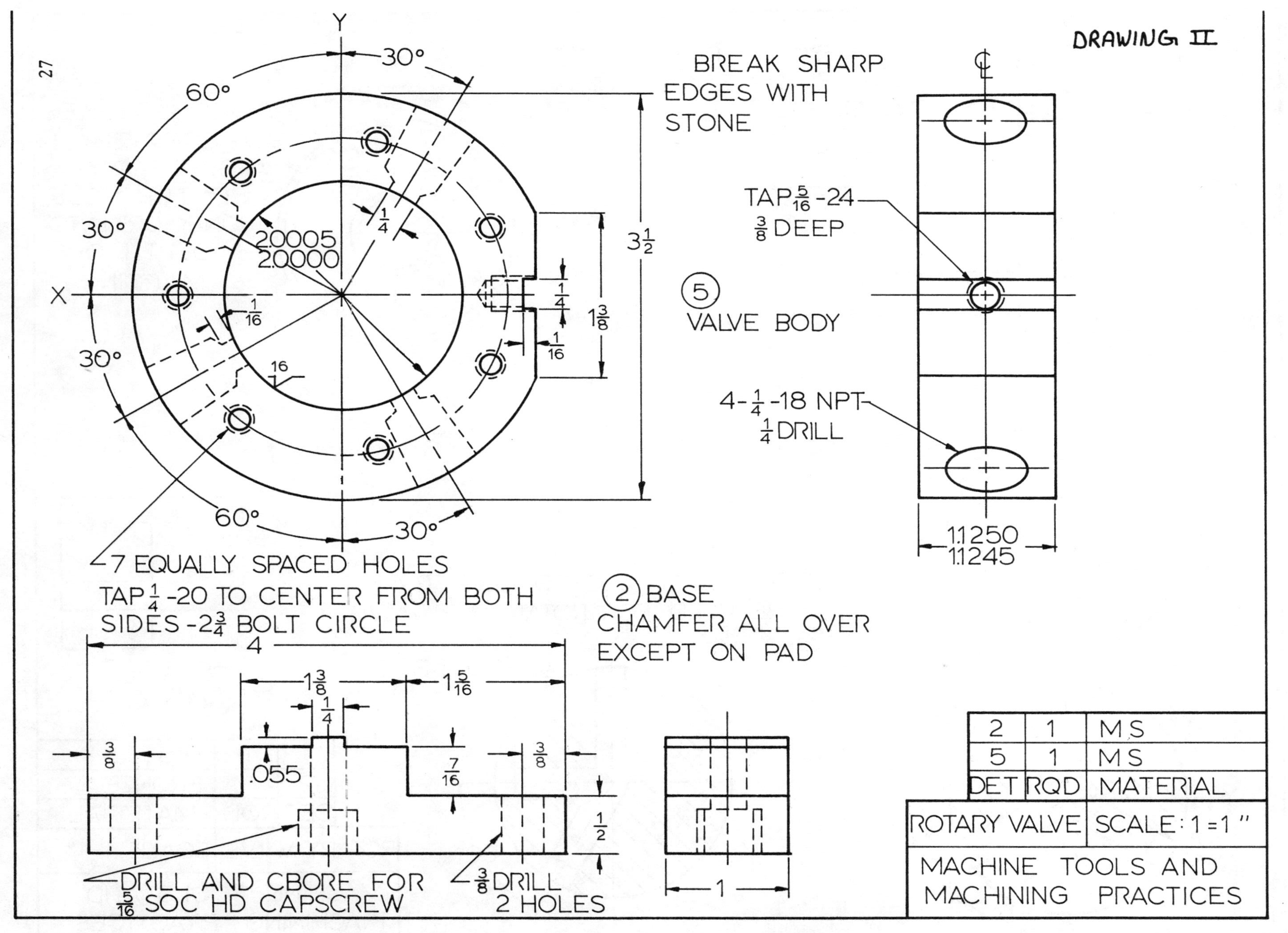
DRAWING II
BREAK SHARP EDGES WITH STONE
TAP 5/16 -24
3/8 DEEP
(5) VALVE BODY
4-1/4-18 NPT
1/4 DRILL
1.1250
1.1245
2.0005
2.0000
3 1/2
1 3/8
30°
60°
7 EQUALLY SPACED HOLES
TAP 1/4 -20 TO CENTER FROM BOTH SIDES -2 3/4 BOLT CIRCLE
(2) BASE
CHAMFER ALL OVER EXCEPT ON PAD
1 5/16
.055
DRILL AND CBORE FOR 5/16 SOC HD CAPSCREW
3/8 DRILL 2 HOLES
2 | 1 | M.S
5 | 1 | M.S
DET | RQD | MATERIAL
ROTARY VALVE | SCALE: 1 =1"
MACHINE TOOLS AND MACHINING PRACTICES

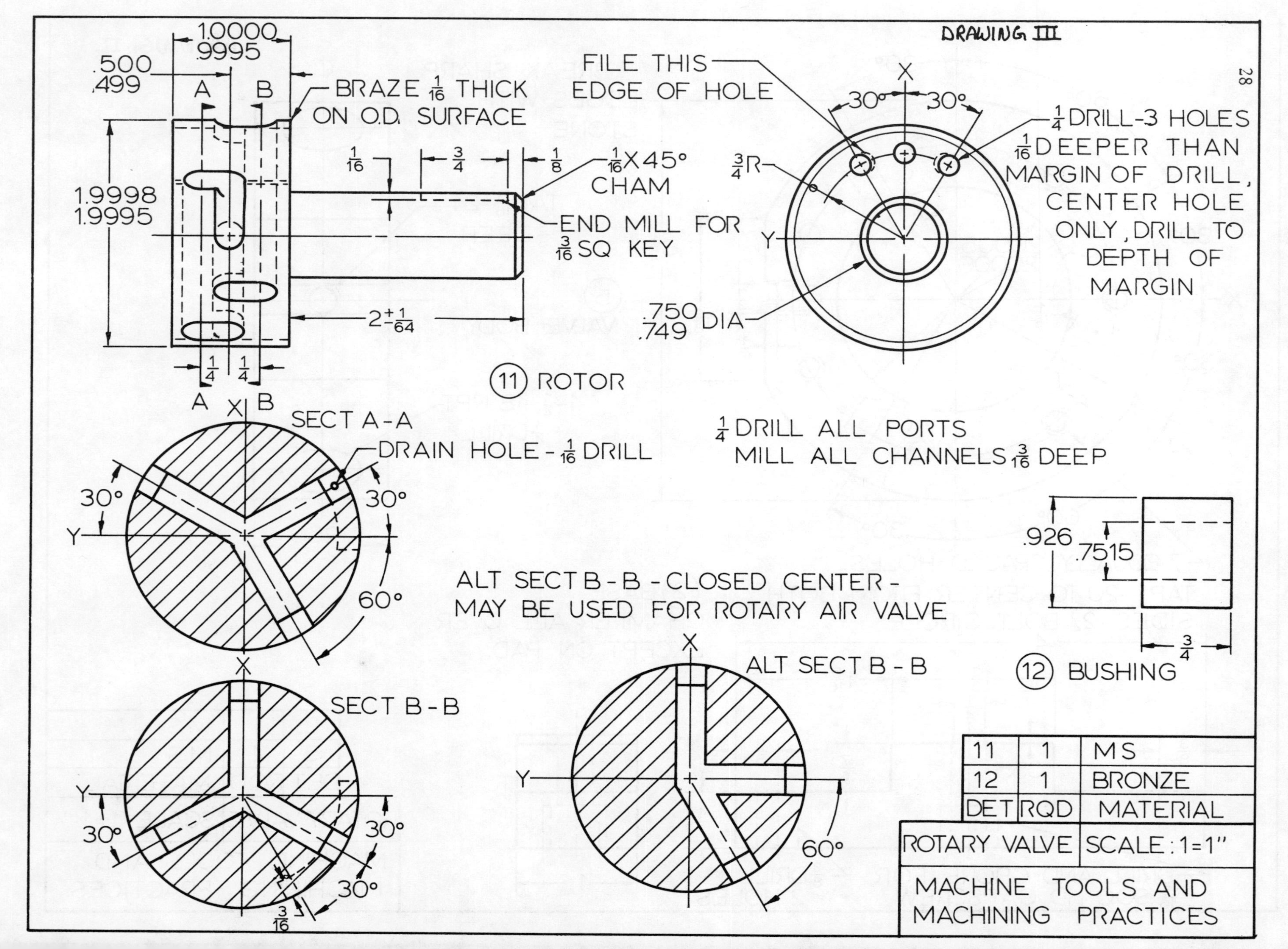

11	1	MS
12	1	BRONZE
DET	RQD	MATERIAL

ROTARY VALVE	SCALE: 1=1"
MACHINE TOOLS AND MACHINING PRACTICES	

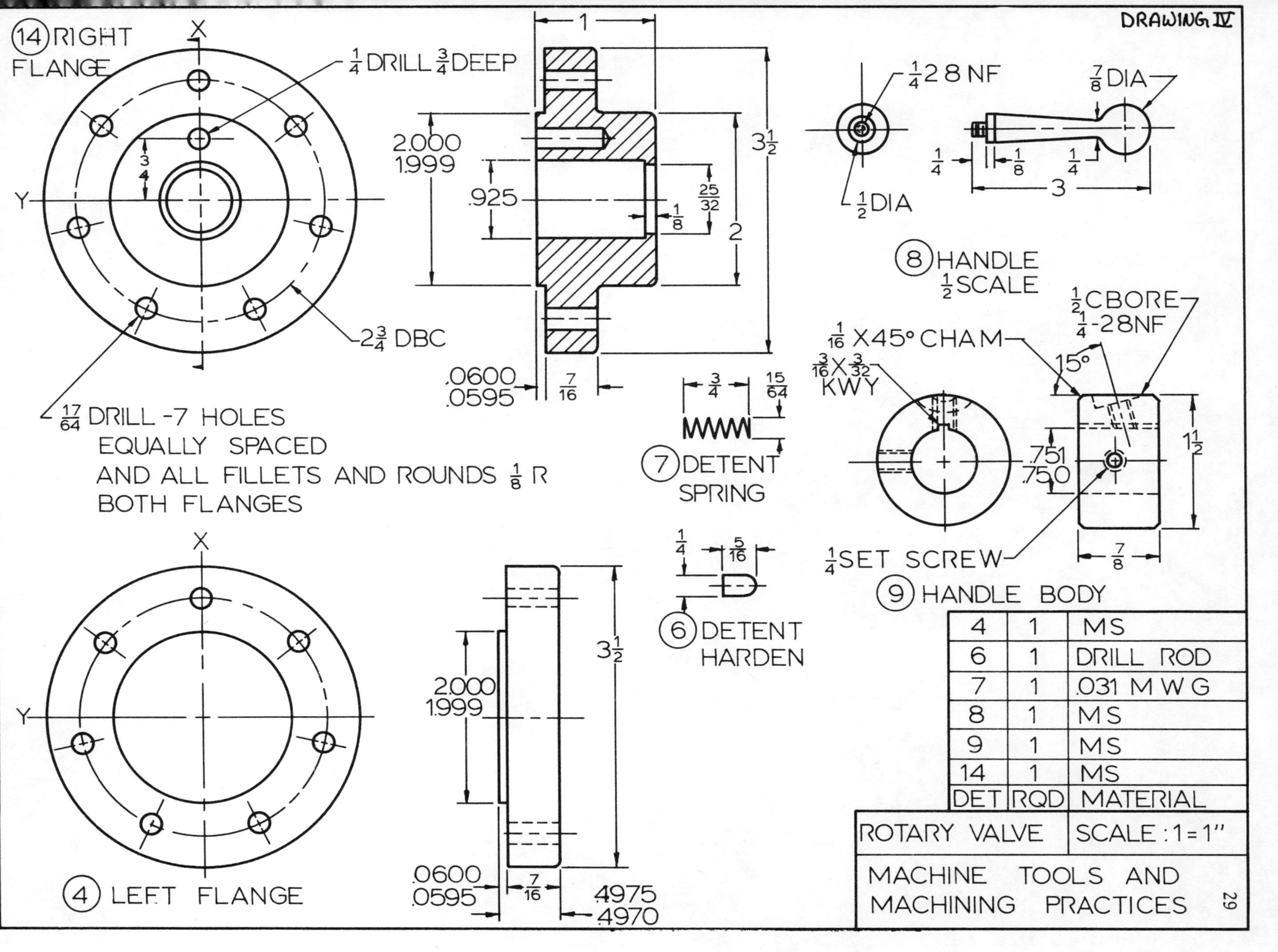

DET	RQD	MATERIAL
4	1	MS
6	1	DRILL ROD
7	1	.031 M W G
8	1	MS
9	1	MS
14	1	MS

ROTARY VALVE	SCALE : 1=1"
MACHINE TOOLS AND MACHINING PRACTICES	

PROCESS SHEET FOR WHEEL PULLER

Making the Body

1. Saw the material for the body from $3\frac{1}{2}$ in. MS round stock. Cut off a piece about $\frac{7}{8}$ in. long.

2. Set up a three-jaw chuck with the jaws set to grip the outside of this piece. Place the material in the chuck with the jaws gripping about $\frac{1}{8}$ in. True up the piece by measuring from the chuck face with a rule.

3. Take a facing cut to clean up one side.

4. Turn the OD to the size given in the drawing. Machine as close to the chuck jaws as possible. Chamfer the edge.

5. Remove the part from the chuck and apply layout dye to the finished surface.

6. To lay out the part, find the center and scribe a centerline (a) across the surface (Figure 1). Prick punch the center.

7. Set the dividers to approximately $1\frac{1}{2}$ in. Put one leg in the prick punch mark and scribe an arc of about 180 degrees.

8. With the dividers at the same setting, place one leg where the centerline and the arc coincide. This will mark points 60 degrees on either side of the centerline (Figure 2).

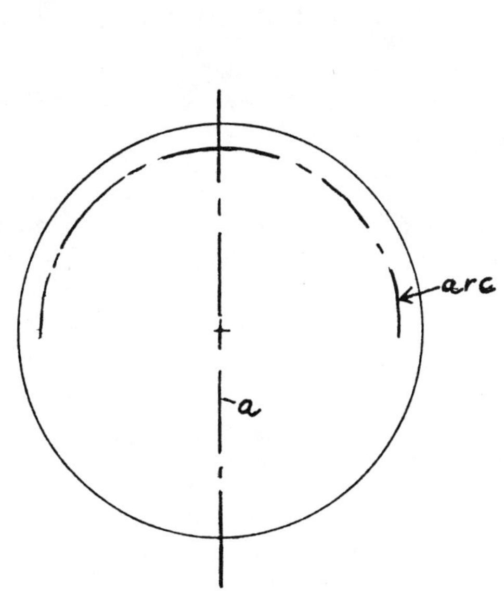

Figure 1

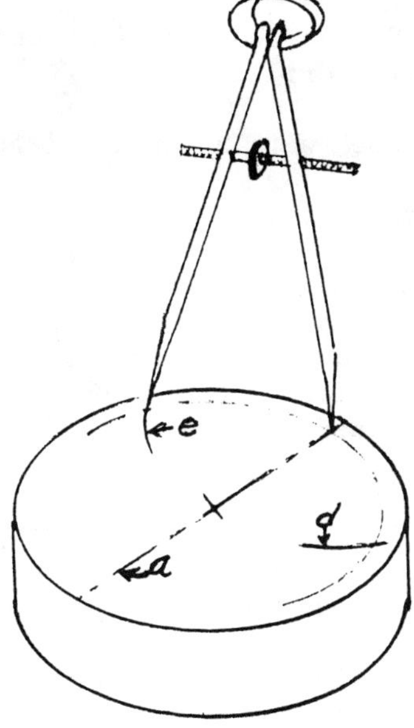

Figure 2

9. Scribe a centerline (b and c, Figure 3) through the center to the two short arcs (d and e).

10. On the four lines that now extend to the outside edge of the circle, measure in $\frac{7}{8}$ in. and scribe a short line perpendicular to the center line to outline the bottom of the slots.

11. Measure $\frac{1}{8}$ in. on either side of the centerlines and scribe parallel lines to meet the short cross line (Figure 3).

12. Scribe parallel lines $\frac{1}{4}$ in. on either side of the slots. Mark their length from the outside $\frac{11}{16}$ in.

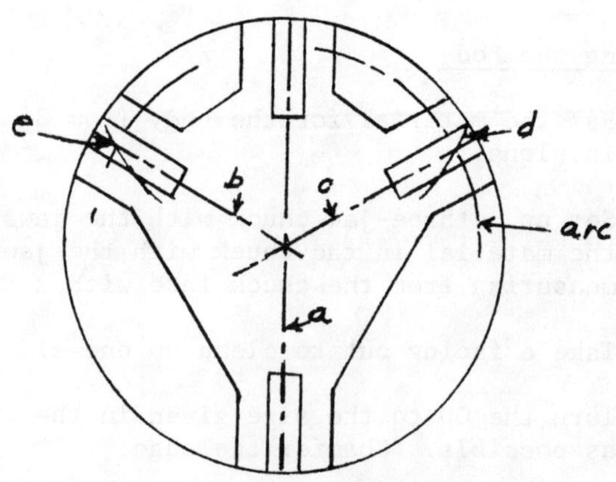

Figure 3

13. Connect the ends of these lines to form the remainder of the outline of this part. The layout is now complete.

14. Replace the part in the lathe chuck with the finished face in. Grasp it this time as far back into the jaws as it will go. Be sure the seating surfaces of the jaws are clean and free from chips.

15. Face to the thickness given in the drawing. This should remove the $\frac{1}{8}$ in. section where the jaws were holding the part in the last operation. Chamfer the OD.

16. Centerdrill and then drill through with a pilot drill or a drill slightly smaller than the tap drill.

17. Drill through with a tap drill for $\frac{3}{4}$-16 NF thread.

18. Chamfer the hole.

19. Set up the tap with the dead center supporting it and the tap handle resting on the carriage or on the compound. Release the spindle so it is free wheeling. Turn the chuck by hand to make the thread while following with the dead center by gently turning the tailstock handwheel. <u>Do not turn on the machine for this operation</u>. Use sulfurized cutting oil. Remove the work when finished and clean the machine.

20. To continue with this project, you should be familiar with the use of a small horizontal milling machine. You will need to be able to set up the cutter, vise, and work. You must also set your speeds and feeds. If you are not ready for this operation, your instructor may help you to set up.

21. Cut a slot first, then make the two cuts on each side of the slot (Figure 4). Use cutting oil.

22. Turn the work and set up the next centerline with a square head. Repeat the cutting procedure in step 21.

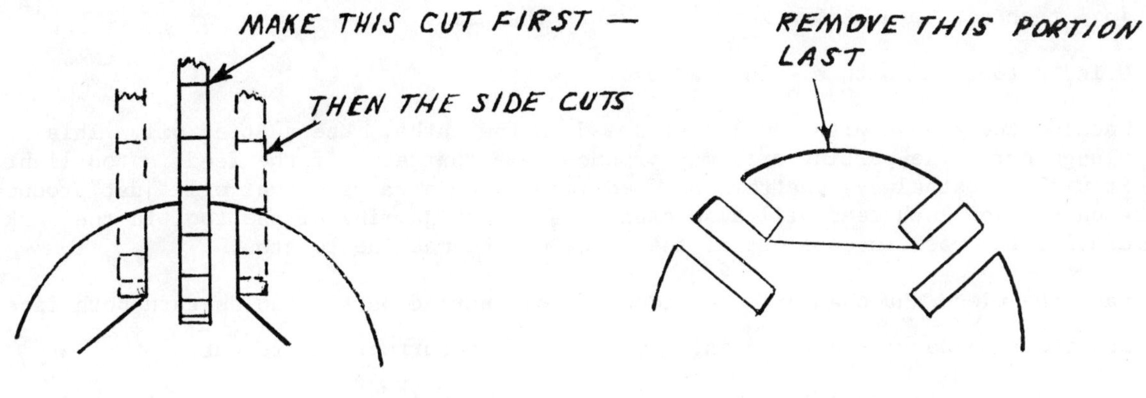

Figure 4

Figure 5

23. When all four slots and side cuts have been made, rotate the work so that the line on the spaces in between is level or parallel with the solid jaw of the vise.

24. Remove all excess material by taking cuts with the same milling cutter (Figure 5), or by sawing on a vertical bandsaw.

25. When the milling is finished, remove the part, deburr and chamfer all edges.

26. Lay out for the four bolt holes in the ears, and center punch.

27. Set up in the drill press with one ear level with the table.

28. Drill through both halves of the ear with a $\frac{1}{4}$-20 tap drill.

29. Drill through the <u>top ear only</u> with a $\frac{1}{4}$ in. drill

30. Rotate the piece to the next ear and repeat steps 27 through 29.

31. After all four ears are drilled, deburr and tap through the ears with a $\frac{1}{4}$-20 tap. Clean and apply a light film of oil.

Making the Nut

32. Cut off a piece of mild steel slightly larger than $2\frac{1}{4}$ in. diameter. The next size larger may be $2\frac{7}{16}$ in. CF shafting. The length should be about $1\frac{1}{4}$ in.

33. Since there are some very heavy tool pressures in this operation such as knurling, grooving, and drilling, it is best to set up the work in a four-jaw chuck. Leave about $\frac{7}{8}$ in. extending out of the chuck and roughly true up the work with no more than .010 in. runout.

34. The operation with the greatest work force should be done first so that if the work moves it can be more easily corrected. Therefore, the knurling should be done first, but the part must first be machined to the knurl diameter.

35. When you have turned the nut to the knurl diameter in as far as the shoulder ($\frac{9}{16}$) in., then set up a medium knurl and knurl the part.

36. Grind a tool bit with a $\frac{1}{8}$ in. radius.

37. Machine the groove with the lowest speed on the lathe. Use cutting oil. This plunge cut, like parting off, may produce some chatter. If the feed is too light, it will almost always chatter, so feed in by hand at a rate that will just produce a chip. Too much feed will also cause chatter or jamming of the tool in the work causing the work to come out of the chuck or the machine to stop.

38. Face the piece and chamfer both sides of the knurled part. Finish turn both faces and the shoulder again to $\frac{9}{16}$ in. from the end to correct any runout.

39. Centerdrill, pilot drill, and tap drill as with the body.

40. Tap $\frac{3}{4}$-16 as before.

41. Remove the nut from the chuck and change to a three-jaw chuck.

42. Chuck a threaded stub mandrel (spud) having a $\frac{3}{4}$-16 NF thread.

43. Screw on the nut with the knurled part next to the chuck.

44. Turn the OD to $2\frac{1}{4}$ in. Face the $\frac{13}{16}$ in. length. Mark a 2 in. diameter line on the face.

45. Free hand machine a slight radius from the OD to the 2 in. line as shown in the drawing.

46. Finish the radius with a file and deburr the edge nearest the chuck. Chamfer the threaded hole. Clean and apply a light film of oil.

Making the Screw

47. Cut off a piece of 1 in. hexagon stock $7\frac{1}{2}$ in. long. The extra length is for turning off the center.

48. Chuck the piece in a three-jaw chuck and face both ends. Chamfer one end to a point slightly below the flats on the hexagon stock. Center drill the other end. Chuck $\frac{1}{2}$ in. of the chamfered end and support the other end in the tailstock center.

49. Turn the diameter to size. Check for tapering and correct if needed.

50. Set up for threading and cut the $\frac{3}{4}$-16 thread. Check for fit with the nut you have just finished. Turn the $\frac{1}{2}$ in. diameter. This should now be about $\frac{3}{8}$ in. longer than it will be when finished.

51. With one end still in the chuck, set up a steadyrest on the other end at the $\frac{1}{2}$ in. diameter. Move the tailstock away. Be sure the carriage is to the right of the steadyrest so you can turn the end of the piece.

52. Machine off the center hole and face to length, being careful to leave material in the center for the point.

53. Remove the part from the lathe and caseharden.

54. Clean up the part and apply light oil.

Making the Legs

55. Cut off three pieces of $\frac{1}{4}$ x 1 in. MS $6\frac{1}{16}$ in. long.

56. Lay out as shown on the drawing.

57. Drill the $\frac{1}{4}$ in. holes. Chamfer.

58. Saw along the layout lines with the vertical band saw, leaving a minimum of material to file. Use a push stick for safety when sawing.

59. Finish file the lets and chamfer all edges.

60. Caseharden all three legs. Clean and apply a light film of oil.

Assembly

61. Obtain three $\frac{1}{4}$-20 socket head capscrews $\frac{3}{4}$ in. long. Assemble the legs on the body.

62. Install the nut on the screw and turn the screw into the body.

63. This tool may also be used in the alternate position with two legs opposed.

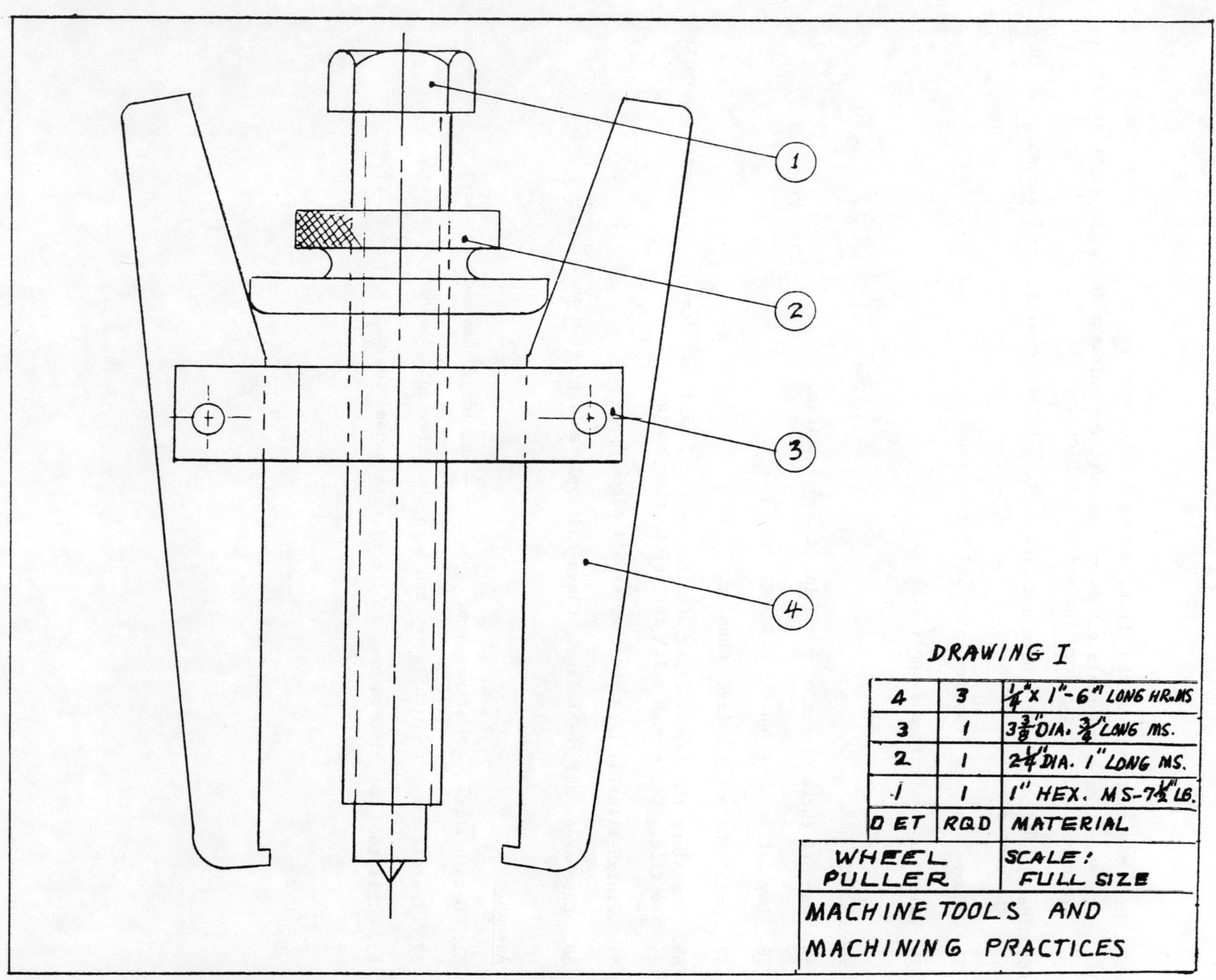

1
2
3
4
DRAWING I
4 | 3 | 1/4" X 1"-6" LONG HR. MS
3 | 1 | 3 3/8" DIA. 3/4" LONG MS.
2 | 1 | 2 1/4" DIA. 1" LONG MS.
1 | 1 | 1" HEX. MS-7 1/2" LB.
DET | RQD | MATERIAL
WHEEL PULLER
SCALE: FULL SIZE
MACHINE TOOLS AND MACHINING PRACTICES

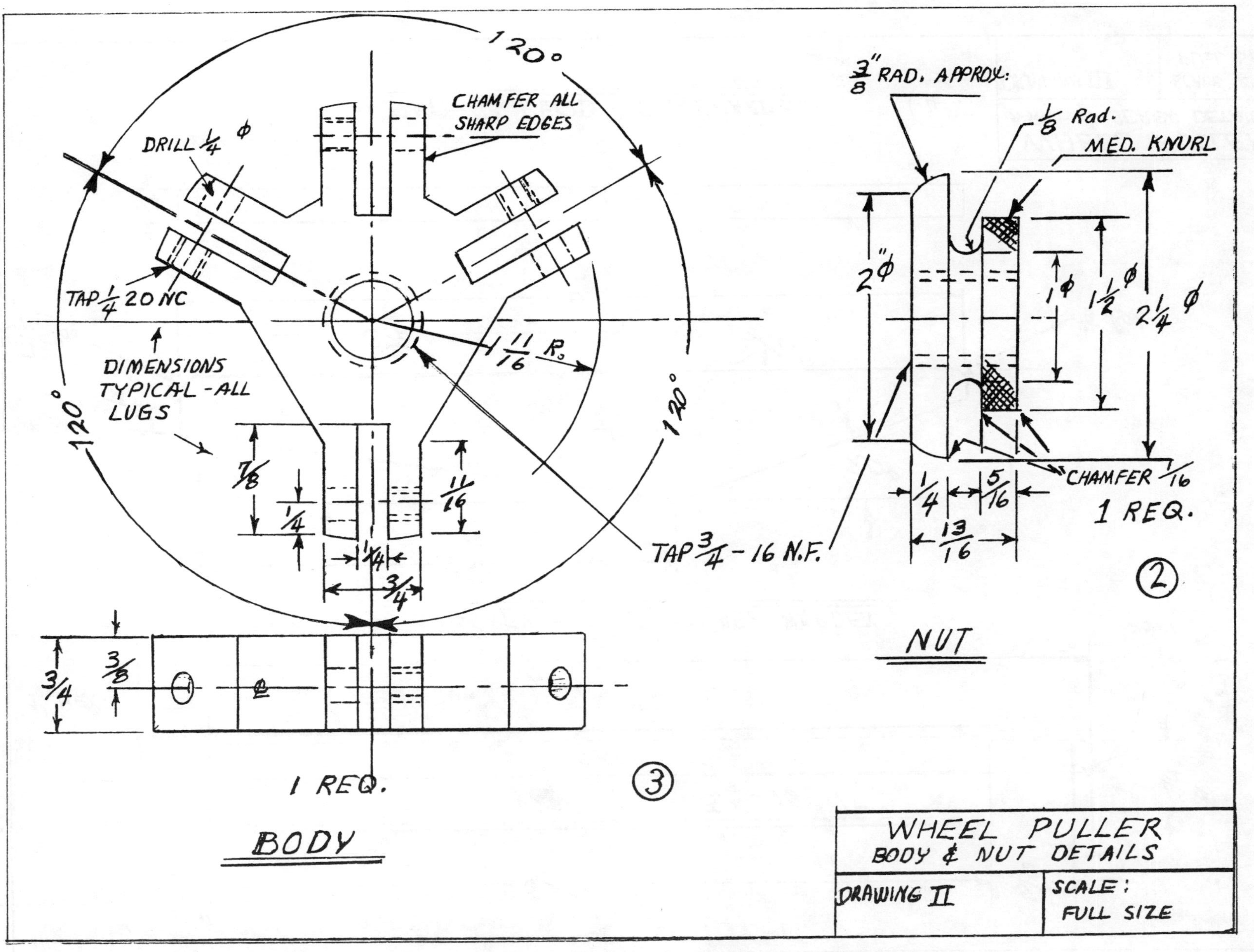

120°
CHAMFER ALL SHARP EDGES
DRILL 1/4 ϕ
TAP 1/4 20 NC
DIMENSIONS TYPICAL - ALL LUGS
1 11/16 R
7/8
1/4
11/16
1/4
3/4
TAP 3/4 - 16 N.F.
3/4
3/8
1 REQ.
③
BODY
3/8" RAD. APPROX.
1/8 Rad.
MED. KNURL
2" ϕ
1 ϕ
1 1/2 ϕ
2 1/4 ϕ
CHAMFER 1/16
1/4
5/16
13/16
1 REQ.
②
NUT
WHEEL PULLER
BODY & NUT DETAILS
DRAWING II
SCALE: FULL SIZE

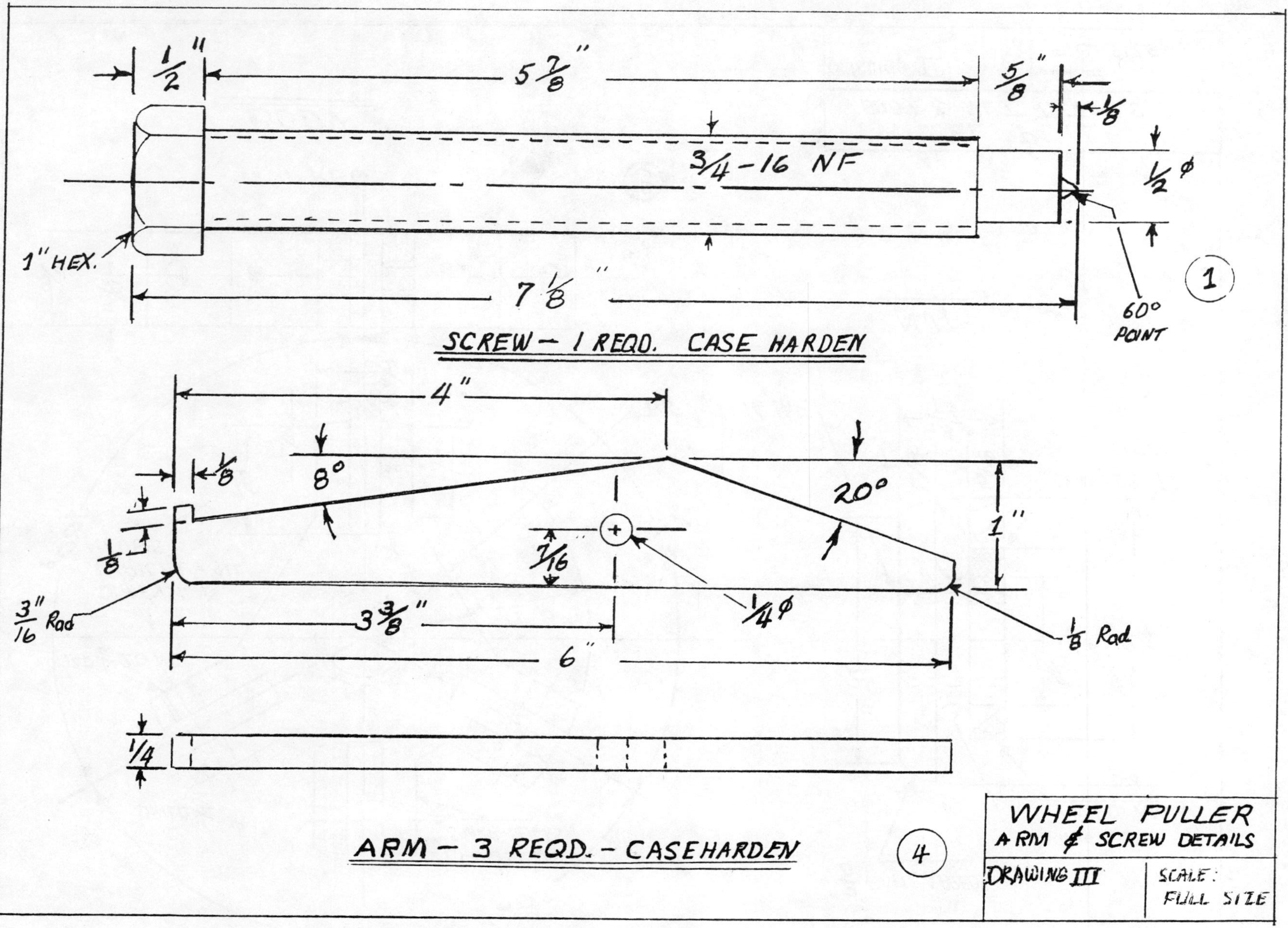
1/2"
5 7/8"
5/8"
1/8
3/4-16 NF
1/2 φ
1" HEX.
7 1/8"
1
60° POINT
SCREW - 1 REQD. CASE HARDEN
4"
1/8
8°
20°
1"
1/8
7/16
3/16" Rad
1/4 φ
3 3/8"
1/8 Rad
6"
1/4
ARM - 3 REQD. - CASEHARDEN
4
WHEEL PULLER
ARM & SCREW DETAILS
DRAWING III
SCALE: FULL SIZE

PROCESS SHEETS FOR TAP WRENCH

Making Part No. 1

1. Cut off a piece of hot rolled mild steel $\frac{1}{2}$ x 1 x $5\frac{1}{2}$ in. long.
2. Clean the lathe spindle nose and mount a four-jaw chuck on it.
3. Fasten your workpiece in the chuck and let approximately 1 in. extend out from it.
4. Center your work to within .003 in.
5. Mount a No. 3 centerdrill in the tailstock drill chuck.
6. Select and set the speed for center drilling.
7. Center drill the end. Use cutting oil.
8. Use a right hand turning tool and face the end with a good finish. Do not remove more material than necessary.
9. Take the workpiece out of the chuck, reverse it, and repeat steps 4 through 8.
10. Remove the workpiece from the chuck.
11. Remove the chuck and substitute a driving plate and center in the headstock.
12. Fasten the dog on your workpiece and set it up for turning between centers.
13. Select the speed for roughing. Record here. _______
14. Select the feed for roughing. Record here. _______
15. Mark your workpiece 2 in. from the tailstock end and take roughing cuts to this mark until the diameter is approximately .800 in.
16. Now mark your workpiece $\frac{7}{16}$ in. from the tailstock end and turn that portion to approximately .560 in.
17. Reverse you workpiece end for end, clamping the dog on the end you have just turned.
18. Mark your workpiece $1\frac{9}{16}$ in. from the <u>headstock</u> end and rough turn to that mark until the diameter is approximately .560 in.
19. Now make a mark $2\frac{1}{6}$ in. from the <u>headstock</u> end and turn your piece to approximately .430 in. diameter to that mark.
20. Resharpen you tool so it can be used for finishing, or make a finishing tool.
21. Select a speed for finishing. Record your RPM here. _______
22. Select a feed for finishing. Record your feed here. _______

23. Mark the work at 2 in. from the <u>headstock</u> end.

24. Finish turn the $\frac{3}{8}$ in. diameter with a tolerance of .377 to .373 in. Machine to the mark.

25. Finish turn the $\frac{1}{2}$ in. diameter from .500 to .494 in. It should end exactly $1\frac{1}{2}$ in. from the headstock end.

26. Set up a medium diamond knurling tool in the tool post.

27. Use a low speed and a feed of about .010 to .015 in.

28. Make a mark $2\frac{13}{16}$ in. from the <u>headstock end</u>; this is how far your knurl will go.

29. Bring the knurls to the work and feed in until you can see a definite diamond pattern develop. If there is one solid line one direction and short broken lines in the other, either raise the tool up, lower it, or turn it slightly sideways so it will "bite" in better. If that doesn't work, find a different knurling tool and try that. Use lube or cutting oil on the knurls and on the work. When a full diamond pattern develops, stop knurling, since further working will ruin the job. Two passes should be sufficient; however, this workpiece will spring in the middle so more passes may be necessary at the center of the workpiece. Remove the knurls while the work rotates to avoid bending the work.

30. Reverse you workpiece; protect the knurled section with some soft material such as aluminum when you put the dog on.

31. Change speed and feed for a finishing cut and set up your right hand turning tool again.

32. Turn the large diameter from .750 to .748 in.

33. Turn the $\frac{1}{2}$ in. diameter nearest the <u>tailstock</u> end from .500 to .494 in. and $\frac{1}{2}$ in. long.

34. Set the compound rest so it will cut the 30 degree angle; also set up the tool for the cut (Figure 1).

35. Lock the carriage in place and cut the taper. Make sure you get a smooth transition between the $\frac{1}{2}$ in. diameter and the taper.

36. Swivel the compound rest to cut the other 30 degree bevel (Figure 2).

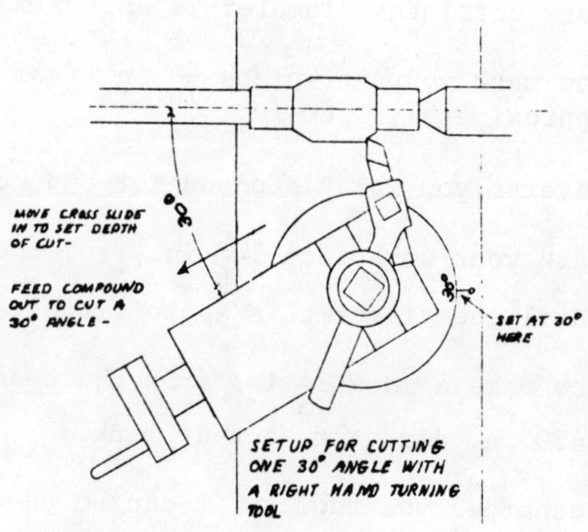

Figure 1

37. Turn this taper, being careful also to make a smooth transition between the taper and $\frac{1}{2}$ in. diameter.

38. Set the cutting edge of the tool at 45 degrees to the work and make the two required chamfers.

39. Remove the dog from the workpiece and change to a four-jaw chuck on the spindle.

40. Mark you workpiece 5 in. long. Use a protective aluminum sleeve and chuck the workpiece with the small end out. Allow approximately 1 in. to extend from the chuck.

41. Adjust the chuck jaws until the workpiece runs true.

42. Face off the excess material (to your mark).

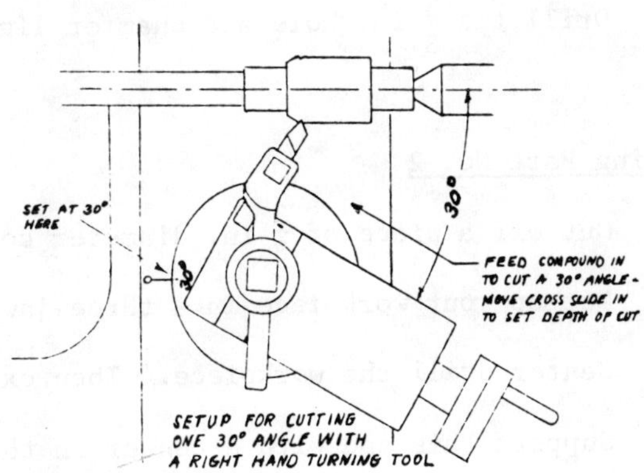

Figure 2

43. Rough turn the $\frac{3}{16}$ in. radius and use a file to complete the shape and to finish it.

44. Remove your workpiece from the chuck and chamfer.

45. Chuck the workpiece on the $\frac{3}{8}$ in. diameter using the protective sleeve; let the large part extend out from the chuck.

46. Adjust the jaws until the work runs concentric. Center drill.

47. Find the size of the tap drill for $\frac{5}{16}$-24 NF threads and record here. _______

48. Hold this drill in the tailstock drill chuck and drill your piece. The center drilled hole will act as a guide.

49. Remove the drill and fasten a $\frac{5}{16}$-24 NF tap in the drill chuck.

50. Loosen the tailstock clamp so it slides freely on the ways.

51. Put cutting oil on the tap and turn the chuck with the workpiece in it by hand; after you bring the tap in contact with the work it will pull itself into the work.

52. When the tap has reached full depth, turn the chuck in reverse. This will push the tap out.

53. Lay out for the $\frac{3}{8}$ drilled hole on the flat side of the large diameter. Center punch.

54. Clamp the large diameter in a drill press vise using soft protective material on the jaws. Use a level on the part to make sure it is set up square to the spindle after the vise is tightened.

55. Spot drill with a small center drill.

56. Drill the $\frac{3}{8}$ in. hole and chamfer lightly on both sides with a countersink.

Making Part No. 2

57. Cut off a piece of $\frac{3}{8}$ in. diameter cold rolled mild steel $4\frac{3}{4}$ in. long.

58. Set up your workpiece in a three-jaw chuck. Check it for concentricity.

59. Center drill the workpiece. Then extend it 3 in. from the chuck.

60. Support this end with a center in the tailstock.

61. Put a mark on your workpiece $2\frac{9}{16}$ in. from the tailstock end. This is how far the knurl will extend.

62. Repeat steps 26 to 29.

63. Use a protective sleeve to hold the knurled piece so that the end with the center hole extends 1 in. out from the chuck.

64. Use your right hand tool and cut $\frac{3}{8}$ in. off the end of the workpiece. This should remove the center hole.

65. Rough turn and use a file to make the $\frac{3}{16}$ in. radius.

66. Remove your workpiece from the chuck and mark it $2\frac{11}{16}$ in. from the rounded end.

67. Chuck the workpiece so your mark is $\frac{1}{2}$ in. from the chuck.

68. Center drill the end and support it with a center.

69. Turn the $\frac{5}{16}$ in. diameter from .312 to .310 in diameter to your mark.

70. Turn the $\frac{1}{4}$ in. diameter at the end from .250 to .248 in. diameter so that 1 in. remains of the $\frac{5}{16}$ in. diameter.

71. Make a small undercut $\frac{3}{32}$ in. wide to the minor diameter of your thread.

72. Set up your threading tool and thread the workpiece. Make sure your tool is sharp.

73. Use your right hand tool to cut the $\frac{1}{4}$ in. diameter back so it will be $\frac{5}{16}$ in. long. If an aluminum protective sleeve is used on the knurl, the end may be turned off while set up as a chucking operation (without the dead center).

74. Chamfer the $\frac{1}{4}$ in. diameter to the specifications on the drawing.

75. This completes the turning of part 2.

Assembling the Tap Wrench

76. Use a small square file and make the Vee in part 1. It should be symetrical to the center line.

77. Assemble both pieces. Use oil as a rust preventative.

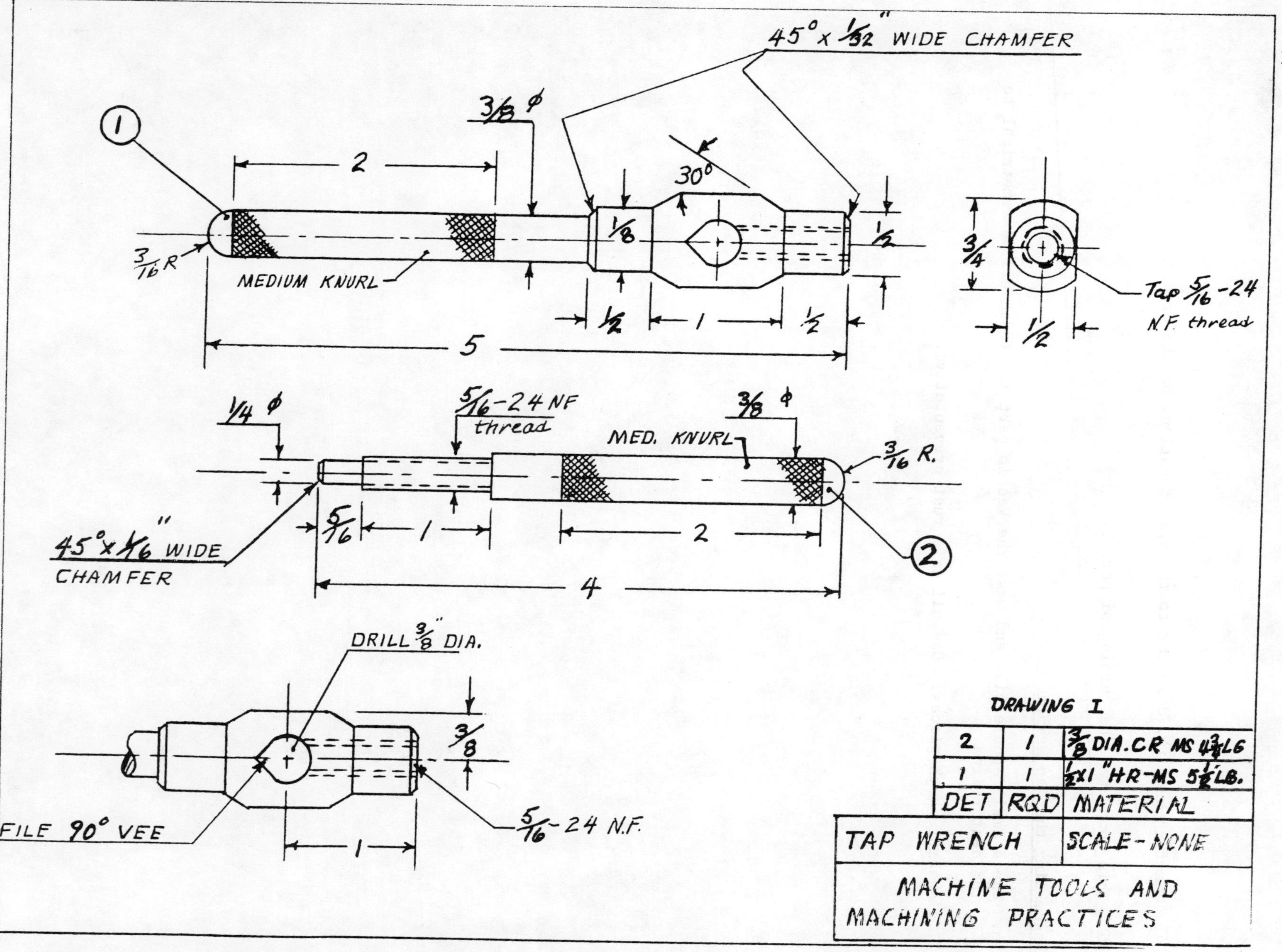
45° x 1/32" WIDE CHAMFER
1
3/8 ⌀
2
30°
1/8
1/2
3/4
3/16 R
MEDIUM KNURL
Tap 5/16-24
N.F. thread
1/2
1
1/2
1/2
5
1/4 ⌀
5/16-24 NF
thread
3/8 ⌀
MED. KNURL
3/16 R.
45° x 1/16" WIDE
CHAMFER
5/16
1
2
2
4
DRILL 3/8" DIA.
3/8
FILE 90° VEE
5/16-24 N.F.
1
DRAWING I
2 | 1 | 3/8 DIA. CR MS 4 3/8 LG
1 | 1 | 1/2 x 1" HR-MS 5 1/2 LB.
DET | RQD | MATERIAL
TAP WRENCH
SCALE - NONE
MACHINE TOOLS AND
MACHINING PRACTICES

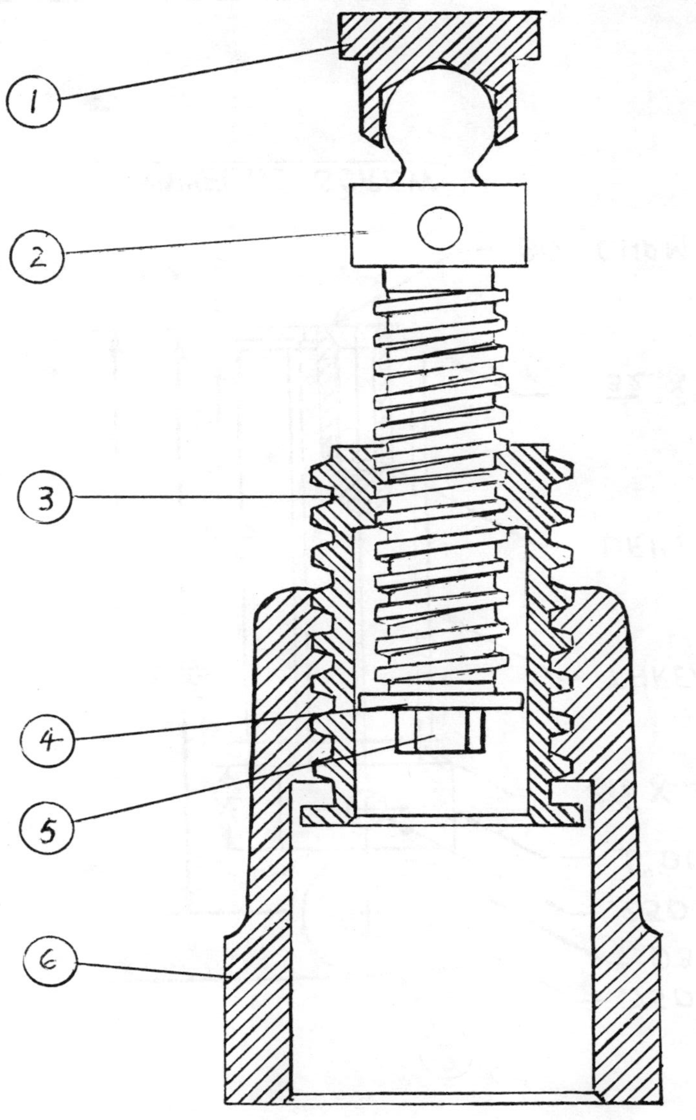

DRAWING I

DET	RQD	MATERIAL
6	1	$2\frac{1}{2}$" DIA. - 3" LG. MS
5	1	$\frac{1}{4}$-20 - $\frac{3}{4}$" LG
4	1	$\frac{15}{16}$" DIA. X 1 $\frac{5}{32}$" MS.
3	1	$1\frac{5}{8}$" DIA. - 3" LG MS
2	1	1" DIA. - 4" LG. MS.
1	1	$1\frac{1}{4}$" C.R. - $\frac{7}{8}$" LG

SCREW JACK	SCALE - NONE
MACHINE TOOLS AND MACHINING PRACTICES	

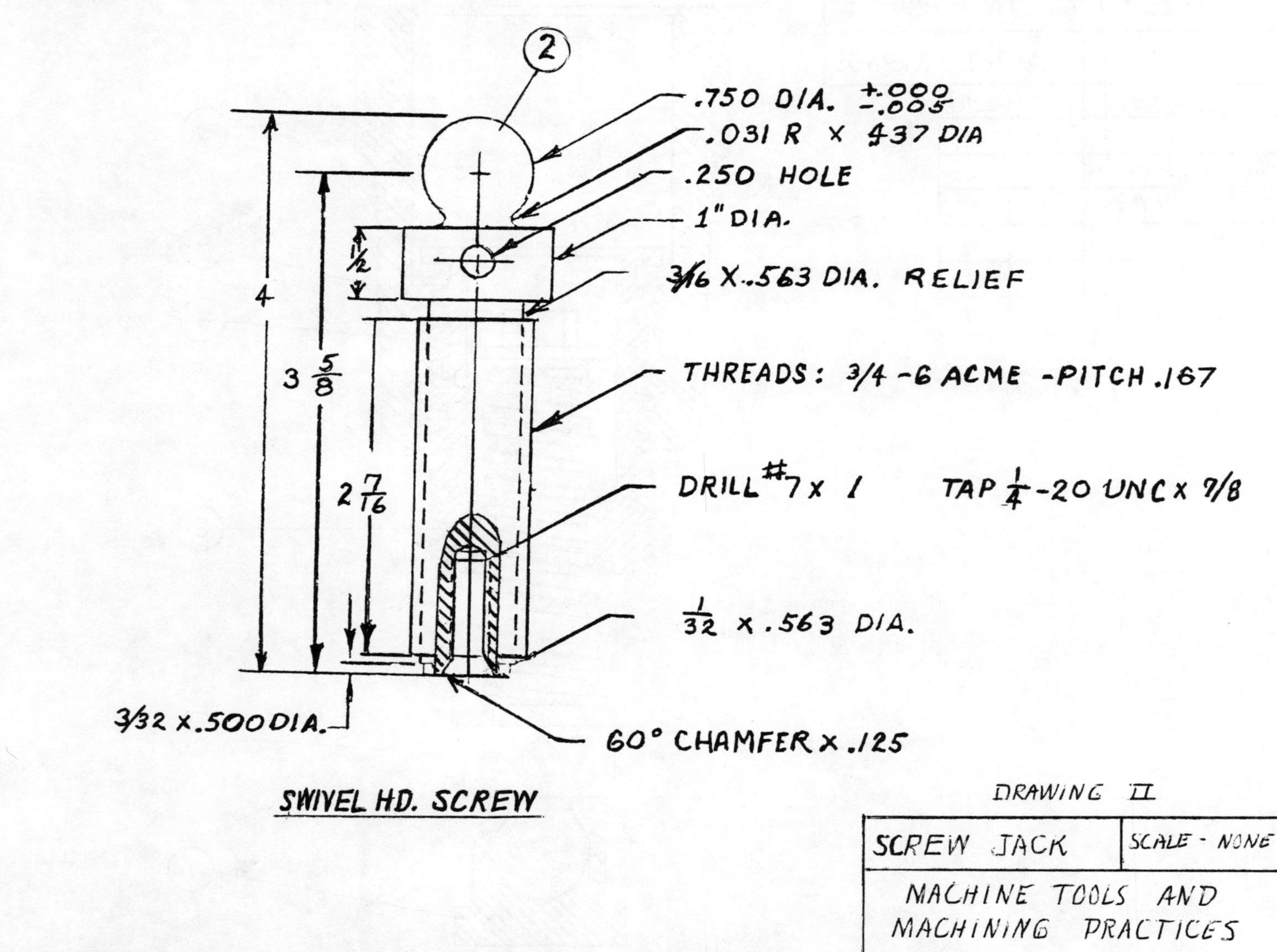
2
.750 DIA. +.000 -.005
.031 R x .437 DIA
.250 HOLE
1" DIA.
3/16 X .563 DIA. RELIEF
THREADS: 3/4 -6 ACME -PITCH .167
DRILL #7 x 1
TAP 1/4 -20 UNC x 7/8
1/32 x .563 DIA.
60° CHAMFER x .125
3/32 x .500 DIA.
1/2
4
3 5/8
2 7/16
SWIVEL HD. SCREW
DRAWING II
SCREW JACK
SCALE - NONE
MACHINE TOOLS AND MACHINING PRACTICES

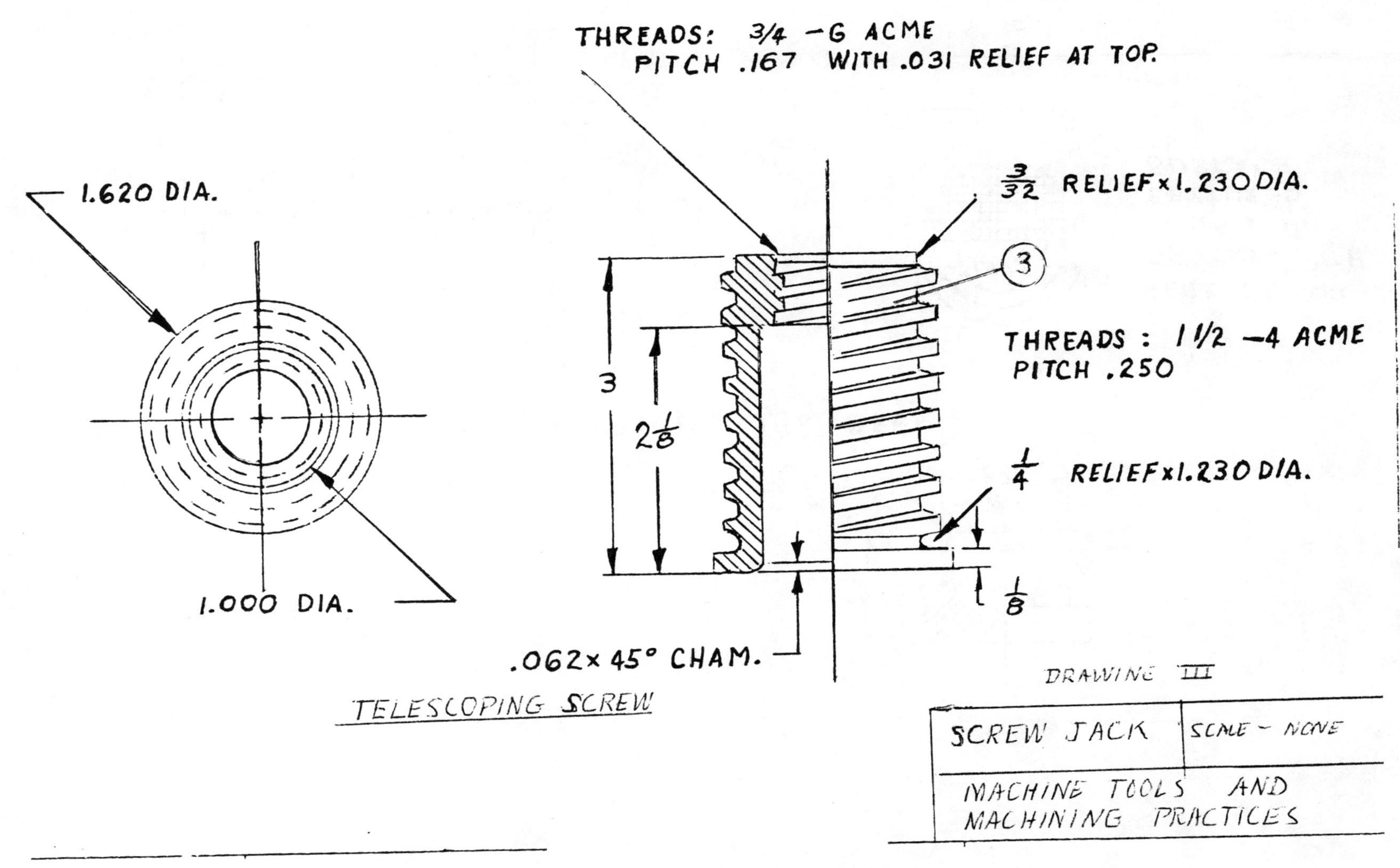
THREADS: 3/4 -6 ACME
PITCH .167 WITH .031 RELIEF AT TOP.
3/32 RELIEF x 1.230 DIA.
3
THREADS : 1 1/2 -4 ACME
PITCH .250
1/4 RELIEF x 1.230 DIA.
1/8
1.620 DIA.
1.000 DIA.
3
2 1/8
.062 x 45° CHAM.
TELESCOPING SCREW
DRAWING III
SCREW JACK
SCALE - NONE
MACHINE TOOLS AND
MACHINING PRACTICES

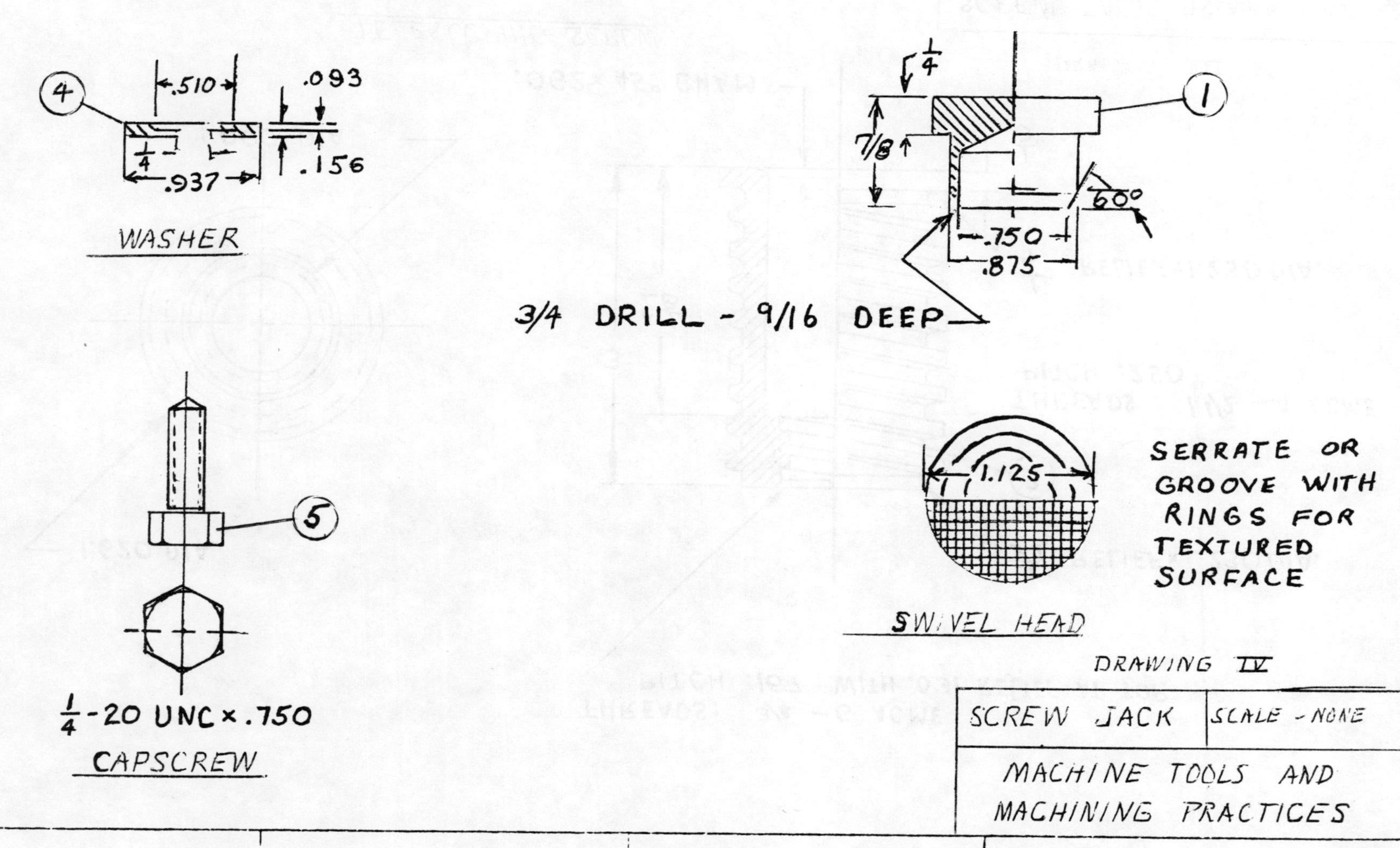
4
.510
.093
1/4
.937
.156
WASHER
1/4
7/8
1
60°
.750
.875
3/4 DRILL - 9/16 DEEP
5
1/4-20 UNC × .750
CAPSCREW
1.125
SERRATE OR GROOVE WITH RINGS FOR TEXTURED SURFACE
SWIVEL HEAD
DRAWING IV
SCREW JACK
SCALE - NONE
MACHINE TOOLS AND MACHINING PRACTICES

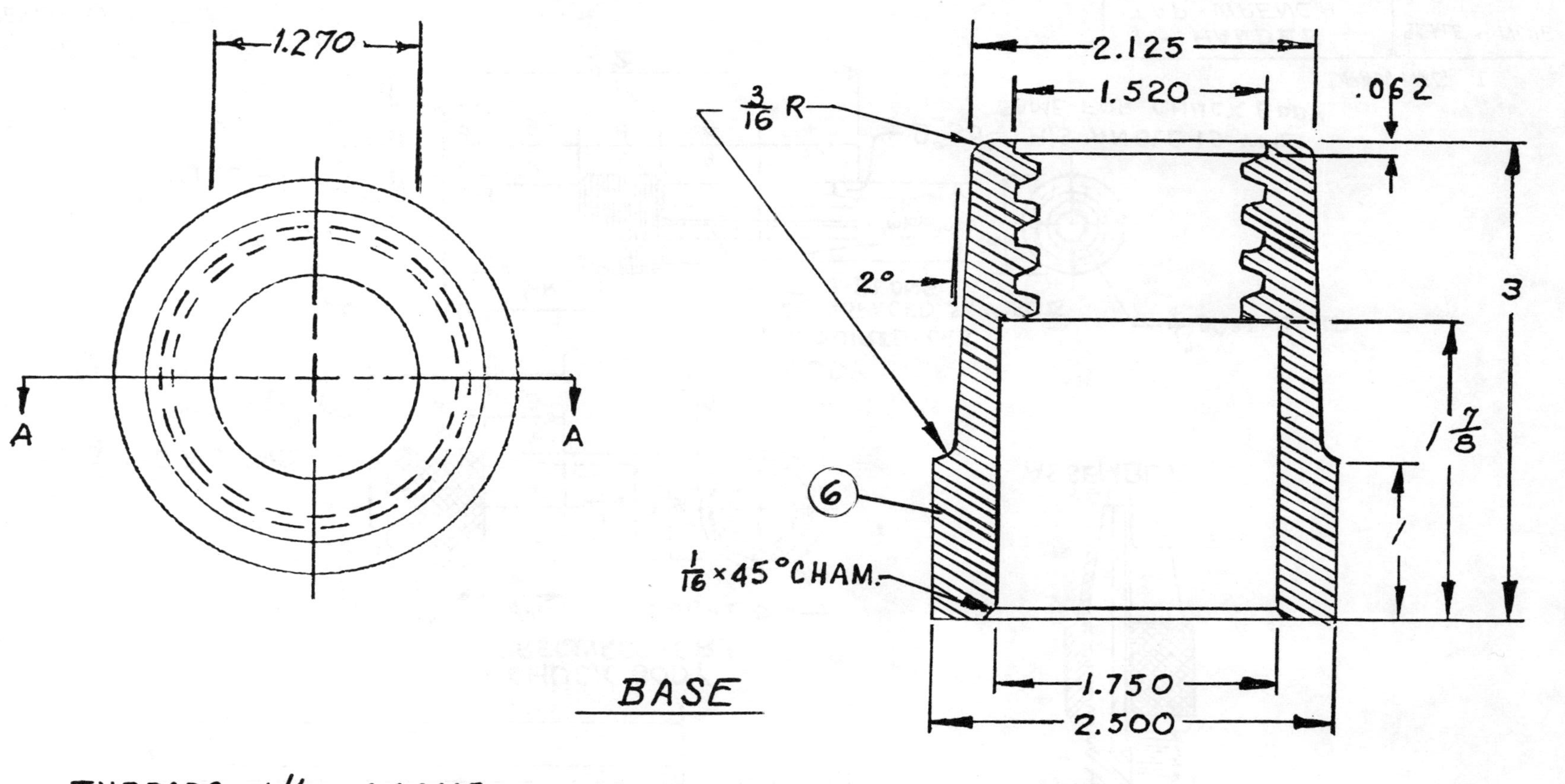

SECTION AA

DRAWING V	
SCREW JACK	SCALE - NONE
MACHINE TOOLS AND MACHINING PRACTICES	

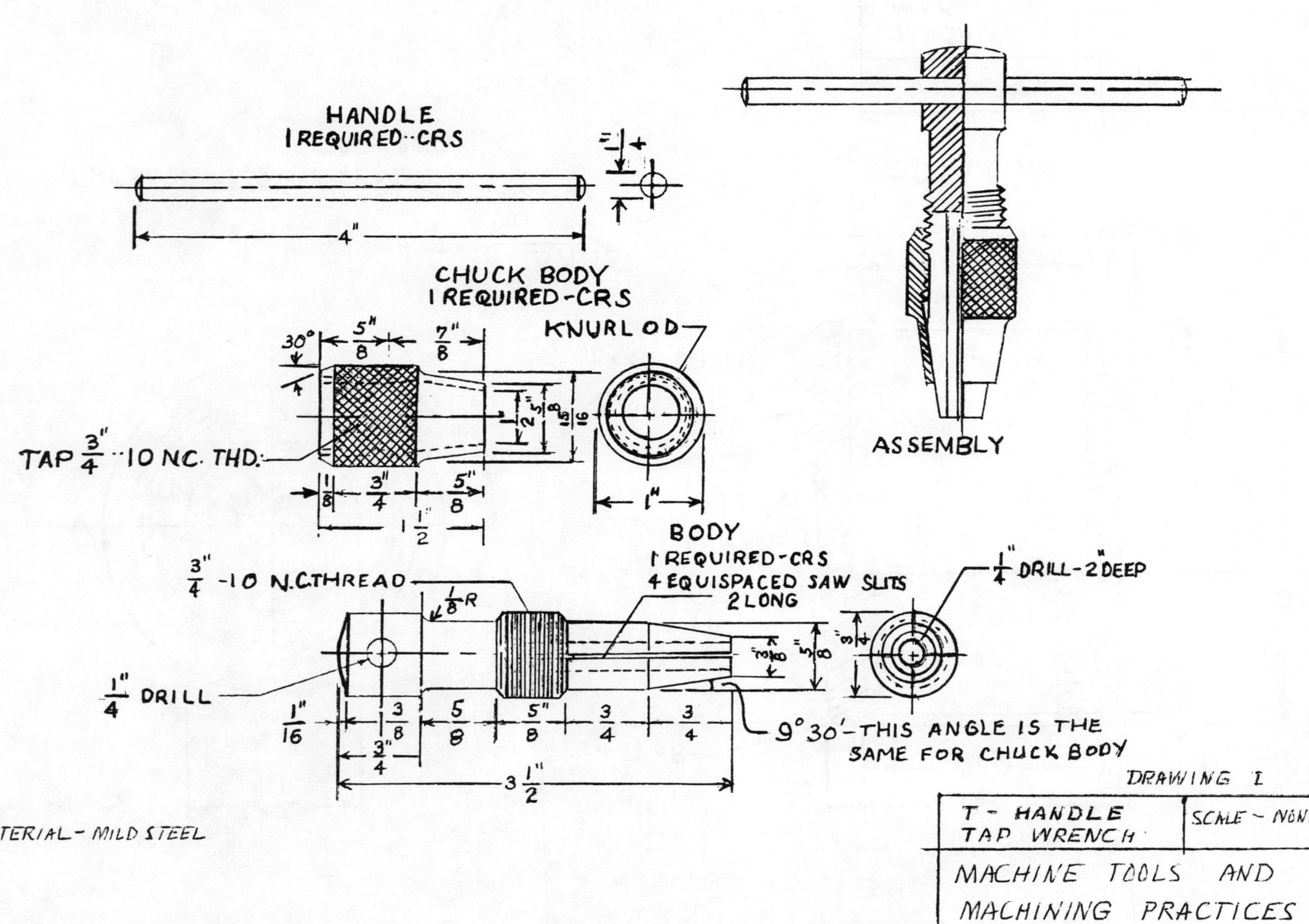
TAP WRENCH
HANDLE
1 REQUIRED-CRS
4"
CHUCK BODY
1 REQUIRED-CRS
KNURL OD
TAP 3/4" -10 NC. THD.
30°
1"
ASSEMBLY
BODY
1 REQUIRED-CRS
4 EQUISPACED SAW SLITS
2 LONG
3/4" -10 N.C.THREAD
1/8 R
1/4" DRILL-2" DEEP
1/4" DRILL
9° 30'-THIS ANGLE IS THE
SAME FOR CHUCK BODY
3 1/2"
DRAWING I
T - HANDLE
TAP WRENCH
SCALE - NONE
MACHINE TOOLS AND
MACHINING PRACTICES
MATERIAL - MILD STEEL

Steam engine. This model is machined from a set of castings produced by Stuart Turner Ltd., Henley-on-Thames, England. It provides intermediate level students with a large variety of machine tool setups and workpiece materials (Courtesy of Lloyd R. Larson).

Steam engine. This model is machined from a set of castings produced by Stuart Turner Ltd., Henley-on-Thames, England. It provides intermediate level students with a large variety of machine tool setups and workpiece materials. (Courtesy of Lloyd R. Larson)

MEASURING KITS FOR POST TESTS

For conventionally organized lecture-laboratory situations, it is useful to have a carefully made set of test pieces. These test pieces (Figure 1a) are out of a set of 20, each made to slightly different dimensions, hardened and ground. Each test piece has a master sheet of carefully determined measurements. As each student completes his exercise (Figure 1b), his results are compared with the master sheet while the student is present. This procedure gives rapid feedback in order to correct reading or procedural errors, and the student continues to work until his results meet standards.

With programs that permit individual student entry at any time, kits of various types are useful to supplement instructional units (Figures 2 to 9). Only one kit of each kind is necessary unless there is a heavy student usage; in this case, two identical kits may be needed.

Figure 1a. Serial numbered test pieces. Each block is slightly different from the others. Each has a master sheet of dimensions (DeAnza College).

The purpose of the exercise in measurement (Figure 1b) is to acquaint the student with a variety of measuring devices. Measure each feature with the number of measuring devices indicated. Measure to the limit of resolution of the instrument. Where metric measurement is indicated, use a selection of instruments with differing calibrations. Specify the measuring instruments used next to each recorded measurement.

BLOCK NUMBER ______________________

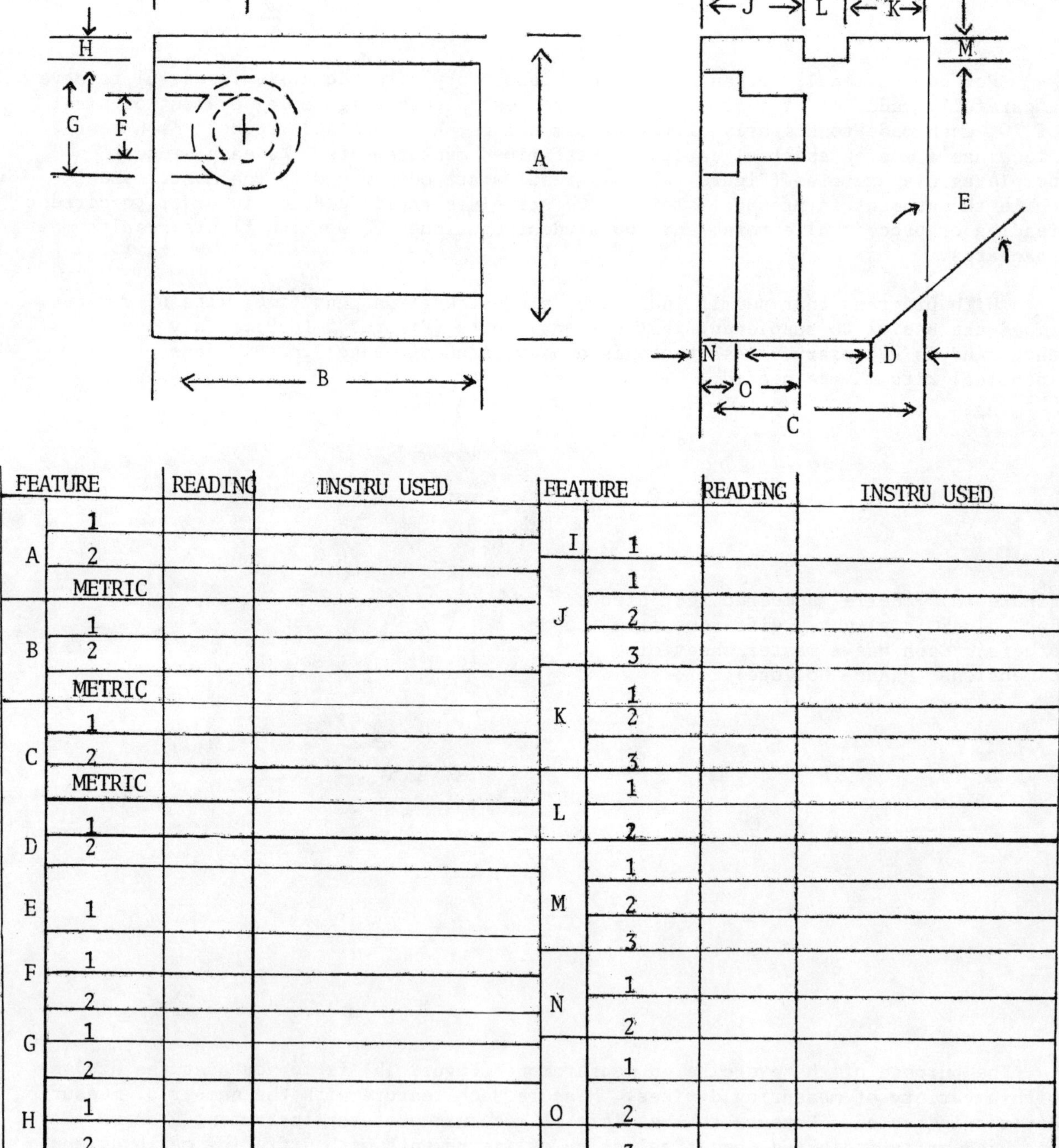

FEATURE		READING	INSTRU USED	FEATURE		READING	INSTRU USED
A	1			I	1		
	2			J	1		
	METRIC				2		
B	1				3		
	2			K	1		
	METRIC				2		
C	1				3		
	2			L	1		
	METRIC				2		
D	1			M	1		
	2				2		
E	1				3		
F	1			N	1		
	2				2		
G	1			O	1		
	2				2		
H	1				3		
	2						

Figure 1b. Chart for recording test measurements

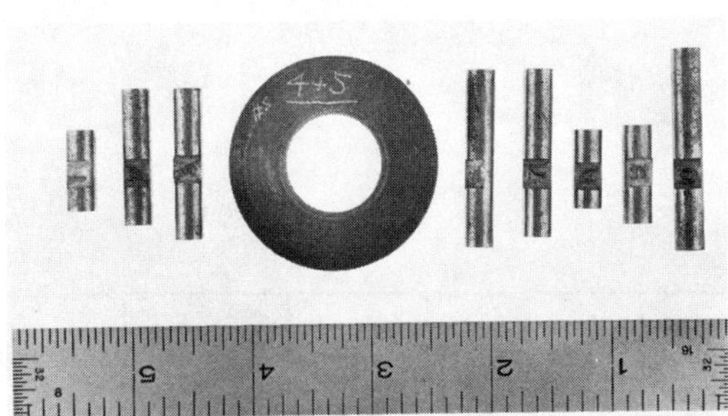

Figure 2. Steel rule test kit for $\frac{1}{8}$ and $\frac{1}{16}$ in. measurements (DeAnza College).

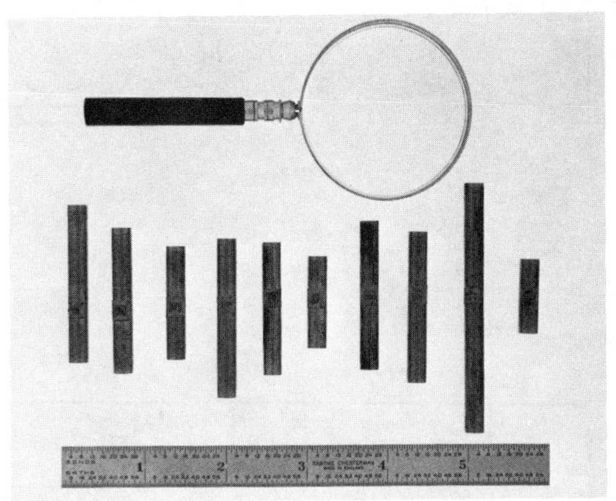

Figure 3. Steel rule test kit for $\frac{1}{32}$ and $\frac{1}{64}$ in. measurements. A similar kit is easily made up for decimal inch and metric use (DeAnza College).

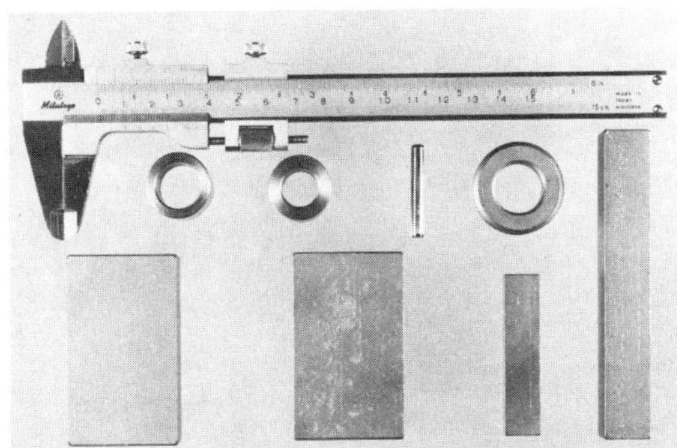

Figure 4. Vernier caliper test kit made up for .02 mm and .001 in. measurements (DeAnza College).

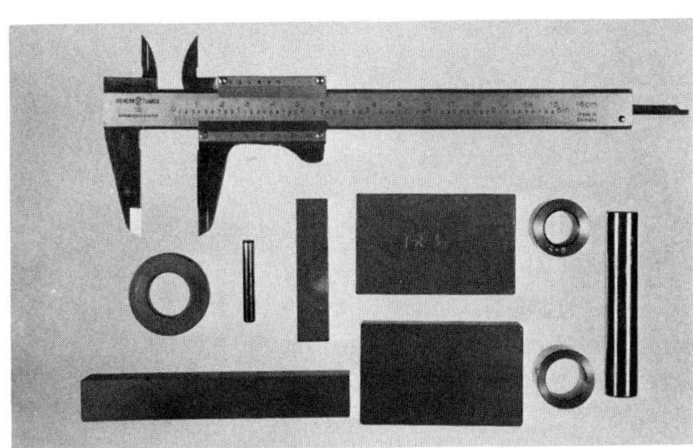

Figure 5. Vernier caliper test kit made up for .05 mm and .001 in. measurements (DeAnza College).

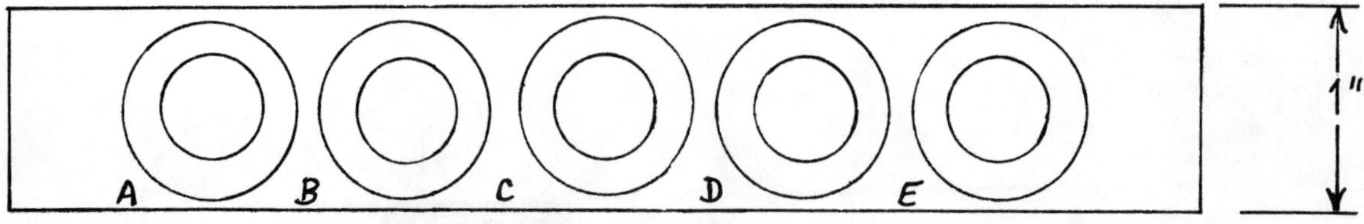

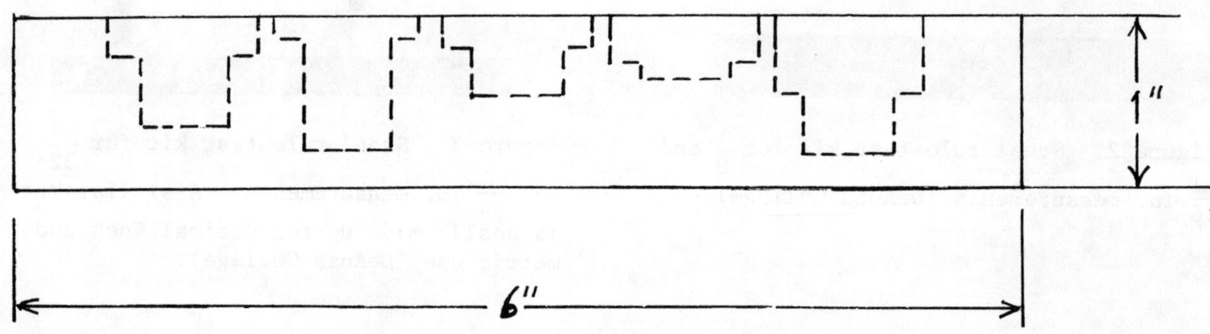

$\frac{7}{8}$ in. diameter counterbore, various depths

$\frac{1}{2}$ in. diameter flat bottom drill,

Material: mild steel

Figure 6. Suggested test piece design for use with vernier depth gages.

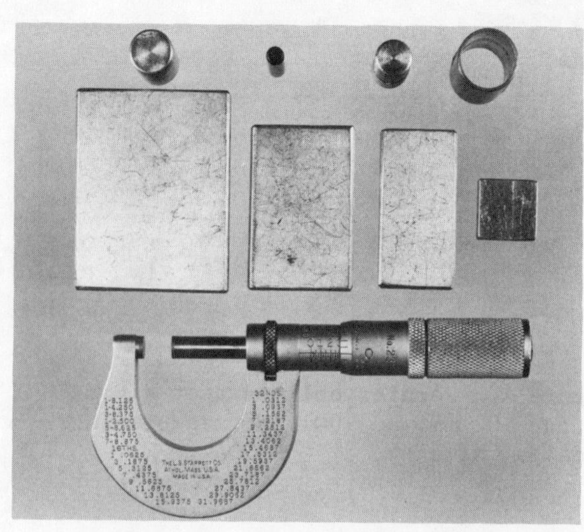

Figure 7. Micrometer test kit. A similar kit is useful for use with a metric micrometer (DeAnza College).

Figure 8. Test kit for telescoping and small hole gages. The pieces are hardened and the inner surfaces honed to an accurate cylindrical form (DeAnza College).

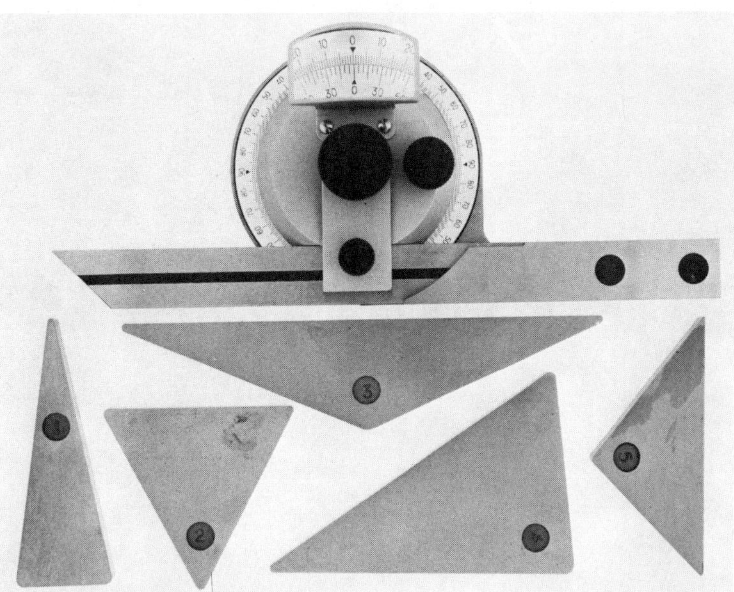

Figure 9. Angular test kit with universal vernier bevel protractor. The test pieces are hardened and ground (DeAnza College).

POST TEST QUESTIONS

Volume I, Section A Date _____________ Name ________________________________

UNIT 1. REVIEW OF SHOP MATHEMATICS

POST TEST

Circle the letter preceding the correct answer.

1. Express the fraction $\frac{33}{64}$ in decimal form to the nearest thousandth place.
   A. .513
   B. .515
   C. .517
   D. .540

2. If the fraction $\frac{27}{64}$ were divided into 7 parts, each part would be equal to:
   A. .0602
   B. .0590
   C. .003
   D. .0612

3. What is the reciprocal of 35?
   A. .2850
   B. .00285
   C. .0295
   D. .0285

4. Express $\frac{7}{8}$ in decimal form to the thousandth place.
   A. .780
   B. .750
   C. .875
   D. .870

5. If A equals the reciprocal of B, then B equals:
   A. $\frac{1}{A}$
   B. Cannot be determined from data given
   C. 1 over the reciprocal of A
   D. $\frac{B}{A}$ (B over A)

6. The number .001 would be read as:
   A. 1 tenth
   B. 1 ten thousandth
   C. 1 thousandth
   D. 1 millionth

7. The sum of $\frac{3}{8}$ and $\frac{19}{64}$ is equal to:
   A. $\frac{57}{64}$
   B. $\frac{43}{64}$
   C. $\frac{56}{64}$
   D. $\frac{25}{32}$

8. The square root of 90 is equal to:
   A. About 9
   B. 10
   C. 9.487
   D. 9.5

9. What is the reciprocal of .025?
   A. 40
   B. $\frac{1}{25}$
   C. $\frac{1}{40}$
   D. 25 thousandths

10. If $\frac{59}{64}$ were divided into 8 parts, three of these parts would equal:
    A. .3457
    B. .4537
    C. .1152
    D. .1512

11. Add the following: $\frac{3}{8} + \frac{7}{32} + \frac{9}{32}$

A. .875

B. $\frac{7}{16}$

C. .873

D. $\frac{8}{7}$

12. Reduce $\frac{355}{1725}$ to lowest terms.

A. $\frac{355}{1725}$ is already at lowest terms

B. $\frac{71}{345}$

C. .874

D. 4.859

13. Divide $\frac{9}{32}$ by $\frac{1}{8}$.

A. $\frac{6}{5}$

B. $\frac{9}{256}$

C. $2\frac{1}{8}$

D. 2.25

14. The decimal equivalent of $\frac{1}{2}$ of $\frac{3}{4}$ is:

A. $\frac{3}{2}$

B. .35700

C. .37500

D. $\frac{3}{8}$

15. The square root of 4 squared is:

A. 4

B. 16

C. 2

D. 1.414

16. What is the decimal equivalent of the pitch of a bolt with 20 threads per inch?

A. $\frac{1}{20}$

B. .005

C. .05

D. Pitch is 20

17. Add the following decimals: .003 + .0003 + .00003.

A. .00333

B. .000333

C. .003333

D. .0333

18. The decimal equivalent of $\frac{5}{16}$ is:

A. .0312

B. .3215

C. .3125

D. .2135

19. What is $\frac{1}{2}$ of $\frac{7}{16}$?

A. .2187

B. $\frac{3}{16}$

C. .2817

D. .02187

20. The decimal equivalent of $\frac{59}{64}$ is:

A. .9219

B. .9128

C. .9218

D. .9217

Volume I, Section A Date ___________ Name ______________________________________

UNIT 3. REVIEWING PLANE GEOMETRY

POST TEST

Circle the letter preceding the correct answer.

1. A right triangle with two equal sides is known as which kind of triangle?
   A. Equilateral
   B. Equal sided
   C. Isosceles
   D. Oblique

2. The diameter of a circle with a circumference of 10 units is:
   A. 3.1416
   B. 3.183
   C. 3.813
   D. 31.14

3. The area of the circle in question 2 is how many square units?
   A. 7.843
   B. 10 pi
   C. 7.597
   D. 7.957

4. The intersection of two planes forms a:
   A. Line
   B. Third plane
   C. Right angle
   D. Point

5. If angle X plus angle Y equals 180 degrees, the angles are:
   A. Complementary
   B. Supplementary
   C. Oblique
   D. Elementary to each other

6. To establish six equal circumference spacings, what is layed off as a chord around the circumference?
   A. Diameter
   B. One half the radius
   C. Radius
   D. One and one half times the radius

7. Find the area of a triangle in which base and altitude are equal to 5 units.
   A. 12.5
   B. 25
   C. 5
   D. Cannot be determined from the data given

8. The center of a circle can be located by:
   A. Approximating the diameter
   B. Laying off the radius as a chord around the circumference
   C. Arc measurement
   D. The intersection of the perpendicular bisector of two chords

9. The circumference of a circle is about equal to what times the diameter?
   A. Pi
   B. Three and one half
   C. Three
   D. Four

10. If a triangle has all 60-degree angles, what can be said of the sides?
    A. At least two of the sides are equal in length
    B. Both C and D
    C. All sides are equal in length
    D. The triangle is equilateral

Volume I, Section A Date ____________ Name ________________________________

UNIT 4. REVIEWING RIGHT TRIANGLE TRIGONOMETRY

POST TEST

Figure 17. Right Triangle KLM

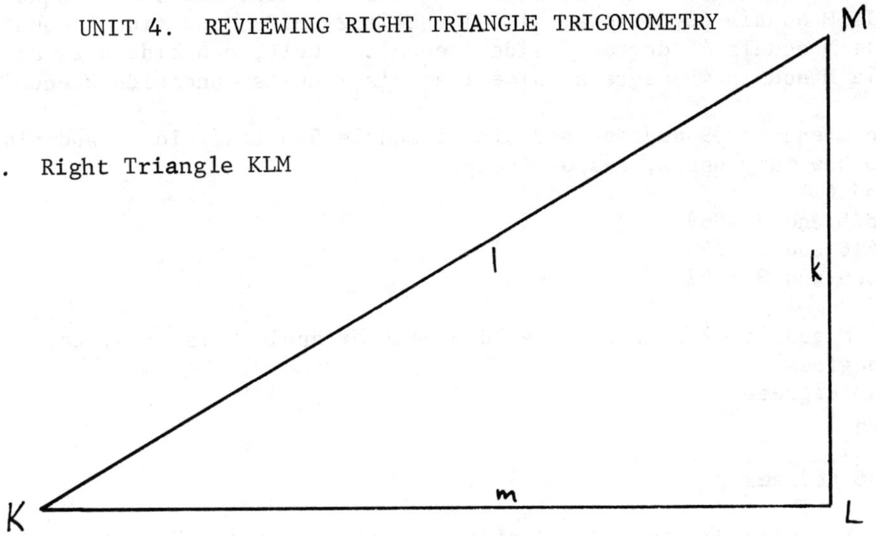

Solve the following right triangles (Figure 17). Use the trigonometric function table in the appendix.

Circle the letter preceding the correct answer.

1. If angle K equals 15 degrees and side k equals 7 units, side m is equal to:
   A. 26.1234 units
   B. k x sinM
   C. 6.7614 units
   D. 11.9206 units

2. If angle K equals 50 degrees, what is the cosecant of angle M?
   A. $\frac{1}{\sin K}$
   B. 1.5556
   C. sinK
   D. Both A and B

3. If side l equals 2.828 units and side k equals 2 units, then:
   A. The triangle is equilateral
   B. Angle K and angle M are equal to 45 degrees
   C. Side m equals 1 unit
   D. Side m equals 4 units

4. Angle K plus angle M equal how many degrees?
   A. 80
   B. 180
   C. 90
   D. 900

5. If angle K equals 30 degrees and side m equals 3.4641 units, it can be said that:
   A. Angle M equals 60 degrees, side l equals 4 units, and side k equals 2 units
   B. Angle M equals 60 degrees, side l equals 2 units, and side k equals 4 units
   C. Angle M equals 45 degrees, side l equals 1 unit, and side k equals .5 unit
   D. Angle M equals 45 degrees, side l equals 2 units, and side k equals 1.414 units

6. If angle M equals 39 degrees and side l equals 5 units, side m and side k are equal to how many units, respectively?
   A. 5 and 6
   B. 2.9875 and 3.8869
   C. 3.1416 and 1.4142
   D. 3.1466 and 3.8857

7. If angle M equals 42 degrees, the cotangent of angle K is equal to:
   A. 48 degrees
   B. tan48 degrees
   C. .9004
   D. $\frac{1}{\text{cot48 degrees}}$

8. If angle K equals 35 degrees and side l equals 4 units, the area of triangle KLM is equal to how many square units?
   A. 3.2766
   B. 3.7587
   C. 2.2943
   D. The area cannot be determined from the data given

9. Angle K minus angle M equals 10 degrees. Angle K is equal to:
   A. Angle K cannot be determined from the data given
   B. 80 degrees
   C. 90 degrees
   D. Angle L

10. What is the length in inches of the side of the largest square that can be made from a 2 inch diameter round bar?
   A. .875
   B. 1.141
   C. 1.414
   D. 2.828

Volume I, Section A Date ____________ Name ______________________________

UNIT 5. READING SHOP DRAWINGS

POST TEST (Refer to Figure 21)

Circle the letter preceding the correct answer.

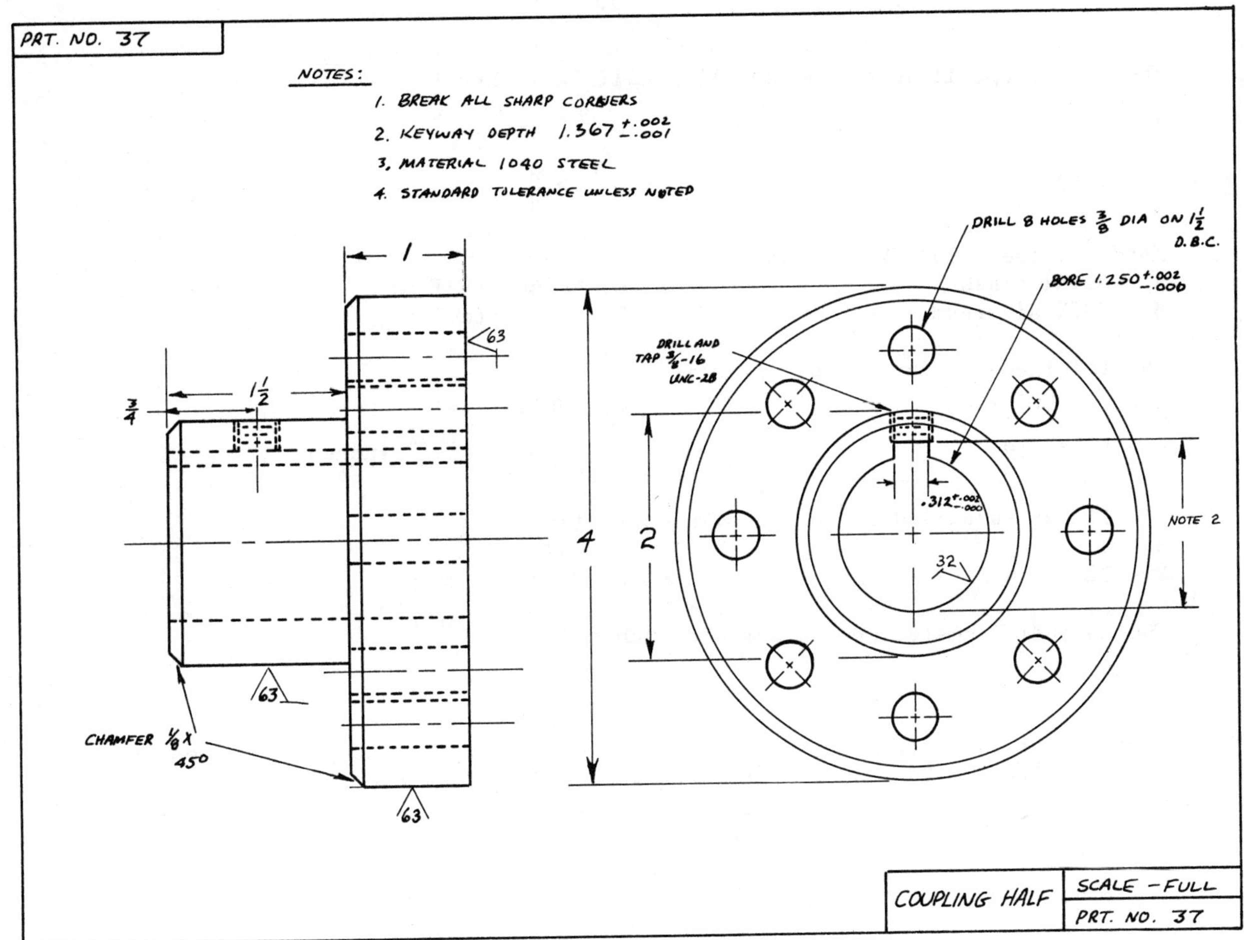

Figure 21

1. The drawing is shown in what format?
   A. Orthochromatic
   B. Orthographic
   C. Right angular
   D. Two view

2. The tolerance of the bore through the coupling half is:
   A. Bilateral
   B. Unilateral
   C. Standard
   D. Not specified

3. After boring the hole through the coupling half, a machinist determines the diameter to be 1.251 inches. It can then be concluded that the diameter of the bore is:
   A. Too small
   B. Too large
   C. Exactly as specified by the drawing
   D. Within acceptable tolerance

4. The distance to the center of the set screw hole from the small end of the coupling half in inches is:
   A. $\frac{3}{8}$
   B. $\frac{3}{4}$
   C. 1
   D. $1\frac{3}{4}$

5. The D.B.C. specified on the coupling half in inches is:
   A. $1\frac{1}{2}$
   B. 1.597
   C. 2
   D. $8\frac{3}{8}$

6. Material specified for the part is:
   A. Naval brass
   B. 7075 aluminum
   C. 4140 steel
   D. 1040 steel

7. The tolerance of the keyway width is:
   A. $\pm$ .001 inch
   B. Bilateral
   C. Unilateral
   D. $1.367 \begin{smallmatrix} +.002 \\ -.001 \end{smallmatrix}$ inches

8. The finish specified in the coupling bore is:
   A. 4
   B. 32
   C. 63
   D. 500

9. The largest diameter on the part in inches is:
   A. 2
   B. 4
   C. 5
   D. 4.500

10. A machinist is assigned the job of producing a number of coupling halves on a chucking lathe. The job specifications call for a piece of stock which is $2\frac{1}{4}$ inches longer than the finished part. Knowing this, how many inches in length should he request that the stockroom cut the material?
    A. $4\frac{3}{4}$
    B. 5
    C. 7
    D. $4\frac{1}{2}$

Volume I, Section A Date ____________ Name ________________________________

UNIT 6. INTRODUCTION TO MECHANICAL HARDWARE

POST TEST

Circle the letter preceding the correct answer.

1. The difference between a screw and a bolt is the:
   A. Application
   B. Head shape
   C. Length
   D. Class of thread

2. Cap screws are:
   A. The same as machine screws
   B. Also called machine bolts
   C. Precision screws
   D. Square headed

3. Set screws are used:
   A. To secure pulleys to shafts
   B. In place of machine screws
   C. Because they are soft
   D. Because they have hex heads

4. Thread forming screws are used because:
   A. They are small
   B. Of their appearance
   C. They are light
   D. They are convenient in sheet metal assemblies

5. A regular nut is:
   A. Slotted
   B. Thicker than a jam nut
   C. Thinner than a jam nut
   D. Hardened

6. To protect the end of a threaded rod, use a
   A. Cap nut
   B. Jam nut
   C. Pipe cap
   D. Thread protector

7. An external tooth lock washer:
   A. Is used with flat head screws
   B. Provides less friction than an internal tooth lock washer
   C. Provides more friction than an internal tooth lock washer
   D. Provides the same friction as an internal tooth lock washer

8. Dowel pins are:
   A. Made from dowel stock
   B. Made from brass
   C. Painted
   D. Hardened

9. A bearing is often held on a shaft with a:
   A. Retaining ring
   B. Bearing holder
   C. Set screw
   D. Lock washer

10. When a heavy load is transmitted between a shaft and a pulley, use a:
    A. Heavy duty woodruff key
    B. Tapered key
    C. Feathered key
    D. Heavy duty square key

11. Identify the 20 pieces of mechanical hardware in the kit obtained from your instructor. Match the number of the item with the list of names.

_____ Square head machine bolt

_____ Socket head cap screw

_____ Socket head set screw, dog point

_____ Square head set screw

_____ Thread forming screw

_____ Thread cutting screw

_____ Hex jam nut

_____ Slotted nut

_____ Helical spring lock washer

_____ Dowel pin

_____ Taper pin

_____ Roll pin

_____ Retaining ring

_____ Square key

_____ Internal tooth lock washer

_____ Woodruff key

_____ Tapered key

_____ Cotter pin

_____ Flat washer

_____ Wing nut

Volume I, Section A Date ___________ Name ____________________________________

UNIT 8. SHOP SAFETY

POST TEST

Circle the letter preceding the correct answer.

1. Safety is:
   A. An attitude that should be considered in everything you do
   B. Something that pertains only to machine tool operations
   C. Something that pertains only to being inside the machine shop
   D. Really only important to beginners

2. Compressed air can:
   A. Injure ears
   B. Injure skin
   C. Cause metal chips to fly
   D. Cause all of the above

3. Grinder operation requires that:
   A. Dust be controlled
   B. Side shield safety glasses be worn and dust controlled
   C. Plain safety glasses be worn and dust controlled
   D. Side shield safety glasses be worn

4. Proper dress includes:
   A. Solid shoes and a shop coat
   B. Any shoes, short hair and short sleeves
   C. Solid shoes, shop apron or short sleeve shop coat, short or secured hair, and a short sleeve shirt
   D. Short hair and short sleeve shirt

5. To protect hands:
   A. Keep them out of danger by thinking about safety
   B. Wear gloves
   C. Clear chips with a brush instead of hands
   D. Both A and C

6. Grinding dust can:
   A. Be a hazard to health
   B. Cause damage to other machines
   C. Be controlled by a vacuum dust collector
   D. All of the above

7. The first step in lifting is to:
   A. Bend knees and squat down
   B. Size up the load to determine if it is within your lifting capacity
   C. Lean over the load and lift it slightly to see how heavy it is
   D. Weigh the load to see if it is over 57 pounds

8. You are going to do maintenance on a permanently wired machine tool. You should first:
   A. Turn the machine switch to off
   B. Have another person stand by the machine switch while you work
   C. Switch off the circuit breaker to the machine and tag with an appropriate warning
   D. Call an electrician to disconnect the machine wiring

9. When cleaning a machine tool after use:
   A. Blow chips with compressed air as long as the air pressure is not over 10 pounds
   B. Use a brush to remove chips from the machine
   C. Use a rag to remove chips from the machine
   D. Wash the entire machine with a non-flammable cleaning solvent

10. Oil soaked rags:
   A. Can be a health hazard
   B. Should be stored in approved safety cans
   C. Both B and D
   D. Can be a fire hazard

Volume I, Section B Date ____________ Name ______________________________

UNIT 2. ARBOR AND SHOP PRESSES

POST TEST

Circle the letter preceding the correct answer.

1. Two basic principles always taken into consideration by persons familiar with the proper use of shop presses are:
   A. Personal safety and care of the workpiece to keep it from being damaged
   B. Care to not overload the press by trying to press an oversized part. Personal safety.
   C. Care should be taken not to press too fast, as this creates friction which produces heat causing the part to expand and not fit properly. Personal safety.
   D. Always use the largest press available for every job, as the part being pressed might stick half way through with a small press. Personal safety.

2. You can use the arbor press or shop press to:
   A. Drill holes in metal parts
   B. Make keyways on shafts
   C. Install and remove mandrels, bushings, bearings and shafts
   D. All of the above

3. An arbor press designed with a rack and pinion is what type?
   A. Gear driven
   B. Hydro-mechanical
   C. Hydraulic
   D. Mechanical

4. To avoid failures from seizing when pressing a shaft or mandrel, you should:
   A. Apply high pressure lubricant to the bore and shaft
   B. Use sulfurized cutting oil on both parts
   C. Use a good grade of lubricating oil on both parts and don't stop after you start pressing
   D. Press them together dry

5. A loose arbor press ram may cause:
   A. A keyway broach to "hog" in or a bushing to twist out of alignment
   B. A keyway broach to twist and cause an excessively wide keyway and a mandrel to "hog" in half way through the bore
   C. A loss of pressure making it difficult to force a broach through the work
   D. None of the above

6. The amount of pressure you should apply to a bushing in an arbor press would be:
   A. Between 10 and 30 tons
   B. Just the amount needed to push it through the bore and then considerable more force applied to make sure it is seated
   C. Just the amount needed to push it through the bore and when slight additional resistance is felt, stop pressing
   D. About 5 tons

7. A ball bearing that is on a shaft or in a housing should be removed:
   A. By pushing on and supporting any part of the bearing that is accessible
   B. By applying pressure only to that race that is supported securely by the press plate
   C. Only by pushing on the inner race when the outer race is in a housing or by pushing on the outer race when the inner race is on a shaft
   D. B and C above

8. A mandrel will slip into a bore on one of its ends. Why then does it press tightly in the bore?
   A. It has been made rough by a knurling process in the center thus enlarging it slightly
   B. The high pressure lubricant applied to its surface causes the bore to tighten up on it
   C. It is made in a "barrel" shape so that it is slightly larger in the center than at the ends.
   D. It is made very slightly tapered so that it is somewhat larger at one end

9. What two important things should be done before pressing in a bushing?
   A. Chamfer and lubricate the bore
   B. Clean all the oil off the bushing and wash your hands so you won't get it contaminated
   C. Oil the bushing and start it in the bore with a hammer before you start pressing
   D. None of the above

10. When using broaches in the arbor press, you should avoid:
    A. Loose press rams and lack of clearance for the broach through the press plate
    B. Lack of lubrication of the broach and using the broach on hard materials
    C. Using an ill fitting bushing and having less than two teeth contacting the work
    D. All of the above

Volume I, Section B   Date __________ Name ______________________________

UNIT 3. NONCUTTING HAND TOOLS

POST TEST

Circle the letter preceding the correct answer.

1. A machinist's bench vise is measured by:
   A. The height of the vise
   B. The width of the jaws
   C. How far it will open
   D. Its overall length

2. "Soft" jaws are sometimes put on a vise to:
   A. Protect the workpiece
   B. Protect the vise jaws
   C. Provide a new gripping surface
   D. Give more gripping power

3. C-clamps are mostly used by machinists for:
   A. Holding delicate measuring and layout setups
   B. Clamping workpieces on the bench for filing and sawing
   C. Clamping workpieces on machines such as drill presses
   D. Holding vises on milling machines and shapers

4. Large water pump pliers can be used:
   A. To loosen arbor nuts
   B. For any bolt or nut it will extend to fit
   C. For unfinished packing nuts, pipe and pipe fittings
   D. All of the above

5. One type of tool is least likely to slip when holding small parts. It is the:
   A. Lever jawed wrench
   B. Slip joint plier
   C. Water pump plier
   D. Parallel jaw cutting plier

6. What should a 2½ or 3 pound ball peen hammer be used for?
   A. Layout work
   B. Reposition work in a machine vise
   C. Hammering on wrench handles to break loose stubborn threads
   D. General heavy bending and hammering

7. When disassembling a machine, a few light blows are needed on the end of a shaft to remove it. Which is the proper tool to use?
   A. 3 pound ball peen hammer
   B. Plastic or rawhide mallet
   C. 8 ounce ball peen hammer
   D. Mall

8. An advantage of the adjustable wrench is that one tool can be used for many sizes. What are its disadvantages?
   A. If it is adjusted too loosely, it will slip and round off the nut or bolt head. This is also hard on the user's knuckles.
   B. It is bulkier than end wrenches and will not fit in some places
   C. A and B above
   D. There are no disadvantages

9. Besides pipe and pipe fittings, pipe wrenches can be used on:
   A. Ground and polished shafting
   B. Nuts and bolt heads
   C. Cold finished round stock
   D. None of the above

10. Standard screwdrivers will slip and may damage the slot if:
    A. The blade is too narrow or too wide
    B. The hardness or temper has been drawn out by overheating
    C. The point is misshapen
    D. All of the above

Volume I, Section B Date ____________ Name ______________________________

UNIT 4. CUTTING HAND TOOLS: HACKSAWS

POST TEST

Circle the letter preceding the correct answer.

1. The pitch of a hacksaw blade is the same as the:
   A. Set of the blade
   B. Thickness of the blade
   C. Number of teeth per inch
   D. Kerf cut by a blade

2. To start a hacksaw cut easily:
   A. Use short, quick strokes
   B. Draw the saw backwards
   C. Mark the starting point with a center punch
   D. Mark the starting point with a file

3. The speed for sawing is generally how many strokes per minute?
   A. 30
   B. 50
   C. 70
   D. 90

4. Which of the following conditions is most likely to cause a hacksaw blade to break?
   A. Pressure on the return stroke
   B. Sawing too fast
   C. A new blade in an old cut
   D. Tubing cut with a 32 tooth blade

5. Set on a hacksaw blade can be:
   A. Wavy
   B. .025 inch
   C. $\frac{1}{2}$ inch
   D. 18 teeth per inch

6. How many teeth per inch should a hacksaw blade have to cut off a piece of aluminum from a 1 inch square bar?
   A. 14
   B. 18
   C. 24
   D. 32

7. How many teeth per inch should a hacksaw blade have for cutting off thin wall tubing?
   A. 14
   B. 18
   C. 24
   D. 32

8. Which of the following conditions will cause a hacksaw blade to dull quickly?
   A. Too slow sawing speed
   B. Too fast sawing speed
   C. No pressure on the return stroke
   D. Too short a saw blade

9. A new hacksaw blade should not be used to finish a cut started with an old hacksaw blade because:
   A. The kerf would wear rapidly
   B. The set would wear rapidly
   C. It would take too long
   D. The pitch is too coarse

10. A general rule when selecting a hacksaw blade is use a:
   A. Coarse pitch saw for hard materials
   B. Fine pitch saw for soft materials
   C. Blade with at least three teeth in contact with the cutting area
   D. Blade with the greatest number of teeth per inch

Volume I, Section B Date ____________ Name ________________________________

UNIT 5. CUTTING HAND TOOLS: FILES

POST TEST

Circle the letter preceding the correct answer.

1. A mill file is:
   A. Square
   B. Milled
   C. Double cut
   D. Single cut

2. The edge on a file without teeth is called a:
   A. Straight edge
   B. Safe edge
   C. Smooth edge
   D. Flat edge

3. Files are cleaned with a:
   A. File cleaner
   B. Brush card
   C. File card
   D. Bench brush

4. Soft materials should be filed with which kind of file?
   A. Knife
   B. Coarse
   C. Tapered
   D. Flat

5. To get a smooth finish on a workpiece, which kind of file is used?
   A. Single cut
   B. Double cut
   C. Crosscut
   D. Smooth cut

6. File coarseness is designated by numbers on which files?
   A. Mill
   B. Curved tooth
   C. Machine
   D. Needle

7. The life of a file is shortened by:
   A. Too much pressure on the file while filing
   B. Filing too fast
   C. Letting one file lay on top of another
   D. All of the above

8. A file cuts:
   A. Only on the forward stroke
   B. Only on the return stroke
   C. On the forward and return strokes
   D. Better with short strokes

9. Files do not make good pry bars because they are:
   A. Too tough
   B. Too brittle
   C. Not long enough
   D. The wrong shape

10. File handles are used to:
    A. Protect the file
    B. Extend the file
    C. Protect the file user
    D. Extend the file life

Volume I, Section C Date ____________ Name ________________________________

UNIT 1. SYSTEMS OF MEASUREMENT

POST TEST

Circle the letter preceding the correct answer.

1. 2.73 cm is equal to:
   A. .1074 inch
   B. 1.074 inches
   C. .01074 inch
   D. 107.4 inches

2. Knowing inches, to find cm, multiply inches by:
   A. 25.4
   B. .03937
   C. 2.54
   D. 10

3. Knowing mm, to find cm:
   A. Multiply by 10
   B. Divide by 100
   C. Divide by 10
   D. Multiply by 100

4. .0625 inch equals how many mm?
   A. 1.58
   B. .002
   C. 6.25
   D. .625

5. A certain machined part has a length of 1257 mm. Expressed in terms of meters, the part would be how long?
   A. 12570
   B. 1.257
   C. .1257
   D. 125.7

6. Express the tolerance $\pm$ .05 mm in terms of inches to the nearest thousandth.
   A. $\pm$ .127
   B. $\pm$ .005
   C. $\pm$ .050
   D. $\pm$ .002

7. Express the tolerance $\pm$ .125 inch in terms of mm to the nearest $\frac{1}{100}$ mm.
   A. $\pm$ 3
   B. $\pm$ 1.25
   C. $\pm$ 3.17
   D. $\pm$ .05

8. 17.27 cm is equal to how many inches?
   A. 43.865
   B. 6.799
   C. 172.7
   D. .06799

9. A cutting speed of 80 feet per minute is equal to approximately how many cm per minute?
   A. 800
   B. 38
   C. 960
   D. 2438.4

10. During a certain machining operation, 12 cubic inches of material are removed. This amount expressed in terms of cubic centimeters would be equal to how many cm^3?
    A. 196
    B. 1966
    C. 16.38
    D. 163.8

Volume I, Section C Date ____________ Name ________________________________

UNIT 2. USING STEEL RULES

POST TEST

Obtain the rule measuring kit from your instructor. The kit will contain 10 objects to be measured with the six-inch fractional rule, six-inch decimal rule, and 150 mm metric rule. Measure the objects accurately and record the dimensions of each in the following table.

Part	Fractional Dimension	Decimal Dimension	Metric Dimension
1. Length of bar A	________	________	________
2. Length of bar B	________	________	________
3. Length of bar C	________	________	________
4. Length of bar D	________	________	________
5. Outside diameter of E	________	________	________
6. Inside diameter of E	________	________	________
7. Outside diameter of F	________	________	________
8. Inside diameter of F	________	________	________
9. Outside diameter of G	________	________	________
10. Inside diameter of G	________	________	________

Volume I, Section C Date ____________ Name ________________________________

UNIT 3. USING VERNIER CALIPERS AND VERNIER DEPTH GAGES

POST TEST

Part 1. Measuring with the Inch Vernier Caliper

Obtain the inch vernier caliper measuring test kit from your instructor. Measure and record the dimension indicated on the objects in the kit to the nearest .001 inch.

A. _____ Outside diameter of washer

B. _____ Outside diameter of pin

C. _____ Width of square stock

D. _____ Length of flat stock

E. _____ Length of square stock

F. _____ Width of flat stock

G. _____ Outside diameter of bushing

H. _____ Inside diameter of bushing

I. _____ Length of pin

Part 2. Measuring with the Metric Vernier Caliper

Obtain the metric vernier caliper measuring test kit from your instructor. Measure and record the dimensions indicated on the objects in the kit to the nearest .02mm.

A. _____ Inside diameter of bushing

_____ Outside diameter of bushing

B. _____ Inside diameter of bushing

_____ Outside diameter of bushing

C. _____ Diameter of pin

D. _____ Outside diameter of washer

E. _____ Width of flat stock

F. _____ Length of flat stock

G. _____ Length of square stock

H. _____ Width of square stock

Part 3. Measuring with the Vernier Depth Gage (Inch)

Obtain the inch vernier depth gage measuring test kit from your instructor. The test piece has five flat bottomed holes with counterbored recesses. Measure the depth of the holes and counterbores to the nearest .001 inch and record the results.

A. _____ Hole depth

_____ Counterbore depth

B. _____ Hole depth

_____ Counterbore depth

C. _____ Hole depth

_____ Counterbore depth

D. _____ Hole depth

_____ Counterbore depth

E. _____ Hole depth

_____ Counterbore depth

Volume I, Section C Date ____________ Name ________________________________

UNIT 5. USING MICROMETER INSTRUMENTS

POST TEST

Circle the letter preceding the correct answer.

1. A standard micrometer has a discrimination of what part of an inch?
   A. .100
   B. .010
   C. .001
   D. .0001

2. The distance between the graduations on the sleeve is what part of an inch?
   A. .001
   B. .025
   C. .040
   D. .050

3. The part of the micrometer which carries the .001 inch graduations is called:
   A. Sleeve
   B. Carrier
   C. Spindle
   D. Thimble

4. How many threads per inch are on a micrometer spindle?
   A. 10
   B. 25
   C. 40
   D. 100

5. A two-inch micrometer measures from:
   A. 1 to 2 inches
   B. 2 to 3 inches
   C. 0 to 2 inches
   D. 2 inches and up

6. The part of the micrometer which supports the anvil is called the:
   A. Support
   B. Spindle
   C. Brace
   D. Frame

7. The scale which permits reading a micrometer to .0001 inch is called the:
   A. Decimal
   B. Vernier
   C. Micro
   D. Milli

8. What part of a micrometer assures repeated equal measuring pressure?
   A. Friction spindle
   B. Spindle lock
   C. Ratchet stop
   D. Pressure regulator

9. In order to be certain of the dimension when measuring with a micrometer:
   A. Take at least one reading
   B. Take at least two readings
   C. Show the mike to a friend
   D. Show the mike to your instructor

10. When measuring a workpiece still hot from machining:
    A. Take a quick measurement
    B. Do not let the anvil touch the work
    C. Warm up the micrometer
    D. Cool off the workpiece

POST TEST EXERCISE

Obtain the measuring kits from your instructor and follow his instructions on their use.

Volume I, Section C Date ____________ Name ________________________________

UNIT 7. USING COMPARISON MEASURING INSTRUMENTS

POST TEST

Circle the letter preceding the correct answer.

1. To measure a $\frac{5}{16}$ inch inside round corner, you would use a:
   A. Fillet gage
   B. Inside corner gage
   C. Radius gage
   D. Curbometer

2. You wish to measure 1500 parts produced on an automatic screw machine. The tolerance is $\pm$ .005 inch. This measurement could be best done:
   A. On an electronic comparator with .00005 inch discrimination
   B. With a dial indicator comparator with .001 inch discrimination
   C. With a vernier micrometer with .0001 inch discrimination
   D. On an optical comparator

3. A common comparison measuring system for holes ranging from approximately ½ to 6 inches would be a:
   A. Telescoping gage and micrometer
   B. Binocular gage and scale
   C. Dial bore gage
   D. Small hole gage

4. A certain workpiece in a lathe chuck must be adjusted so that it runs on center. A suitable tool for this would be a:
   A. Concentricity gage
   B. Dial comparator gage
   C. Center gage
   D. Dial indicator

5. A precise square that has the ability to indicate the amount of deviation from true perpendicularity is a:
   A. Cylindrical square or micrometer square
   B. Precision beveled edge square
   C. Combination square
   D. Solid beam square

6. You wish to check the outline of a form lathe cutter to determine whether it has been properly ground. This could be done on:
   A. A dial comparator
   B. A profilometer
   C. A radius gage
   D. An optical comparator

7. A type of fixed precision square that provides a single line of contact with the workpiece is a:
   A. Solid beam square
   B. Cylindrical square
   C. Precision beveled edge square
   D. Micrometer square

8. You have just drilled and reamed a one-fourth inch diameter hole. In order to check the size, you could use a:
   A. Telescoping gage
   B. Small hole gage and micrometer
   C. Dial bore gage
   D. Dial test indicator

9. When transferring height measurements using a precision height gage micrometer, what should always be used?
   A. Planer gage
   B. Height gage scriber
   C. Dial test indicator
   D. Dial comparator

10. Assuming a dial indicator misalignment of 10 degrees from the axis of measurement, the cosine error in .200 inch of movement along the axis of measurement would amount to what part of an inch?
   A. .202
   B. .209
   C. .205
   D. .203

Volume I, Section C Date ____________ Name ______________________________

UNIT 8. USING GAGE BLOCKS

POST TEST

Circle the letter preceding the correct answer.

1. An AA set of gage blocks has a size tolerance of ± .000002 inch. This set is:
   A. A shop grade set
   B. An inspection grade set
   C. A laboratory grade set
   D. An always accurate set

2. A conditioning stone is:
   A. Used to bevel gage block edges
   B. A fine abrasive
   C. Used as a gage block heat sink
   D. Used sparingly for deburring gage blocks

3. As gage blocks are disassembled and replaced, they are:
   A. Thoroughly cleaned
   B. Coated with preservative
   C. Handled only with cloth or tissue
   D. All of the above

4. Wear blocks are used:
   A. For machine setups involving cutting tools only
   B. To determine the accuracy of optical flats
   C. To protect the gage blocks on the end of the stack from damage by direct contact
   D. To gain additional measuring capacity with the gage block set

5. Corrosion mainly is a problem with gage blocks and is caused from:
   A. Leaving blocks wrung for extended periods of time
   B. Handling gage blocks
   C. Using incorrect preservatives
   D. Using impure solvents

6. A heat sink, in regard to gage blocks, is:
   A. Used to maintain the temperature in the gage lab at a constant level
   B. Used to restore gage block temperature to the surrounding temperature
   C. A device to calibrate thermometers used to check gage block temperature
   D. Used to keep gage blocks from warping due to heat

7. When assembling a gage block stack with assembly screws:
   A. A torque screwdriver should be used
   B. Tighten one and one-half turns to displace any air in the wringing interval
   C. Use any available screwdriver
   D. Gage blocks need not be wrung as the screw will hold them together

8. Make up a minimum gage block stack for the dimension 3.3947 inches without wear blocks. Use the space below.

9. Make up a minimum gage block stack for the dimension 3.3947 inches using a .050 inch wear block on each end of the stack. Use the space below.

10. A good wringing interval is what part of an inch per interval?
    A. .00004
    B. .00002
    C. .000003
    D. .000002

Volume I, Section D   Date ____________ Name ________________________________

UNIT 1. SAFETY IN MATERIAL HANDLING

POST TEST

Circle the letter preceding the correct answer.

1. When lifting, use your:
   A. Back
   B. Legs
   C. Best arm
   D. Total strength

2. The advantages of an electric hoist over hand lifting and carrying are:
   A. Maneuverability and lifting power
   B. Speed of lifting and moving from place to place
   C. You never have to wait to move something
   D. Unlimited lifting power

3. When operating a hoist or crane:
   A. Always stand clear of the load
   B. Watch out for someone else who might be in the way
   C. Use a spreader bar on long loads
   D. All of the above

4. To avoid serious cuts for yourself and others when cutting off steel:
   A. Don't pick up the saw chips
   B. Speed up the saw to avoid a burr
   C. Deburr the saw cut
   D. Don't carry stock material by hand

5. Continuous noise above 85 decibels without ear protection can contribute to:
   A. A gradual impairment of vision or deafness
   B. Hearing loss
   C. Speech and hearing loss
   D. Loss of hair

6. Hot metals can cause bad burns. What can you do to help avoid such accidents when working with them?
   A. Wear heavy gloves and face shield
   B. Identify hot metals with a mark
   C. Keep sand on the floor when pouring molten metals
   D. All of the above

7. What will extinguish burning magnesium chips?
   A. Water
   B. Soda-acid fire extinguisher
   C. Sand
   D. Oxygen gas

8. Burning and welding on galvanized steel makes a person ill if there is not adequate ventilation. This is caused by what kind of poisoning?
   A. Zinc metal
   B. Radiation
   C. Lead
   D. Cyanide

9. Mercury is one of several metals whose vapors and compounds are not only poisonous to animal life, but have another bad characteristic in that they are:
   A. Radioactive
   B. Cumulative
   C. Known to be contagious
   D. None of the above

10. A carburizing compound that is very deadly to use without adequate ventilating equipment is:
    A. Carbo-nitriding compound
    B. Carbonaceous compounds
    C. Kasenite
    D. Potassium cyanide

Volume I, Section D   Date __________ Name ______________________________

UNIT 2. PIG IRON AND STEEL MAKING

POST TEST

Circle the letter preceding the correct answer.

1. The major element that needs to be removed from iron ore in order to produce pig iron is:
   A. Sulfur
   B. Oxygen
   C. Phosphorus
   D. Carbon

2. Pig iron is the basis for such products as:
   A. Cast aluminum and bronze
   B. Coke and limestone
   C. Cast iron and steel
   D. None of the above

3. Three essential raw materials are needed to produce cast iron. What are they?
   A. Limestone, coke and iron ore
   B. Iron ore, limestone and gangue
   C. Scrap steel, iron ore and coke
   D. Limestone, scrap steel and iron ore

4. The carbon content of pig iron is:
   A. Between 20 and 45 percent
   B. Between .05 and 2 percent
   C. Between 2 and 4.5 percent
   D. None of the above

5. Iron ore is enriched before shipment to the smelter by a process called:
   A. Glomming
   B. Ore dressing
   C. Salting
   D. Reduction

6. What major changes take place in the pig iron in the steel making furnace?
   A. Carbon is added to it to give it a higher carbon content so it will cast in the ingot without porosity.
   B. The carbon is removed; a small amount is added in the ladle. Most impurities are removed.
   C. Nothing is changed except that some things like manganese and silicon are added.
   D. None of the above

7. What kind of steels do electric furnaces mostly produce?
   A. Stainless and special alloy
   B. Open hearth
   C. Rimmed
   D. Cold rolled

8. "Killed" steel is:
   A. Decarburized steel
   B. Deoxidized steel
   C. Steel lanced with an oxygen lance
   D. None of the above

9. What does the basic oxygen furnace use to produce steel?
   A. Hot air blasts
   B. Oxygen lances
   C. Cold air blasts
   D. Electrodes

10. One major drawback of the Bessemer converter as compared to other steel making processes is:
    A. It doesn't get hot enough
    B. It is too slow
    C. It cannot utilize large quantities of scrap steel
    D. It wears out too soon

Volume I, Section D Date ___________ Name ______________________________

UNIT 3. STEEL FINISHING PROCESSES

POST TEST

Circle the letter preceding the correct answer.

1. Which one of the following does the soaking pit uniformly heat and bring to rolling temperature?
   A. Bloom
   B. Ingot
   C. Billet
   D. Slab

2. The grain structure of the ingot is improved by:
   A. Teeming
   B. Soaking
   C. Stripping
   D. Rolling

3. What percent of carbon does ordinary mild steel contain?
   A. 0.05 to 0.20
   B. 0.20 to 1.00
   C. 0.50 to 1.00
   D. 0.05 to 1.7

4. How do the distorted grains in cold finished steel make it different than an equivalent hot rolled steel?
   A. Softer
   B. More ductile
   C. Stronger
   D. Rougher

5. Cold finished steels have a black, scaly surface.
   A. True
   B. False

6. How is a forged part different than an equivalent cast or machined part?
   A. Stronger
   B. Weaker
   C. Better looking
   D. More accurate

7. Tubing that is made by piercing a billet and rolling over a mandrel is called:
   A. Butt welded
   B. Billet
   C. Electric
   D. Seamless

8. Small pipe and tube are cold formed. How are they welded?
   A. Arc
   B. Resistance
   C. Submerged
   D. Pressure

9. Tin plating and galvanizing prevents rusting.
   A. True
   B. False

10. Wire is made by:
   A. Pulling it through sets of rolls
   B. Extruding it through a die
   C. Pulling it through sets of dies
   D. None of the above

Volume I, Section D   Date ____________   Name ______________________________

UNIT 4. SELECTION AND IDENTIFICATION OF STEELS

POST TEST

Circle the letter preceding the correct answer.

1. What numerical system is used to designate carbon and alloy steels?
   A. Color based
   B. SAE - AISI
   C. ISAE - AES
   D. U.S.A.

2. Three basic types of stainless steel are:
   A. Martensitic, Ferritic and Austenitic
   B. Troositic, Martensitic and Ferritic
   C. Graphitic, Normalized and Resulfurized
   D. Electric, Basic and Open hearth

3. Which of the following is a resulfurized, free machining steel?
   A. AISI C4140
   B. AISI C1040
   C. AISI C8620
   D. AISI B1113

4. A soft form of iron that can be readily cast into molds and is very machinable is called:
   A. Wrought iron
   B. White cast iron
   C. Grey cast iron
   D. Low carbon steel

5. The letter "O" as assigned to tool steels designates:
   A. Oil hardening steels
   B. Over stressed steels
   C. Steels annealed in ovens
   D. Steels that were made from selected ores

6. The weight of one square foot of steel one inch thick is 40.80 lbs. A steel bar ½ inch x 6 inches x 8 feet long is rated at 30 cents per pound. What is the cost of the bar?
   A. $ 8.16
   B. $81.60
   C. $ 2.45
   D. $24.48

7. The file hardness test is useful to determine:
   A. Brinell or Rockwell hardness numbers exactly
   B. The machinability and relative hardness of metals
   C. The carbon content of steels
   D. All of the above

8. Austenitic steels are always:
   A. Harder than ferritic steels
   B. Weaker than ferritic steels
   C. Nonmagnetic when annealed
   D. None of the above

9. Certain nonferrous metals are magnetic; among these is:
   A. Copper
   B. Aluminum
   C. Titanium
   D. Nickel

10. When selecting steel some things you should keep in mind are:
    A. Pliability, friability and its amorphous structure
    B. Hardness, machinability, strength
    C. Point of origin, lot number
    D. Age of steel, color

Volume I, Section D   Date ____________   Name ____________________________________

UNIT 5. SELECTION AND IDENTIFICATION OF NONFERROUS METALS

POST TEST

Circle the letter preceding the correct answer.

1. A good construction material for a bridge across a river would be:
   A. Magnesium
   B. Aluminum
   C. Steel
   D. Titanium

2. The letter "T" following the four digit number designating aluminum represents:
   A. Temper
   B. Solution heat treatment
   C. Strain hardened and tested
   D. Titanium alloyed with aluminum

3. How is magnesium different than aluminum?
   A. Brighter
   B. Stronger
   C. Heavier
   D. Lighter

4. Copper wire is basically pure copper that has been hardened by:
   A. Strain hardening
   B. Precipitation hardening
   C. Heating to 1200° F. (649° C.) and quenching in water
   D. Alloying with tin and zinc

5. What does an alloy of tin and copper make? An alloy of zinc and copper?
   A. Brass, bronze
   B. Bronze, die cast
   C. Bronze, brass
   D. High temperature solder, galvanizing compound

6. Unalloyed nickel is the metal used for:
   A. United States nickel coins
   B. Electroplating
   C. Electric power lines
   D. All of the above

7. Galvanizing, sherardizing and tin plate are all familiar uses of zinc, lead and tin. On what are these processes usually performed and what do they resist?
   A. Die cast, deformation
   B. Pipe joints, leaking
   C. Babbitt bearings, wear
   D. Steel, corrosion

8. Steels are often alloyed with planned amounts of nonferrous metals such as:
   A. Aluminum and magnesium
   B. Molybdenum and tungsten
   C. Hydrogen, nitrogen and oxygen
   D. Sulfur, phosphorus and hydrogen

9. Babbitt metals are made in three basic types. They are:
   A. Tin, lead and cadmium
   B. Lead, gold and silver
   C. Tin, cadmium and silver
   D. Zinc, lead and tin

10. Molding with high pressures uses various metal bases. What are these metals called?
    A. Babbitt type
    B. Investment casting
    C. Die cast
    D. Permanent mold

Volume I, Section D Date ____________ Name ______________________________________

UNIT 6. HARDENING, TEMPERING AND CASE HARDENING

POST TEST

Circle the letter preceding the correct answer.

1. Quenching high carbon tool steel (about 1.0 percent carbon) from 1200° F. (649° C.) causes:
   A. Martensite to form
   B. No increase in hardness
   C. Annealing of the metal
   D. None of the above

2. If wrought iron or very low carbon steel (.10 percent carbon) is quenched from a red heat about 1500° F. (815° C.), it will:
   A. Remain soft
   B. Crack or split
   C. Get hard
   D. Need to be tempered

3. The severity of water quench sometimes causes:
   A. One inch thick sections to harden clear through
   B. Lack of hardening in W1 steels
   C. Bubbles to form inside the steel
   D. Distortion and cracking

4. The greatest advantage of case hardening processes is that:
   A. A case hardened part can remain as hard as Rc60 all the way through without the need for tempering and still be just as tough as a similar tempered part
   B. Low carbon steels can be made very hard on the surface only while the core remains soft and tough
   C. It makes possible the hardening of thicker sections completely through while using an oil quench to avoid distortion
   D. Surface hardening can be done on any ferrous metal that contains sufficient carbon. Induction heating and flame hardening are two methods used. Lathe ways and gear teeth are examples.

5. The correct temperature for quenching carbon steels is how many degrees above the upper critical limit?
   A. 1450
   B. 100
   C. 50
   D. 200

6. High carbon steel is tempered after being hardened to:
   A. Toughen and soften it
   B. Anneal it
   C. Give it a good color
   D. Make the grains smaller

7. Which of the following would require the highest tempering temperature?
   A. Steel cutting tool
   B. Wood chisel
   C. Cold chisel
   D. Spring steel part

8. Which oxide color will show when tempering a steel cutting tool?
   A. Blue
   B. Light straw
   C. Violet
   D. Grey

9. When a carbon steel cutting tool such as a drill is heated to a blue color, it has:
   A. Lost its temper
   B. Been retempered and is harder
   C. Been retempered and is softer
   D. Not been affected at all

10. After hardening, tempering should be done:
   A. Within 24 hours
   B. Whenever time permits
   C. Immediately
   D. If one feels it is needed for his particular job

Volume I, Section D Date ____________ Name ________________________________

UNIT 7. ANNEALING, NORMALIZING AND STRESS RELIEVING

POST TEST

Circle the letter preceding the correct answer.

1. Castings and forgings with a nonuniform grain structure need to be:
   A. Annealed
   B. Process annealed
   C. Normalized
   D. Spheroidized

2. The normalizing temperature is:
   A. 100° F. (38° C.) above the upper critical T line
   B. 50° F. (10° C.) above the upper critical T line
   C. Close to 1300° F. (704° C.)
   D. 950° F. (510° C.) to 1250° F. (677° C.)

3. The spheroidizing temperature is:
   A. 100° F. (38° C.) above the upper critical T line
   B. 50° F. (10° C.) above the upper critical T line
   C. Close to 1300° F. (704° C.)
   D. 950° F. (510° C.) to 1250° F. (677° C.)

4. Which type grain structure is mostly affected by stress relief anneal?
   A. Hard carbides and pealite grains
   B. Cold worked ferrite grains
   C. All grains are recrystallized
   D. Intermetallic compounds and martensite

5. The stress relief temperature is:
   A. Close to 1300° F. (704° C.)
   B. 50° F. (10° C.) above the upper critical T line
   C. 100° F. (38° C.) above the upper critical T line
   D. 950° F. (570° C.) to 1250° F. (677° C.)

6. What is sometimes done to high carbon steels to give them free machining qualities?
   A. Spheroidizing
   B. Stress relieving
   C. Normalizing
   D. Process annealing

7. What is the term used by the wire and sheet industry for stress relieving?
   A. Full anneal
   B. Process anneal
   C. Spheroidize anneal
   D. Normalizing

8. After heating to the normalizing temperature, how should the piece be cooled?
   A. By quenching in oil
   B. By cooling to 1300° F. (704° C.), holding for several hours, and then air cooling.
   C. By cooling in still air
   D. By cooling slowly in the furnace

9. After heating to the full annealing temperature, how should the piece be cooled?
   A. By cooling in still air
   B. By slowly cooling in the furnace
   C. By quenching in oil
   D. None of the above

10. Low carbon steels that are spheroidized tend to be:
   A. Work hardening
   B. Free machining
   C. "Gummy"
   D. More likely to produce good finishes

Volume I, Section D Date ____________ Name ____________________________________

UNIT 8. OTHER METALS USED IN MACHINING

POST TEST

Circle the letter preceding the correct answer.

1. What makes wrought (worked) aluminum different than cast aluminum?
   A. Lower strength
   B. Higher strength
   C. More alloying elements
   D. Less hardness

2. A built up edge on a lathe tool bit can be avoided when machining aluminum by using:
   A. Large back rake angles
   B. Cutting oils
   C. Correct cutting speeds
   D. All of the above

3. Water based coolants should not be used for machining magnesium because:
   A. They would tend to increase a fire in the event the chips ignited and burned
   B. They tend to contaminate the metal
   C. They do not do an adequate job of cooling and a rough finish is produced
   D. All of the above

4. The rake angle for tools used on brasses and bronzes should be:
   A. Positive
   B. Negative
   C. Zero
   D. Variable

5. Besides iron, stainless steels contain large amounts of:
   A. Aluminum
   B. Chromium
   C. Manganese
   D. Copper

6. Since stainless steels tend to work harden, a good general rule to follow when machining them is:
   A. Slow speeds, heavy feeds
   B. Light feeds, fast speeds
   C. Very steep back rakes and high speeds
   D. High speed tools with light feeds

7. One way to tap a thread in work hardening stainless steel is to select a tap drill that will produce what percent of thread?
   A. 100
   B. 80
   C. 60
   D. .05

8. Which is the most difficult one of the following types of cast iron to machine?
   A. Malleable
   B. Chilled
   C. Nodular
   D. Gray

9. The machinability of gray cast iron is more or less affected by·
   A. Coolant
   B. Feeds
   C. Welds
   D. All of the above

10. Some chilled cast irons can be machined by using:
   A. High speed steel tools
   B. The proper carbide tool
   C. Carbon steel tools
   D. All of the above

Volume I, Section D Date ___________ Name ________________________________

UNIT 9. CASTING PROCESSES

POST TEST

Circle the letter preceding the correct answer.

1. Two types of sand casting are:
   A. Shell molding and green sand molding
   B. Investment casting and rammed castings
   C. Green sand molding and dry sand molding
   D. Flask molding and core molding

2. Patterns are made of:
   A. A refractory material
   B. Aluminum oxide or silicon carbide
   C. Wood, metal or wax
   D. Baked sand which contains organic resins or linseed oil

3. Cores are made by:
   A. Hollowing out the patterns so the rammed green sand will be formed inside
   B. Making separate cores of green sand and baking them in an oven
   C. The shell molding process using dry molding sand
   D. Ramming dry molding sand into a mold and baking the green cores in an oven

4. A device placed in a mold to control or increase the cooling rate of the casting is called a:
   A. Chill
   B. Thermocouple
   C. Match plate
   D. Cold sheet

5. Shell molds are made by:
   A. Using a mixture of ground up oyster shells and sand to form a mold around a pattern
   B. Bringing a heated metal pattern into contact with a dry molding sand
   C. Casting a thin "shell" of plaster of paris around a wax pattern which is then removed by heating the mold
   D. Blowing dry molding sand into a core box

6. When molten metal is poured into a rapidly rotating mold, the method of casting is called:
   A. Metal spinning
   B. Centripetal casting
   C. Centrifugal casting
   D. Gravity casting

7. Investment casting molders use a:
   A. One-piece mold with a wax pattern
   B. Two-piece mold with a metal pattern
   C. Two-piece mold with wooden patterns having match plates between them
   D. Two-piece metal die

8. Permanent molds:
   A. Are used over and over and never wear out
   B. Must be discarded after a few thousand castings
   C. Produce a poor finish and low precision on the product as compared to sand castings
   D. Are shells of dry molding sand formed and baked on a metal pattern

9. Molten metal is:
   A. Poured into dies in a die casting machine or injected under pressure into a permanent mold
   B. Kept in a melting pot which has a plunger and gooseneck on the cold-chamber machine
   C. Injected under pressure in a die casting machine or poured into a permanent mold
   D. B and C above

10. Die casting produces:
   A. Intricate precision castings at high production rates
   B. Very small to very large precision castings
   C. Precision castings, but with poor mechanical properties
   D. All of the above

Volume I, Section D   Date __________ Name ______________________________

UNIT 10. ROCKWELL AND BRINELL HARDNESS TESTERS

POST TEST

Circle the letter preceding the correct answer.

1. The Rockwell and Brinell Hardness Testers utilize the specific property of hardness known as:
   A. Elastic hardness
   B. Resistance to abrasion
   C. Resistance to penetration
   D. Hardenability

2. The Rockwell Hardness Tester measures:
   A. The rebound
   B. The depth of penetration
   C. Wear
   D. The amount of pressure required to penetrate to major depth

3. When hardness increases, what else also increases?
   A. Ductility
   B. Depth of penetration
   C. Tensile strength
   D. Plasticity

4. What will happen to the Rockwell steel ball penetrator, if it is used for testing hard steels?
   A. It will flatten and become inaccurate
   B. It will become embedded in the specimen
   C. It will roll and cause the specimen to fly out
   D. None of the above

5. On the Brinell tester, how much load should be used for testing steel?
   A. 10 mm.
   B. 500 kg.
   C. 3000 kg.
   D. 150 kgf.

6. Which of the following penetrators should be used for testing thin brass sheet?
   A. "A" Brale
   B. One-sixteenth inch ball penetrator
   C. "N" Brale
   D. "C" Brale

7. Which anvil, because of its hardness, will not become indented when used for superficial testing?
   A. Spot anvil
   B. V anvil
   C. Plane anvil
   D. Diamond spot anvil

8. The test results can be affected by the specimen having:
   A. Excessive roughness on the surface
   B. A curved surface
   C. Been tested too near an edge
   D. All of the above

9. Hardened tool steel that has been decarburized while in the furnace is:
   A. The same hardness throughout the piece
   B. Harder just under the surface "skin".
   C. Case hardened, having only a hardened surface
   D. Impossible to test in the Rockwell or Brinell testers

10. Testing of angular surfaces such as knife blades is permissible if the angle does not exceed how many degrees from the horizontal?
    A. 10
    B. 2
    C. 5
    D. 3

Volume I, Section D Date ____________ Name ____________________________________

UNIT 11. NONDESTRUCTIVE TESTING

POST TEST

Circle the letter preceding the correct answer.

1. Nondestructive testing is used for:
   A. Measuring physical properties of metals without going past the point of rupture or failure
   B. Determining discontinuities in lattice structures of metals by the use of X-ray diffraction technique
   C. Determining metal alloy content
   D. None of the above

2. Magnetic particle inspection may be used on:
   A. Iron, steel and all nonferrous metals
   B. Any material
   C. Only iron and steel or other ferromagnetic metals and alloys
   D. None of the above

3. New magnetic poles are formed at a crack in a part if it is magnetized:
   A. Lengthwise for a crosswise crack and circular for a lengthwise crack
   B. Circular for a crosswise crack and lengthwise for a lengthwise crack
   C. Lengthwise on one end only, where the crack is located, to concentrate the magnetic field
   D. None of the above

4. Fluorescent penetrants are:
   A. Used only on ferromagnetic metals such as iron and steel since the dye is attracted to the defect by magnetic capillary action
   B. Used on all metals and many nonmetals
   C. Able to locate the defect by showing it with a colored dye
   D. Only available in very small test kits

5. Dye penetrant types have the advantage of:
   A. Being able to detect deep flaws and inclusions not exposed to the surface
   B. Making the defect show up clearer than with any other method
   C. Detecting physical and composition changes on a coninuous moving strip of material
   D. Being portable, easy to use and low in cost

6. Two systems of ultrasonic testing are:
   A. The through-transmission and pulse-echo systems
   B. The transducer-reciever and two-transducer systems
   C. The dry and wet methods
   D. None of the above

7. What kind of defects can be found with ultrasonic testing?
   A. Surface defects only
   B. Internal flaws, porosity, laminations and weld bonds
   C. Differences in alloy composition and in heat treatment
   D. Surface defects stand out with a bright color so they can be easily detected

8. X-rays can help us to detect flaws in materials by:
   A. Reflecting off the part and then going into a transducer, which shows on an oscilloscope screen as a "pip"
   B. Being reflected off the part and onto a photographic plate. This is then developed to reveal any flaws
   C. Going through the part and onto a photographic plate which is then developed to reveal any flaws
   D. None of the above

9. X-rays and gamma ray inspections are similar except that:
   A. X-rays are directed and gamma rays go in all directions
   B. Gamma rays are liable to damage steel
   C. You don't need any shielding or protection from X-rays like you do with gamma radiation
   D. None of the above

10. Eddy current inspection is limited to:
   A. Ferromagnetic metals
   B. Dielectric materials only
   C. Piezoelectric materials
   D. Electrically conducting materials

Volume I, Section D Date ____________ Name ________________________________

UNIT 12. NONMETALLIC MATERIALS

POST TEST

Circle the letter preceding the correct answer.

1. Thermosetting plastics such as phenolics and epoxies:
   A. Harden when cooled and soften when heated
   B. Harden by a chemical action when heated and will remain hard when reheated
   C. Are used for injection molding and are allowed to "set" in the mold
   D. None of the above

2. Thermoplastics such as nylons, vinyls and acrylics:
   A. Harden when cooled and soften when heated
   B. Harden by a chemical action when heated and will remain hard when reheated
   C. Are all nonorganic materials that are so difficult to machine that diamond tools are advisable
   D. Have a high rate of heat conductivity which keeps the tool point cool

3. Carbon and ceramic materials cause tool wear primarily because:
   A. Of a rate of thermal conductivity that is extremely high
   B. Of hardness and abrasiveness of the workpiece
   C. They should always be ground rather than machined
   D. None of the above

4. What types of cutting tools are used where low heat dissipation and high abrasion tend to break down conventional tools?
   A. High speed steel and high carbon tool steel
   B. High speed steel and carbides
   C. Grinding tools
   D. Ceramic and diamond tools

5. What can be done to machine ceramic material when the surface is too irregular to machine even with diamond tools?
   A. Grind to size
   B. If it is not machinable, chances are that it can't be ground so it should be scrapped
   C. Use EDM (electrical discharge machining)
   D. None of the above

6. How can soft materials cause tool breakdown?
   A. By hogging in and "grabbing" of the tool, which breaks the tool point off
   B. These soft materials are naturally abrasive and they wear out tools
   C. The sand-like foreign materials that are accidentally embedded in plastics when they are made, wear out tools
   D. Heat generated by cutting is not dissipated readily by these materials so the heat is concentrated at the tool edge. This breaks the tool down since it is operating above its thermal capacity.

7. A fiber reinforced plastic material may:
   A. Be extremely difficult to machine
   B. Cause tool wear as a result of the abrasive fiber material
   C. Be nonmachinable
   D. Need to be machine with a tool shaped like a knife

8. Drills for plastics:
   A. Should have an included point angle of 60 degrees and a zero rake
   B. Should have an included point angle of 140 degrees and a positive rake
   C. Are all carbide tipped
   D. Are all high speed steel

9. The types of cutting tool material used for plastics are:
   A. Low carbon steel, high speed steel, ceramic and diamond tools
   B. High speed steel, ceramics and diamond tools
   C. High speed steel, carbides, ceramics and diamond tools
   D. Drills, tool bits, inserts, carbides and high speed steel

10. Coolants used for machining nonmetallic materials are:
    A. Sulfurized oil, soluble oil, mineral base cutting oils
    B. Air blast, soluble oil, a water-soap solution or plain water
    C. Silicone oils, water soluble oil or lubricating oils
    D. Coolants are not used on any nonmetallic material

Volume I, Section E Date ____________ Name ____________________________________

UNIT 1. CUTOFF MACHINE SAFETY

POST TEST

Circle the letter preceding the correct answer.

1. A primary consideration in cutoff machine safety is:
   A. Ear protection
   B. Eye protection
   C. Foot protection
   D. Use a rag and not your hands to clear chips

2. Bars of material on the roller stock table can:
   A. Possibly bend the rollers
   B. Slide into the moving saw blade
   C. Affect the accuracy of the saw cut
   D. Pinch fingers and hands

3. Overspeeding an abrasive saw can result in:
   A. Increase heat in the cut
   B. Possible blade failure
   C. Faster cutting
   D. No real problems

4. After running a new endless band saw blade, you should:
   A. Stop and see if any teeth are missing
   B. Let the machine run for one hour to break in the blade
   C. Recheck blade tension after a short time
   D. Allow it to cool after each cut

5. When using a cutoff machine with coolant:
   A. Insure that the coolant does not run on the floor
   B. Not use coolant unless absolutely necessary
   C. Shut off the coolant flow when the cut is about two-thirds complete
   D. Insure a coolant flow of at least 5 gallons per minute

Volume I, Section E Date ____________ Name ______________________________________

UNIT 2. USING RECIPROCATING AND HORIZONTAL BAND CUTOFF MACHINES

POST TEST

Circle the letter preceding the correct answer.

1. Saw blade gage is:
   A. Blade thickness
   B. Blade length
   C. Set
   D. Pitch

2. Saw blade pitch is:
   A. The total number of teeth on the blade
   B. The amount of set
   C. A blade coating designed to provide better cutting
   D. The number of teeth per inch

3. You are sawing through a piece of steel tubing with a wall thickness of .250 inch. The pitch of the saw that you use should be at least _____ teeth per inch.
   A. 10
   B. 8
   C. 12
   D. 11

4. The capacity of the horizontal band cutoff machine is determined by the:
   A. Total length of the blade
   B. Largest piece of square material that can be cut
   C. Weight capacity of the roller stock table
   D. Largest piece of round material that can be cut

5. You are sawing a piece of material that has varying shape of cross section. The best blade set for this application is:
   A. Wave
   B. Raker
   C. Straight
   D. Negative

6. Faster cutting can be obtained from what tooth pattern because of the positive rake angle?
   A. Skip
   B. Hook
   C. Standard
   D. Raker

7. Common cutting fluids include:
   A. Water
   B. Soluble oils and synthetic chemicals
   C. Air and oils
   D. Water and oils

8. If the set is gone on one side of a saw blade, the blade will:

   A. Not cut at all
   B. Drift in the direction of the side without set
   C. Drift in the direction of the side with the set
   D. Cut only one-half as fast as if it had set on both sides

9. What is the tooth spacing in inches of a 16 pitch saw blade?

   A. $\frac{1}{16}$

   B. $\frac{1}{32}$

   C. $\frac{1}{8}$

   D. $\frac{1}{64}$

10. Cutting speed is generally:
    A. Fast in tough, hard materials
    B. Slow in soft materials
    C. Fast in soft materials and slow in hard materials
    D. The speed that produces blue chips

Volume I, Section F Date ____________ Name ______________________________

UNIT 1. BASIC SEMI-PRECISION LAYOUT PRACTICE

POST TEST

Layout the tool bit grinding gage (Figure 15) and submit it to your instructor for inspection.

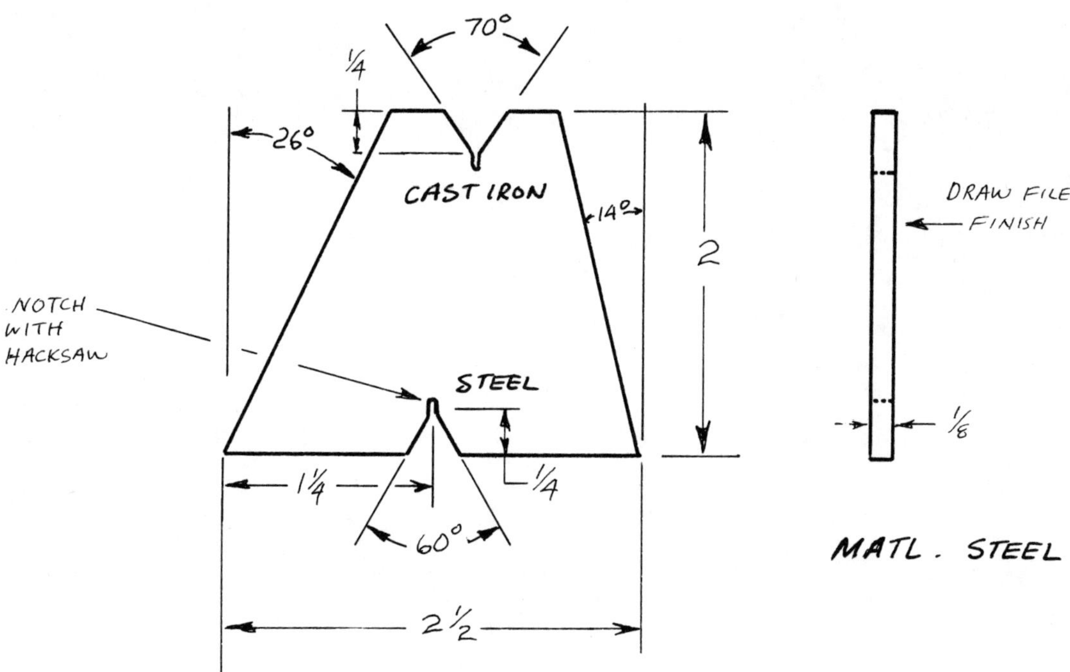

Figure 15. Toolbit Grinding Gage (Lane Community College)

Note: Angles are for tools used in holders with built-in back rake.

Volume I, Section F Date ____________ Name ____________________________________

UNIT 2. BASIC PRECISION LAYOUT PRACTICE

POST TEST

Circle the letter preceding the correct answer.

1. On a 50 division inch vernier height gage, the vernier is coincident at the 23rd line. This means that _____ inch would be ________ to the beam reading.
   A. .023, added
   B. .0023, added
   C. .23, subtracted
   D. .23, added

2. Each one-tenth inch division on the beam scale of a 25 division inch vernier height gage is subdivided into how many parts?
   A. 2
   B. 3
   C. 4
   D. 5

3. Each vernier graduation on a 50 division metric vernier height gage is equal to how many millimeters?
   A. .01
   B. .02
   C. .001
   D. $\frac{1}{50}$

4. The first step in using the height gage after cleaning the layout plate and base is to check the:
   A. Column for perpendicularity
   B. Base for cosine error
   C. Vernier alignment at the top of the beam scale
   D. Alignment of the vernier and beam scale zeros

5. When scribing perpendicular lines, the workpiece must be:
   A. Inverted
   B. Turned 90 degrees
   C. Left as is and the height gage used on an angle plate
   D. Set on a parallel bar

6. Layout lines scribed with a height gage should be:
   A. Only deep enough to remove the layout dye
   B. Scribed so that a permanent mark is left in the work
   C. Short dashed lines
   D. Scribed repeated times to insure a visible mark

7. On a 25 division inch vernier height gage, the vernier is coincident at the 17th line. If the beam scale reads 3.75, the total reading would be:
   A. 3.733
   B. 3.7517
   C. 3.766
   D. 3.767

8. On a 50 division inch vernier height gage, the beam scale reads 7.5 and the vernier is coincident at the first mark. The total reading would be:
   A. 7.499
   B. 7.501
   C. 7.255
   D. 7.500

9. On a 50 division metric height gage, the beam scale reads 151 and the vernier is coincident at the 37th mark. The total reading would be _______ mm.
   A. 151.74
   B. 151.37
   C. 150.26
   D. 150.37

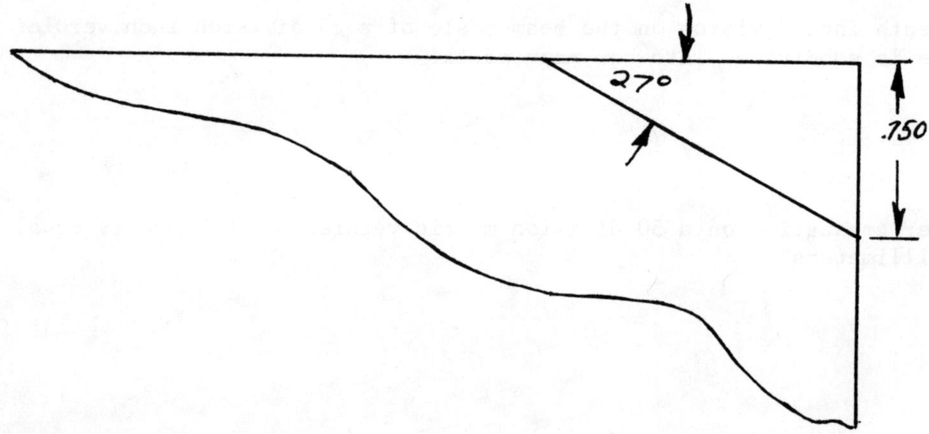

Figure 36.

10. You are laying out an angle of 27 degrees using a 5 inch sine bar. Refer to the example (Figure 36). The sine bar elevation is _______ inch and the vertical distance of the scribe mark below the corner of the workpiece is _____ inch.
    A. 2.269, .750
    B. .667, 2.269
    C. 2.269, .667
    D. .750, 2.269

Volume I, Section G Date __________ Name ________________________________

UNIT 1. DRILLING MACHINE SAFETY

POST TEST

Circle the letter preceding the correct answer.

1. Proper attire for drill press operators would be:
   A. Close fitting clothes without sleeves and having any loose, long hair tied
   B. Loose fitting clothing, light weight shoes and gloves
   C. Short hair, cap, shirt and tie, slacks and oxfords
   D. None of the above

2. If a drill press vise holding the piece being drilled came loose from its clamp and began to spin, what is the first thing you should do?
   A. Call for help and get out of the way
   B. Wait to see if it will fly off the table and, if it does not after a safe interval, shut off the machine
   C. Grab the drill press vise with both hands and hold it while someone near shuts off the machine for you
   D. Quickly shut off the machine

3. Small chips may fly at high speeds toward the drill press operator. How can he protect himself?
   A. Wear leather clothing, heavy boots and a hard hat
   B. He can't; he must just tolerate it as a job hazard
   C. Wear safety glasses
   D. Wear face protection, long, loose sleeves and gloves to keep the small chips from penetrating the arm and hands

4. The best way to clean a Morse taper drill press spindle socket is:
   A. By feeling for nicks and grit with a finger with the machine spindle stopped
   B. By feeling for nicks and grit with a finger, having the machine spindle running
   C. With a stick and a cloth, having the machine running
   D. With a finger and a cloth, having the machine running

5. What is the most important disadvantage of the habit of leaving a chuck key in the drill press chuck?
   A. You can't find the chuck key
   B. It becomes a dangerous missile when the drill press is turned on
   C. When keys are hung on a drill press with a strap or chain, they always get torn off when the drill press is started
   D. All of the above

6. Slowing down a drill press with the hand can cause:
   A. The drill to "grab"
   B. Cuts and abrasions
   C. Chips to wind around the spindle
   D. A "merry-go-round"

7. If both hands are occupied in removing a heavy drill with a drift, how can you keep it from falling to the floor or on your foot?
   A. Catch it in midair
   B. Tie a cord or string to it
   C. You can't, so wear safety toe shoes
   D. Place a block of wood under it

8. You should remove chips from a drill press table by:
   A. Using a brush or stick
   B. Wiping with your hands and a cloth
   C. Using an air jet
   D. The end of the day

9. Oil on the floor can cause:
   A. Your shoes to get messy
   B. You to track oil all over the shop floor
   C. A bad fall, possibly into a running machine
   D. All of the above

10 Sharp edges and burrs should be removed from workpieces as soon as possible because they:
   A. Look unsightly
   B. Weaken the material
   C. Scratch the drill press table
   D. Can cause severe cuts

Volume I, Section G   Date ____________ Name ____________________________________

UNIT 2. THE DRILL PRESS

POST TEST

1. Sensitive drill press. Match the letter of the part in Figure 12 to the correct name listed below.

_____ Guard

_____ Variable speed control

_____ Base

_____ Head

_____ Column

_____ Quill return spring

_____ Motor

_____ Table lock

_____ Depth stop

_____ Quill lock handle

_____ Table lift crank

_____ Power feed

_____ Table

_____ Switch

_____ Spindle

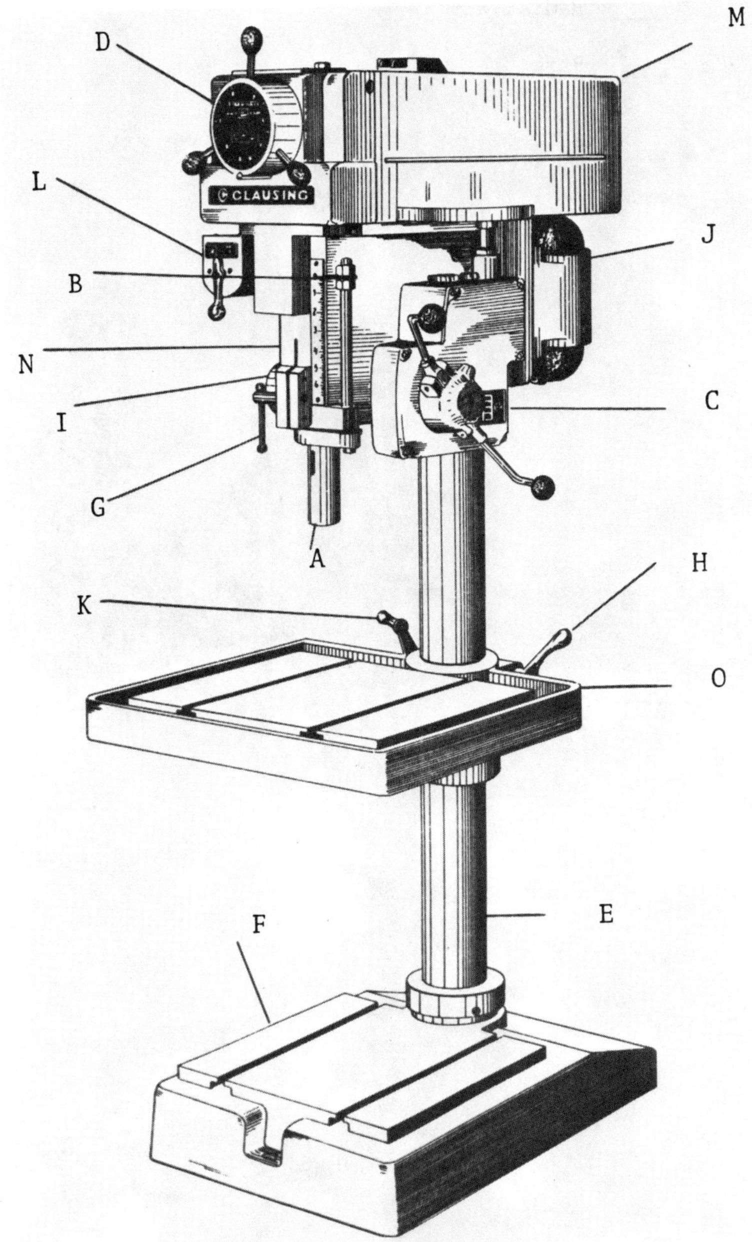

Figure 12 (Courtesy of Clausing Corporation)

2. Radial drill press. Match the letter of the part in Figure 13 to the correct name listed below.

_____ Spindle

_____ Column

_____ Drill head

_____ Radial arm

_____ Base

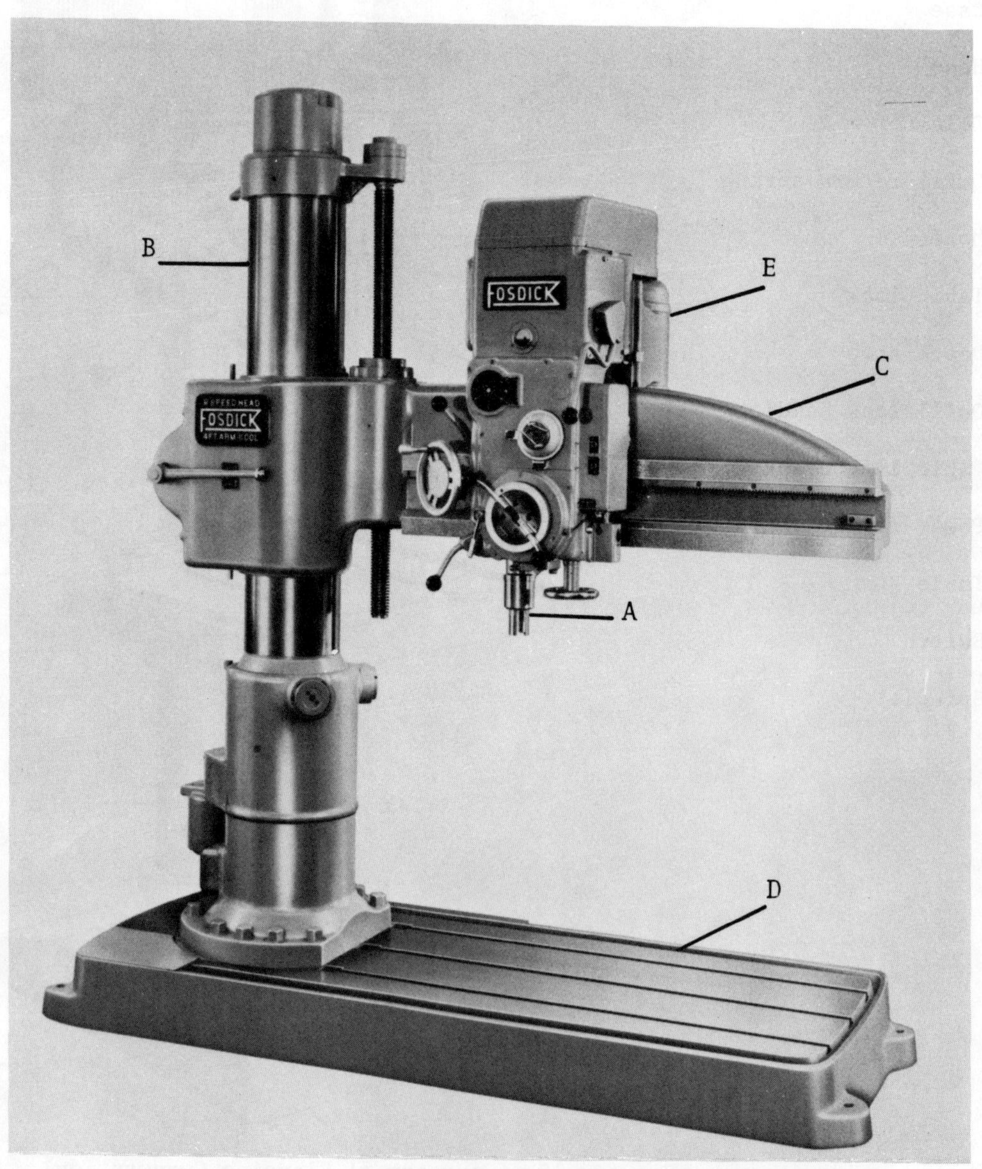

Figure 13 (Courtesy of LeBlond Inc., Cincinnati, Ohio)

Volume I, Section G   Date ____________   Name ____________________________________

UNIT 3. DRILLING TOOLS

POST TEST

Match the letter of the part in Figure 20 to the correct name listed below.

_____ Drill point angle	_____ Web
_____ Body	_____ Cutting lip
_____ Chisel edge angle	_____ Lip relief angle
_____ Axis of drill	_____ Body clearance
_____ Margin	_____ Shank length
_____ Flute	_____ Straight shank
_____ Land	_____ Tang
_____ Helix angle	_____ Taper shank

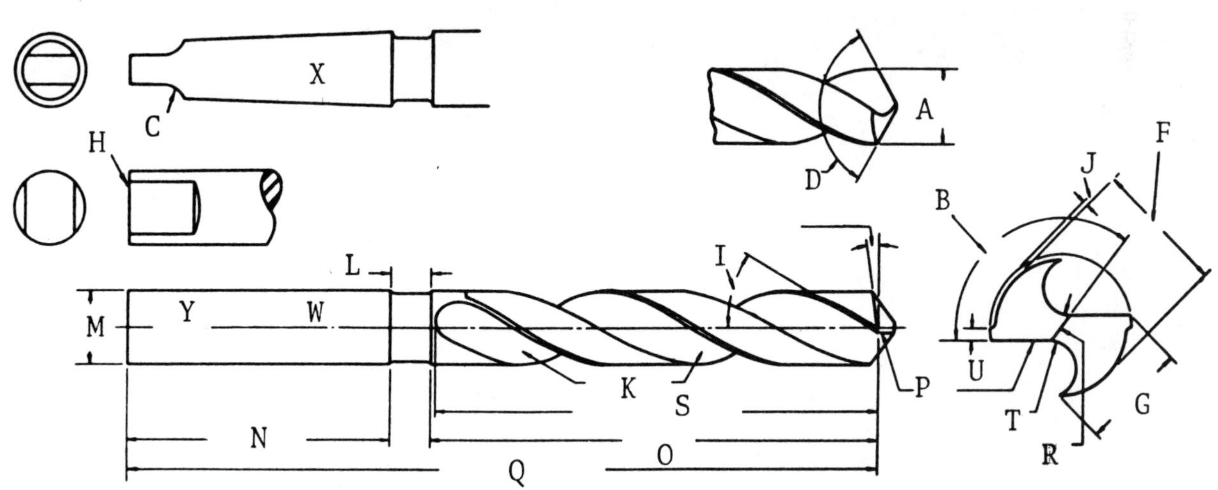

Figure 20 (Courtesy of Bendix Industrial Tools Division)

Volume I, Section G Date ____________ Name ____________________________________

UNIT 4. HAND GRINDING OF DRILLS ON THE PEDESTAL GRINDER

POST TEST

Sharpen a drill and drill a test hole in a piece of scrap steel. The hole should not be more than .010 inch x diameter of the drill. When the drilling operation has been completed, take both the drill and the test block with the drilled hole to your instructor for evaluation.

Volume I, Section G Date ____________ Name ________________________________

UNIT 6. WORK LOCATING AND HOLDING DEVICES ON DRILLING MACHINES

POST TEST

Circle the letter preceding the correct answer.

1. Workholding devices are used on drilling machines because:
   A. They always automatically position the place to be drilled directly under the spindle and guide the drill
   B. They help to keep down the worker fatigue that results from holding the workpieces by hand
   C. They keep the workpiece from turning with the drill and they provide a rigid setup that is safe
   D. All of the above

2. Which of the following are all workholding devices?
   A. Strap clamps, C-clamps, V-blocks, angle plates and drill chucks
   B. V-blocks, angle plates, angular vises, strap clamps and C-clamps
   C. Vises, V-blocks, wigglers, strap clamps and C-clamps
   D. Jigs and fixtures, vises, angle plates, V-blocks, wigglers and C-clamps

3. Parallels are used for:
   A. Spacing workpieces off the drill press table or vise
   B. Aligning a center punch mark on round stock in V-blocks
   C. Scribing a parallel line along a shaft
   D. Heavy, rough drilling

4. When a long workpiece is supported so it can spring down from the drilling pressure, what can be the result?
   A. The work will fly off the machine
   B. The drill may get dull
   C. The drill may get broken
   D. The drill will get overheated and lose its temper

5. Angle drilling is done on:
   A. An angle drill press
   B. Angle iron
   C. An angular workpiece
   D. A tilting type table or an angular vise

6. V-blocks are mostly used on the drill press for:
   A. Holding round stock for cross drilling
   B. Holding round stock in a vertical position to drill deep holes lengthwise of the material
   C. A substitute step block
   D. Quick drilling jobs without the need of clamps or hold downs

7. A wiggler is a:
   A. Device like a fishing lure that indicates approximate rpm of the drill
   B. Hold down device that allows the workpiece to "wiggle" until it is centered under the drill spindle
   C. Spring loaded, scribe-like indicator that can be trued to center by pushing on a ball near its point
   D. Shop term for a workpiece without clamps that has caught in a drill and is spinning around

8. An angular, odd-shaped workpiece cannot be mounted satisfactorily on the drill table or in a vise. It has one machined surface and the hole to be drilled must be parallel to it. How can this work be set up?
   A. It can be clamped in V-blocks
   B. It can be clamped on an angle plate
   C. A special fixture would have to be made
   D. There is no way to clamp it, so you would have to hold it with your hands

9. It is sometimes a good idea to start a tap with a drill press since:
   A. Taps are prone to go in crooked when started by hand
   B. You can put a lot of force on the tap with the drill press feed handle
   C. If you get tired turning the tap by hand, you can always turn on the machine
   D. All of the above

10. Jigs and fixtures are primarily used in:
   A. Small machine shops
   B. Maintenance type machine shops
   C. Manufacturing operations
   D. School shops

Volume I, Section G   Date ___________   Name ________________________________

UNIT 7. OPERATING DRILLING MACHINES

POST TEST

Circle the letter preceding the correct answer.

1. Assuming that a drill press operator has selected the proper tool, assured his own safety and adequately clamped his workpiece, what other considerations should he make before starting the drill press?
   A. Make sure he has his foreman's consent
   B. Set up the correct speed and feed; select a cutting fluid
   C. Get lubricating oil, turn on the machine and make a chip; if it is long and blue, the feed and speed are just right
   D. Consult a drill feed chart and set the drill rpm, then calculate the feed per revolution

2. If drilling speed is too high for the diameter of the drill and for the material being drilled, the result is:
   A. A rough hole
   B. Chips jammed in the flutes
   C. The margins or outer corners are broken down
   D. More feed is required to get the drill to cut and it often breaks

3. Which of the following is the correct rpm for drilling a $\frac{1}{8}$ inch diameter hole in SAE 4140 if CS were 50?
   A. 1600
   B. 25
   C. 250
   D. 160

4. If the drilling speed is too low for the diameter of the drill and the material being drilled:
   A. The margins or outer corners are broken down
   B. More feed is required to get the drill to cut and it often breaks
   C. Chips become jammed in the flutes
   D. The cutting edges become dulled

5. When using a sensitive drill press, you can tell if the feed is approximately right in soft steel if the:
   A. Chips come out long and stringy
   B. Chips come out blue or violet in color
   C. Chip is in short segments
   D. Chip is a tightly rolled helix

6. Which of the following could be an acceptable feed for a $\frac{1}{2}$ inch diameter drill in low carbon steel?
   A. .006 inch per revolution
   B. 90 surface feet per minute
   C. 720 revolutions per minute
   D. 2 inches per minute

7. Coolants may be divided into two groups: the mineral and animal oils and the:
   A. Refrigerants
   B. Water soluble oils
   C. Air coolants
   D. Lubricants

8. Which cutting fluid would be best for reaming or tapping low carbon steel?
   A. Lubricating oil
   B. Soluble oil
   C. Sulfurized cutting oil
   D. Kerosene

9. Jamming of drills when drilling deep holes can be avoided by using a procedure called:
   A. Alternating
   B. Pecking
   C. Withdrawal
   D. Chipping

10. The depth stop on a drill press is used for:
    A. Keeping the quill from falling out by stopping it at full depth
    B. Limiting its stroke and thus preventing the drill from drilling the table
    C. Alerting the operator by ringing a bell when his drilling tool is approaching the depth where he wishes to stop
    D. Detecting when the drill has stopped cutting; it then shuts off the machine

Volume I, Section G Date ___________ Name ______________________________

UNIT 8. COUNTERSINKING AND COUNTERBORING

POST TEST

Circle the letter preceding the correct answer.

1. The best tool to use to chamfer a hole is a:
   A. Chamfer file
   B. Counterbore
   C. Countersink
   D. Reamer

2. To provide a tapered hole for a flat head screw, use a:
   A. Center drill
   B. Counterbore
   C. Countersink
   D. Taper reamer

3. A counterbore is used to:
   A. Make seats for flat head screws
   B. Enlarge holes to recess a bolt head
   C. Make center holes in shafts
   D. All of the above

4. Spotfacing is done with a:
   A. Counterbore
   B. Countersink
   C. Spotfacer
   D. Spotting drill

5. Which inch size pilot should be used in a .500 inch diameter hole?
   A. .505
   B. .502
   C. .498
   D. .494

6. The cutting speed used with a counterbore as compared with an equal size twist drill is:
   A. One-third less
   B. The same
   C. One-third more
   D. None of the above

7. The included angle of a center drill is how many degrees?
   A. 30
   B. 60
   C. 90
   D. 120

8. Most commonly used flat head screws have a head angle of how many degrees?
   A. 52
   B. 60
   C. 72
   D. 82

9. Before starting to counterbore a hole:
   A. Lubricate the pilot
   B. Lubricate the drill press spindle
   C. Reduce the feed by one-third
   D. All of the above

10. The most important factor when counterboring is:
   A. Cutting speed
   B. The feed rate
   C. The kind of coolant used
   D. To fasten the work securely

Volume I, Section G   Date ___________   Name ______________________________

UNIT 9. REAMING IN THE DRILL PRESS

POST TEST

Circle the letter preceding the correct answer.

1. Reaming stock allowance in inches for machine reaming a one-half inch diameter hole should be:
   A. .005
   B. .015
   C. .025
   D. .035

2. Compared with the speed for drilling the same materials, the speed for reaming is __________ that for drilling.
   A. One-fourth
   B. One-half
   C. Equal
   D. Higher than

3. Compared with the feed rate for drilling the same materials, the feed rate for reaming is _________ that for drilling.
   A. One-half
   B. Equal
   C. 2 times
   D. 4 times

4. A high quality surface finish is obtained by:
   A. Using a high cutting speed
   B. Rotating the reamer in reverse
   C. Using a small feed rate
   D. Using a polishing reamer

5. A bell-mouthed hole is caused by:
   A. An oversized reamer
   B. A worn reamer
   C. A slightly tapered reamer
   D. A misaligned reamer

6. An oversized hole is caused by:
   A. The wrong coolant
   B. A built up cutting edge
   C. A bent reamer shank
   D. All of the above

7. Coolant is used while reaming to:
   A. Wash away the chips
   B. Improve the surface finish
   C. Cool the tool
   D. All of the above

8. To eliminate chatter while reaming:
   A. Increase the feed
   B. Decrease the feed
   C. Increase the speed
   D. None of the above

9. A poor quality surface finish is caused by:
   A. Too high a feed rate
   B. Too small a reaming allowance
   C. Too high of a cutting speed
   D. All of the above

10. Obtain a prepared kit of different reamers and identify them by name; also give an example of a common application for each reamer.

	Name of Reamer	Application
A.		
B.		
C.		
D.		
E.		
F.		

Volume I, Section H Date ____________ Name ______________________________

UNIT 1. HAND REAMERS

POST TEST

Circle the letter preceding the correct answer.

1. Hand reamers can be readily identified by the:
   A. Length of the flutes
   B. Length of the body
   C. Markings on the neck
   D. Square on the shank

2. A hole with a slot in it should be reamed with a:
   A. Short starting taper reamer
   B. Spiral flute reamer
   C. Slightly undersized reamer
   D. Straight flute reamer

3. To make a hole .002 inch larger than a nominal size:
   A. Drill with a twist drill
   B. Wiggle the reamer slightly in the hole
   C. Ream with an expansion reamer
   D. Use a spiral flute reamer

4. Coolant is used when reaming:
   A. To obtain a good hole surface finish
   B. To keep the hole from oxidizing
   C. Shallow holes
   D. Undersized holes

5. When a reamer is rotated in reverse, it will:
   A. Leave a very smooth finish
   B. Break long stringy chips
   C. Become dull very quickly
   D. Reduce the heat buildup

6. Stock allowance in inches for hand reaming should be between:
   A. .001 to .005
   B. .006 to .010
   C. .011 to .015
   D. .016 to .020

7. The exact size of a hand reamer is determined by:
   A. Reading the size stamped on the neck of the reamer
   B. Reaming a hole and measuring its size
   C. Measuring the shank diameter and adding .003 inch
   D. Measuring over the margins with a micrometer

8. When hand reaming, the:
   A. Reamer always aligns itself with the existing hole
   B. Reamer alignment is checked with a square
   C. Holes produced by one reamer will vary in size
   D. Length of the flutes determines the depth of the hole

9. To reduce chatter while reaming a hole, which reamer should you select?
   A. High speed steel
   B. Carbon steel
   C. Spiral flute
   D. Straight flute

10. Obtain a prepared kit of different reamers and identify them by name. Also give an example of common application.

	Name of Reamer	Application
A.		
B.		
C.		
D.		
E.		

Volume I, Section H Date ____________ Name ____________________________________

UNIT 2. TAPS, IDENTIFICATION AND APPLICATION

POST TEST

Circle the letter preceding the correct answer.

1. Spiral pointed taps are used:
   A. To tap deep holes
   B. As thread forming taps
   C. To tap shallow blind holes
   D. To tap through holes

2. Fluteless spiral pointed taps are used to tap:
   A. Holes in sheet metal
   B. Deep holes
   C. Tough materials
   D. Nuts

3. Spiral fluted taps are used:
   A. To tap deep blind holes
   B. Because they tend to push chips ahead of them
   C. To cut undersized threads
   D. To cut oversized threads

4. Thread forming taps:
   A. Produce only small chips
   B. Produce no chips
   C. Push the chips ahead of them
   D. Cannot be used on a drill press

5. Serial taps of the same nominal size:
   A. Have different pitch diameters
   B. Have the same pitch diameters
   C. Are used in mass production
   D. Can be used in any sequence

6. The size of a tap is marked on the:
   A. End
   B. Body
   C. Shank
   D. Handle

7. The difference between the taps in a set is found on the:
   A. Shank
   B. Flutes
   C. Pitch diameter
   D. Chamfer

8. Taps are surface treated to:
   A. Improve their appearance
   B. Improve their wear resistance
   C. Keep them from corroding
   D. Be used on automatic machines

9. The rake angle of the cutting edge of a tap varies:
   A. For different materials
   B. To allow lubricant to penetrate
   C. For shallow or deep holes
   D. On thread forming taps

10. Taps can be surface treated by:
   A. Nickel plating
   B. Tempering
   C. Anodizing
   D. Nitriding

VolumeI, Section H Date ____________ Name ________________________________

UNIT 3. TAPPING PROCEDURES

POST TEST

Circle the letter preceding the correct answer.

1. A tap is driven with:
   A. An adjustable wrench
   B. A combination wrench
   C. A tap wrench
   D. Pliers

2. The alignment of a tap is checked with a:
   A. Plumb bob
   B. Square
   C. Level
   D. Dividers

3. The size of the tap drill is important because it:
   A. Determines the size of the thread
   B. Regulates the percentage of thread
   C. Forms the major diameter
   D. Determines the depth of the hole

4. To thread to the bottom of a blind hole, which tap should you use?
   A. Pointed
   B. Taper
   C. Plug
   D. Bottoming

5. The length of a tapped hole should be how many times the diameter of the screw?
   A. One-half
   B. One and one-half
   C. Two and one-half
   D. Three and one-half

6. Taps may break while tapping:
   A. Because the tap drill was too large
   B. If the holes are drilled too deep
   C. If the tap used is too sharp
   D. If chips clog the flutes

7. Dull taps:
   A. Produce polished threads
   B. Should be used with slower cutting speeds
   C. Should be honed more frequently
   D. Produce oversize threads

8. Rough threads in tapped holes can be caused by:
   A. Insufficient lubrication
   B. Dull taps
   C. Chips clogging the flutes
   D. All of the above

9. Cutting speeds which are too high:
   A. May cause tap breakage
   B. May cause burnished threads
   C. Use too much cutting oil
   D. All of the above

10. The strength of a tapped hole is determined by:
   A. The percentage of thread cut
   B. The depth of thread engagement
   C. The material being tapped
   D. All of the above

Volume I, Section H Date ____________ Name ____________________________________

UNIT 4. THREAD CUTTING DIES AND THEIR USES

POST TEST

Circle the letter preceding the correct answer.

1. A die is turned with a:
   A. Die wrench
   B. Die stock
   C. Die plate
   D. Die handle

2. A round split adjustable die is expanded and contracted by a:
   A. Tapered wedge
   B. Nut
   C. Screw
   D. Die adjuster

3. The chamfer on the cutting end of a die:
   A. Distributes the cutting action over a number of threads
   B. Provides space for cutting fluid
   C. Gives extra chip clearance
   D. Is unnecessary

4. You have to choose between four rods to cut a $\frac{1}{2}$ -13NC thread. Which inch size diameter rod will you use?
   A. .489
   B. .497
   C. .503
   D. .515

5. A rod should be chamfered before threading to:
   A. Reduce its diameter
   B. Provide additional chip clearance
   C. Retain cutting oil
   D. Make the die start easier

6. Cutting fluids are used when threading to obtain:
   A. A good surface finish
   B. Close tolerances
   C. A long tool life
   D. All of the above

7. The best die used to cut an undersized thread is:
   A. A round split adjustable die
   B. A hexagon rethreading die
   C. An adjustable two piece die
   D. None of the above

8. While cutting threads with a hand die, the die is frequently reversed or backed off to:
   A. Break the chips
   B. Cool the die
   C. Lubricate the die
   D. All of the above

9. Adjustable two piece dies are assembled:
   A. With the chamfer away from the guide
   B. With the chamfer toward the guide
   C. Without the guide
   D. None of the above

10. Rethreading dies are used to:
   A. Repair damaged threads
   B. Cut occasional new threads
   C. Recut rusty threads
   D. All of the above

Volume I, Section I Date ___________ Name ______________________________

UNIT 1. TURNING MACHINE SAFETY

POST TEST

Circle the letter preceding the correct answer.

1. A chuck wrench can be a potential hazard:
   A. When it is left in the chuck or is placed on top of the headstock
   B. When it is left on a workbench
   C. When placed on a toolboard or lathe backboard
   D. All of the above

2. In lathe operations, burns can be caused by:
   A. Overheated motors, hot gear case oil
   B. Hot handles and handwheels
   C. Hot chips and workpieces
   D. Stopping the lathe by putting your hands on the chuck

3. In lathe operations, the machinist can receive cuts by:
   A. Oiling gears with the guard off while the machine is running
   B. Handling stringy chips with bare hands
   C. Suddenly reversing a threaded nose spindle and chuck
   D. Allowing loose clothing or long hair to dangle near a rough turned, rapidly rotating workpiece

4. What can you do to prevent work from being thrown out of the lathe from workholding devices?
   A. Rotate the work without power to see if it clears the carriage; the chuck jaws should have a secure grip on the workpiece
   B. Workpieces should be securely gripped and not extend more than ten times the diameter of the work; make sure the work clears by slowly rotating the lathe with power
   C. Overtighten the chuck
   D. Undertighten the chuck

5. Electrical power panels or enclosures are accessible to:
   A. Anyone
   B. The machine operator and maintenance personnel
   C. Authorized personnel, maintenance and electrical
   D. Only the foreman

6. What would likely happen to a long slender rod which is chucked and extending out from the lathe spindle and rotating rapidly?
   A. It would fly completely out of the lathe
   B. Nothing would happen as centripetal forces would equal centrifugal forces and it would remain straight
   C. It would simply vibrate considerably
   D. It would immediately begin to fly outward, so if the rod were small and the rpm high, it would bend

7. Clamp bolts and set screws on toolholders and lathe parts are sometimes overtightened by an operator. What can this cause?
   A. It will cause everything to be secure so it won't slip
   B. An overstressed bolt may suddenly break causing the part to come out of the machine
   C. It can cause bent wrenches and the next operator to use the machine to find the bolts difficult to loosen
   D. A waste of energy and it is not necessary

8. To avoid arm and hand injuries when measuring a hole that has been bored, the operator should:
   A. Reverse the boring tool
   B. Use gloves
   C. Cover the boring tool with a rag
   D. Remove the boring tool

9. Tools should be placed on:
   A. The headstock or compound rest
   B. A lathe board or workbench
   C. Chip pan
   D. Ways

10. When filing is done on lathes, the safest way is to:
   A. File right handed
   B. File left handed
   C. Wear gloves while filing
   D. File with one hand only

Volume I, Section I Date ____________ Name ________________________________

UNIT 2. THE ENGINE LATHE

POST TEST

1. Match the names of parts of the lathe with the letters in Figure 13.

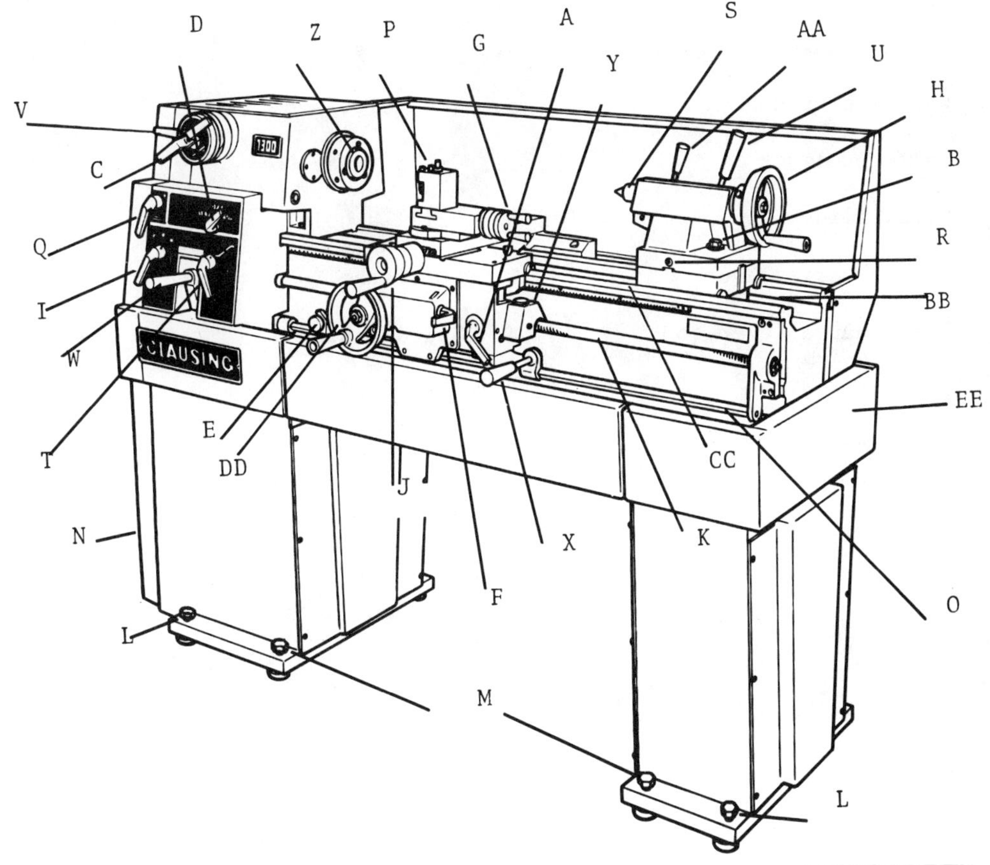

Figure 13. (Courtesy of Clausing Corporation)

1. _____ Variable speed control
2. _____ Tool holder
3. _____ Tailstock lock lever (bed clamp)
4. _____ Half-nut lever
5. _____ Sliding gear lever
6. _____ Carriage handwheel
7. _____ Tailstock spindle (ram)
8. _____ Tailstock handwheel
9. _____ Chip pan
10. _____ Clutch and brake lever
11. _____ Clutch control bar
12. _____ Gear selector lever
13. _____ Spindle
14. _____ Tailstock lock stud (clamp bolt)
15. _____ Gear rack
16. _____ Set over screw
17. _____ Lead screw
18. _____ Ram or spindle lock
19. _____ Bed ways
20. _____ Thread dial
21. _____ Motor switch control
22. _____ Thread/feed selector lever
23. _____ Cross feed handwheel
24. _____ Compound rest feed screw handle
25. _____ Feed (lead screw) reverse lever
26. _____ Power feed lever
27. _____ Speed range selector
28. _____ Clutch kickout

2. Match the following lathe parts or operations with the lathe parts listed.

1. _____ Tailstock adjusting screws	A. Change cross feed to length feed
2. _____ Headstock	B. Change rotation of the lead screw
3. _____ Back gears (on some lathes) or speed range selector	C. Make a facing cut
	D. Move the carriage manually
4. _____ Quick change gear box	E. Cut threads
5. _____ Carriage handwheel	F. Change to a different feed
6. _____ Half-nut lever	G. Cut a taper
7. _____ Cross slide	H. Drill a hole
8. _____ Feed reverse lever	I. Set lathe to low rpm
9. _____ Feed change lever (on some lathes)	J. Spindle nose
10. _____ Tailstock	

Volume I, Section I   Date ____________   Name ________________________________

UNIT 3. ENGINE LATHE MAINTENANCE AND ADJUSTMENTS

POST TEST

Circle the letter preceding the correct answer.

1. What should be used for cleaning the lathe?
   A. Air jet
   B. Floor broom or brush
   C. Small brush and a cloth
   D. Vacuum cleaner

2. Lathe boards and tool boards are used to protect the ways from getting:
   A. Nicks and scratches
   B. Piles of chips
   C. Gritty, oily sludge
   D. Punch marks from layout tools

3. Lathes should be lubricated:
   A. Every other day
   B. Twice a year
   C. Every day
   D. Once a week

4. A lathe having cleaned and oiled ways has not been used for three days. How do you proceed?
   A. You can begin to use it immediately.
   B. The ways may be gritty and should be cleaned and oiled before using
   C. There is no need to worry about it; the coolant will wash off the settled dust
   D. Blow it off with an air hose before using it

5. Two types of gibs used on a lathe are:
   A. The square and rectangular gibs
   B. The lockscrew and thrustscrew gibs
   C. Self-compensating gibs
   D. The straight and tapered gibs

6. How tight should the gib be adjusted on the cross slide?
   A. With just a slight drag
   B. Fairly tight when not in use
   C. Just so a .030 inch feeler gage will slide between the slide and the gib
   D. The adjusting screws should be tightened to 100 pounds per inch

7. The compound slide may be broken or damaged when taking heavy cuts if:
   A. The gibs are too tight
   B. There is too much overhang or it is back in its slide too far
   C. The angle is not set right
   D. The gibs are too loose

8. If a gear lever will not shift into the selected position you can:
   A. Force it into gear
   B. Turn the spindle with power and shift rapidly
   C. Turn the spindle by hand while engaging the gear
   D. With the spindle running, double clutch and it will shift into gear

9. A new lathe should be set in place so that it will make accurate cuts by:
   A. Bolting it to a solid concrete floor
   B. Shimming the headstock and tailstock and bolting them down
   C. Bolting, shimming and checking with a builder's level
   D. Bolting, shimming and checking with a precision level

10. The compound dovetail slide can be nicked and scratched by:
   A. Taking heavy roughing cuts with the dovetail exposed
   B. Having too much overhang
   C. Apprentice machinists and other learners
   D. Using the wrong lubricating oil

Volume I, Section I Date ____________ Name ________________________________

UNIT 4. TOOLHOLDERS AND TOOL HOLDING FOR THE LATHE

POST TEST

Circle the letter preceding the correct answer.

1. Toolholders are used to:
   A. Extend the life of the tool
   B. Protect the tool
   C. Securely clamp the tool
   D. Deflect the cutting pressures

2. Excessive tool overhang:
   A. Causes excessive tool wear
   B. Will result in chatter
   C. Causes tool overheating
   D. Will change top rake and end clearance angles

3. On a standard left hand toolholder:
   A. The cutting tool end is bent to the right
   B. The cutting tool end is bent to the left
   C. There is no back rake angle
   D. No end clearance is provided

4. A standard toolholder with the square hole parallel to the base:
   A. Is used with high speed steel tools
   B. Is used in quick-change tooling
   C. Allows precise tool height adjustments
   D. Is used with carbide tools

5. Tool height adjustments on a quick-change toolholder are made:
   A. With shims
   B. With a rocker
   C. With a micrometer collar
   D. Grinding the tool

6. A turret type tool post normally:
   A. Holds 4 different tools
   B. Holds 6 different tools
   C. Uses standard toolholders
   D. Uses quick-change toolholders

7. A standard right hand toolholder is best used for turning:
   A. Close to the headstock
   B. Close to the tailstock
   C. Small diameter workpieces
   D. For heavy cutting

8. Tool height adjustments on a turret type tool post are made with:
   A. Setscrews
   B. A micrometer collar
   C. A rocker
   D. Shims

9. Tools are secured in a tailstock spindle:
   A. With a spindle clamp
   B. With a setscrew
   C. By their Morse taper shank
   D. With a quick-change holder

10. Straight shank tools are held in a tailstock with:
   A. A collet
   B. A drill chuck
   C. An adapter
   D. Setscrews

Volume I, Section I Date ____________ Name ______________________________

UNIT 5. CUTTING TOOLS FOR THE LATHE

POST TEST

Circle the letter preceding the correct answer.

1. High speed steel tools are:
   A. Used by machinists more often than other kinds
   B. Easily shaped into desired forms of tools
   C. Able to withstand higher temperatures than other kinds of cutting tools such as carbides
   D. Often used on machines that are capable of operating only at high rpm

2. One of the most important aspects of lathe tools is:
   A. The ability to be shaped into desired forms
   B. The fact that they can be resharpened when they wear or break
   C. The tool geometry, including end and side relief and rake
   D. When they get overheated in the cut, they are ruined and must be replaced

3. Form tools produce a specially shaped machined surface by:
   A. Plunging into the workpiece to produce the form of the tool
   B. Using a template of the form and a single point tool
   C. Exerting great pressure on the work and embossing it
   D. The use of special attachments for the lathe

4. What is a "chip trap"?
   A. Too many chips are allowed to accumulate in the chip pan and on the floor making a dangerous "chip trap" for the operator
   B. A "chip trap" is simply a chip disposal device
   C. A wad of stringy chips wrapped around the chuck or workpiece is known as a "chip trap"
   D. An improperly ground tool or one that has been reground many times often has a "chip trap" that prevents a smooth flow of chips across the tool face

5. Back rakes should be ground in the tool:
   A. At the same time the side rake is ground
   B. When the toolholder is of the straight type without a built in back rake
   C. At the angle given in Table 1 for turning various metals
   D. All of the above

6. A threading tool should:
   A. Be ground to offset any built in back rake from the holder, thus giving it zero rake
   B. Be checked with a tool grinding gage for its 60-degree angle
   C. Have no side relief angle
   D. Have a negative rake since it has a tendency to "dig in"

7. The purpose of side and end relief angles is:
   A. To insure uniform even chip flow across the tool face
   B. To carry the chip away from the point of cut
   C. To relieve the pressure of cutting from the point of the tool and divert it to a stronger part of the tool
   D. The side relief allows for feed into the work and the end relief provides clearance for the tool so it will not rub

8. Back and side rakes:
   A. Carry the chip away from the point of cut and insure uniform even chip flow across the face of the tool
   B. Relieve the pressure of cutting from the point of the tool and divert it to a stronger part of the tool
   C. Provide adequate clearances between the workpiece and the tool
   D. Are both the same with different names

9. Chips can be made manageable and safe to the operator by using:
   A. A piece of wood to break them into smaller chips
   B. Feeds and depths of cut that contribute to chip breaking and by using chip breakers on tools
   C. A hook tool to remove them as soon as they are produced and by wearing gloves to protect your hands
   D. Large back rake and side rake angles on tools to contribute to the smooth flow of an even uniform chip

10. A high speed lathe tool would have to be above 1300° F. (704° C.) to be overheated. A temperature of 2000° F. (1093° C.) could be produced on the cutting edge when grinding by:
    A. Getting an edge very thin, similar to a knife blade
    B. Not cooling it off in water frequently
    C. Using a glazed wheel or by forcing the tool into the wheel
    D. Using the roughing wheel for finishing

Volume I, Section I Date ____________ Name ________________________________

UNIT 6. LATHE SPINDLE TOOLING

POST TEST

Circle the letter preceding the correct answer.

1. Chucks and face plates are mounted on the spindle by means of:
   A. Interchangeable spindle noses
   B. Any one of several types of spindle noses
   C. A circle of socket head cap screws
   D. A permanent assembly

2. Threaded, long taper key drive, and camlock are terms used to describe:
   A. Parts of the drive mechanism in the headstock
   B. Screws and slide mechanisms on the carriage of the lathe
   C. Various types of spindle noses
   D. The lead screw and related mechanisms

3. The independent chuck has:
   A. Four jaws, each of which can move without affecting the position of the others
   B. Two, three, or six jaws that all move in or out an equal distance
   C. Three jaws that move independently of each other
   D. A special adjusting system that makes the jaws center round work more accurately

4. The universal chuck has:
   A. Four jaws, each of which can move without affecting the position of the others
   B. Two, three, or six jaws that all move in or out an equal distance
   C. Three jaws that move independently of each other
   D. A special adjusting system that makes the jaws center round work more accurately

5. The combination chuck:
   A. Is a three-jaw chuck held in the jaws of a four-jaw chuck
   B. Is a four-jaw chuck with top jaws
   C. Can be a four-jaw chuck in which the jaws can be moved independently, but are also operated with a scroll plate
   D. Can be a three-jaw chuck with a scroll plate, but each jaw does not have an adjusting screw for independent action

6. Drive plates usually have:
   A. T-slots
   B. T-slots and straight slots
   C. One single slot
   D. One or several slots

7. Live centers are:
   A. Hardened
   B. Hardened and serrated
   C. Soft metal
   D. Made with carbide inserts

8. What are face plates used for?
   A. Mounting fixtures and workpieces
   B. Driving shafts between centers with a lathe dog
   C. Facing operations only
   D. None of the above

9. A drive center or face driver makes possible the:
   A. Driving of a face plate
   B. Driving of work between centers so a cut can be taken the full length
   C. Facing off the rough end of a shaft or in the case of the drive center, the truing up of the center by a kind of reaming
   D. Driving of tubular material without chucking it

10. Steel spring collets are used:
    A. To turn large heavy shafting
    B. For centering and turning irregular shaped parts
    C. For turning small precision parts from standard size bar stock
    D. In automatic machines only

Volume I, Section I Date ____________ Name ______________________________

UNIT 7. OPERATING THE MACHINE CONTROLS

POST TEST

Circle the letter preceding the correct answer.

1. On lathes where speed changes are made by shifting belts on step cone pulleys, the shift to the low range is made by:
   A. Moving the back gear lever forward with the spindle running
   B. Disengaging the bull gear lock pin and moving the back gear lever with the spindle stopped
   C. Engaging both the bull gear lock pin and the back gears
   D. Shifting the belt tightener lever and engaging the back gear

2. Speed changes are made on geared head lathes with:
   A. Automatic transmissions
   B. Single shifter lever mounted on top
   C. Shifting levers with synchro-mesh making possible the shifting up or down with the motor running
   D. Several shifting levers on the headstock

3. The lead screw is reversed by shifting the:
   A. Leadscrew reversing lever
   B. Left hand thread lever
   C. Feed reverse lever
   D. Feed change lever

4. The feed change lever:
   A. Changes the direction of the lead screw
   B. Diverts the feed to either the cross slide or the carriage
   C. Changes the feed to a high or low range
   D. Connects or disconnects the carriage handwheel

5. The sliding gear shifter levers on the quick-change gear box are used for:
   A. Selecting feeds or threads per inch
   B. Quickly changing speeds
   C. Quickly changing feeds during a cut to get a varied finish
   D. Changing the ratio between the longitudinal feed and the cross feed

6. The carriage handwheel:
   A. Has a micrometer dial that is sometimes in metric units as well as English
   B. Is used for a quick approach and return and for delicate operations not requiring power feed
   C. Is used for feeding when coarser feeds are required and when long cuts are made on shafts
   D. Should never be used except in an emergency

7. What affect does the carriage feed-cross feed ratio have on the surface finish if the same feed setting is used for turning both the face and the outside diameter surfaces?
   A. None, they are the same
   B. The facing surface would be coarser and the outside diameter surface would be finer
   C. The outside diameter surface would be coarser and the facing surface would be finer
   D. It would be making threads per inch on the lingitudinal and feeds on the facing surface

8. The half-nut lever is used for:
   A. Engaging the longitudinal feed on the carriage
   B. Taking up the slack in the cross slide nut
   C. Changing from longitudinal to cross feed
   D. Threading

9. Micrometer collars on cross feed and compound feed handles are graduated in:
   A. English and English-metric units
   B. Fractions of inches and in centimeters
   C. Tenths of inches
   D. Degrees and minutes

10. A lathe that is calibrated for single depth:
    A. Will take off the amount turned in on the dial from the diameter of the workpiece
    B. Will take twice the amount turned on the dial from the diameter of the workpiece
    C. Only reads in English units and not in metric
    D. Will take off one-half the amount turned on the dial from the diameter of the workpiece

Volume I, Section I Date ____________ Name ________________________________

UNIT 8. FACING AND CENTER DRILLING

POST TEST

Circle the letter preceding the correct answer.

1. In which kind of chuck is square or rectangular work set up for center drilling and facing?
   A. Universal
   B. Collet
   C. Independent
   D. Six-jaw

2. When taking a facing cut on a workpiece held in a chuck, the point of the tool should be:
   A. Slightly below the center
   B. On center
   C. Slightly above center
   D. Sharp with no radius

3. In order to obtain a facing feed of .010 inch, approximately what inch per revolution feed setting on the quick-change gear box is necessary?
   A. .030
   B. .0033
   C. .010
   D. 10

4. The depth of shoulders and steps machined in workpieces held in a chuck are measured with:
   A. Tape measures and spring calipers
   B. An optical comparator or a bore gage
   C. Inside micrometer and a spring joint caliper
   D. A hook rule or a depth micrometer

5. A right hand facing tool is used for facing:
   A. Centered shaft ends and sharp corners
   B. Chucked shafts and large workpieces in chucks
   C. Rough work where a heavy duty facing tool is needed
   D. Face plates

6. The roughing cutting speed for an alloy steel is 45 sfm, and the workpiece diameter is 5 inches. What is the correct rpm?
   A. 56.25
   B. 360
   C. 36
   D. 562.5

7. A workpiece is center drilled in the lathe for the purpose of:
   A. Turning between centers only
   B. Spotting a hole for drilling or for turning between centers
   C. Placing it on a mandrel and for turning between centers
   D. Facing to the center of the workpiece

8. Round material such as shafts should be laid out on the end for center drilling in a drill press by using a:
   A. Divider
   B. Inside spring caliper
   C. Outside spring caliper
   D. Center head and blade

9. Center drills break as a result of:
   A. Too heavy feed and too low speed
   B. Too light feed and too high speed
   C. Dropping them on the floor
   D. Allowing chips to form a tangle around them

10. Drilling in too far with a center drill:
   A. Makes the taper too large and it heats up
   B. Damages the center drill on the tapered section
   C. Makes a sharp outer edge which is a poor bearing surface
   D. Causes the chips to jam and the drill to heat up

Volume I, Section I Date ____________ Name ______________________________

UNIT 9. TURNING BETWEEN CENTERS

POST TEST

Circle the letter preceding the correct answer.

1. An advantage of turning between centers is that:
   A. It produces less chatter than by other methods
   B. A more positive drive is possible
   C. A shaft can be removed or turned end for end without loss of concentricity
   D. Long work can be supported in a steady rest so facing, drilling or boring can be carried out

2. Driving force is transmitted to the workpiece when turning between centers by means of a:
   A. Three or four jaw chuck
   B. Drive plate and a lathe dog
   C. Trip dog that automatically stops rotation at a predetermined point
   D. Collet and drawbar

3. Three different centers used in the tailstock are:
   A. Pipe, ball bearing and dead centers
   B. Dead, live and drive centers
   C. Dead, soft and ball bearing centers
   D. Hard, soft and pipe centers

4. The dead center is correctly adjusted by turning the tailstock handwheel until a resistance is felt and then:
   A. Stopping
   B. Backing off so there is some end play
   C. Turning in one-fourth turn
   D. Backing off until the dog bent tail clicks freely in its slot

5. The dead center needs to be frequently adjusted between cuts because the:
   A. Lubricating oil runs out
   B. Heat of machining expands the work and tightens it
   C. Machine adjustments often vibrate loose during machining operations, so frequent attention is necessary
   D. Metal in the workpiece center wears and causes the centers to become loose

6. Excessive overhang of the tool and toolholder on roughing cuts can cause:
   A. Chatter and broken tool points
   B. The tool to swing into the lathe dog
   C. The feed rate to change
   D. All of the above

7. If the cutting speed for aluminum is 200 and the workpiece diameter is $2\frac{1}{2}$ inches, what is the rpm setting for the lathe? The formula is $RPM = \frac{CS \times 4}{D}$

A. 3200
B. 2000
C. 320
D. 32

8. The feed rate for roughing should be:
A. From .003 to .005 inch
B. Between .010 and .020 inch
C. One-fifth to one-tenth as much as the depth of cut
D. The one that fives the best surface finish

9. The amount left for finishing on the diameter of a workpiece with a plus or minus .003 inch tolerance should be what part of an inch?
A. .015 to .030
B. .003 to .006
C. $\frac{1}{16}$ to $\frac{1}{8}$
D. .050 to .100

10. When turning to size predictably:
A. A trial cut is taken that looks like the approximate diameter or slightly over and it is checked with a micrometer. This procedure is continued to finishing.
B. A short skim cut is taken and measured, the cross feed collar zeroed, and the roughing depth is dialed. A trial cut is taken, it is checked, and the cut is taken. This procedure is continued to finish size.
C. A trial cut is taken, a spring caliper is set to the size, and it is measured with a rule. This is sufficiently accurate for finishing most outside diameters.
D. A short skim cut is taken and measured, the cross feed collar zeroed, and the roughing depth is dialed. A trial cut is taken and the crossfeed screw backed off after noting the setting. The diameter is checked, the tool returned to the start position, and the dial reset to its former position. The cut is taken. This procedure is continued to finish size.

Volume I, Section I Date ____________ Name ________________________________

UNIT 11. DRILLING, BORING REAMING, KNURLING, RECESSING,

PARTING AND TAPPING IN THE LATHE

POST TEST

Circle the letter preceding the correct answer.

1. Bores of machine parts such as gears and pulleys are not made by drilling in a lathe without further machining, because drills:
   A. Are not made in standard shaft sizes
   B. Tend to produce undersize holes that run eccentric to the work axis
   C. Tend to produce oversize holes that run eccentric to the work axis
   D. Make bell mouthed holes that must be corrected by reaming or boring

2. The main advantage of boring over reaming in the lathe is that:
   A. Boring corrects any eccentricity in the bore and reaming does not
   B. Boring corrects axial misalignment and reaming does not
   C. Better finishes are obtainable
   D. The process of finishing the bore to a precision diameter can be done more quickly

3. The three basic types of boring operations are:
   A. Through boring, countersinking and backfacing
   B. Through boring, counterboring and blind hole facing
   C. Through boring, internal grooving and counterboring
   D. Through boring, thread relief and blind hole boring

4. A machine reamer finish can be improved by:
   A. Boring with a finishing tool
   B. Leaving more material to remove when reaming
   C. Running a hand reamer through the bore
   D. Running a rose reamer through the bore

5. Large internal threads should be made with:
   A. An internal threading tool and boring bar
   B. Tap and tap wrench by hand
   C. Tap and tap wrench with power
   D. All of the above

6. Taps used for lathe tapping are:
   A. Taper, plug and bottoming
   B. National fine, National caorse and taper
   C. Spiral, plug and taper
   D. Plug, bottoming and spiral point

7. Parting tools can jam in the cut and break as a result of:
   A. Cutting speed that is too high
   B. Lack of cutting oil
   C. Feed that is too light
   D. The tool set above center

8. Three ways to prevent chatter when cutting off material with a parting tool are to use:
   A. Coolant, feed in very slowly and use a medium to high speed
   B. Diagonally ground parting tools, use power feed and a slow speed
   C. A light hand feed that makes a chip, low speed and a rigid setup
   D. A heavy feed, low speed and cut off material near the chuck or near the tailstock center

9. Ordinary knurls make a pattern on the workpiece by:
   A. Cutting the material
   B. Displacing the material
   C. Compressing the material
   D. All of the above

10. Three reasons knurling is done on workpieces are:
   A. For tool handles, to provide a gripping surface, and for appearance
   B. For press fits, appearance, and a gripping surface
   C. To cover up errors by increasing the diameter of a part, for tool handles, and press fits
   D. None of the above

Volume I, Section I Date ____________ Name ____

UNIT 12. SIXTY DEGREE THREAD INFORMATION AND CALCULATIONS

POST TEST

Circle the letter preceding the correct answer.

1. The sharp V thread:
   A. Is very durable and will take much abuse without damage
   B. Is seldom used today
   C. Has an included angle of 55 degrees
   D. Does not fit or seal as close as most threads

2. The pitch of the thread is the:
   A. Same as the number of threads per inch
   B. Helix angle
   C. Distance between a point on a screw thread to a corresponding point on the next thread
   D. Distance a nut will travel in one revolution on a two lead screw thread

3. American National and Unified thread systems:
   A. Have the same classes of fits
   B. Are the same thread form in every detail
   C. Are similar in thread form but are not made in the same pitch series
   D. Both have the 60-degree included angle but the depth of thread is different

4. One reason for having thread tolerances and classes of fits is:
   A. To insure interchangeability of threaded parts
   B. So specific threads can be properly labeled
   C. The percent of thread can be more easily determined
   D. That better finishes can be obtained

5. A three-quarter inch diameter, 10 TPI, Unified nut with a Class 2 tolerance would be properly written:
   A. $\frac{3}{4}$ - 10 UNC - 2B
   B. $\frac{3}{4}$ - 10 UNC - 2A
   C. $\frac{3}{4}$ - 10 TPI UNF - 2B
   D. $\frac{3}{4}$ ten TPI Unified - Tol 2

6. What would the flat on the end of a threading tool for a 10 thread per inch Unified thread be in inches if the formula is P x .144 inch?
   A. .144
   B. .0014
   C. .0144
   D. 1.44

7. How many inches will the compound set at 30 degrees move to cut a .100 inch pitch thread if the formula is $\frac{.708}{n}$?
   A. .0708
   B. .708
   C. .007
   D. 7.08

8. The percent of thread:
   A. Refers to the class of fit
   B. Refers to the actual minor diameter of the internal thread
   C. Indicates the depth of the external thread expressed as a percentage
   D. Refers to the allowable limits or tolerances

9. M15x1.25 refers to:
   A. Military specifications for part dimensions
   B. An SI Metric designation for a 15 mm diameter, 1.25 mm pitch thread
   C. Threads per inch and the diameter of the part
   D. ISO Metric designation for a 15 mm diamter, 1.25 mm pitch thread

10. Which of the following metric threads would have the closest tolerance?
   A. M12x1.25-4H
   B. M18x1.5-6H/6g
   C. M6x0.75-3H
   D. M10x1.5-5H

Volume I, Section I Date ____________ Name ____________________________________

UNIT 13. CUTTING UNIFIED EXTERNAL THREADS

POST TEST

Circle the letter preceding the correct answer.

1. Threads are cut or chased on a lathe with a single point tool by:
   A. Making a series of cuts in the same groove
   B. Using a threading die
   C. Moving the carriage by means of the rack that is located under the front way
   D. Setting the correct feeds on the quick-change gearbox

2. Sixty degree thread cutting is best done with the compound set at 29 degrees so that:
   A. It will be swung out of the way to make the cross feed micrometer dial more visible
   B. When the cross feed is brought back to zero after each cut and the compound is fed in, a slightly smaller amount is removed from the trailing side of the tool for finishing
   C. Threads can be made more quickly than with straight infeed
   D. Most of the cutting is done on the leading edge of the tool as it is fed in, but the compound is brought back to zero at the end of each cut causing some cutting on the trailing edge on the next pass

3. Threading tools are checked for accuracy on the 60-degree angle by using a:
   A. Thread gage
   B. Center gage
   C. Screw pitch gage
   D. Tool angle gage

4. The tool is aligned with the work:
   A. With a center gage
   B. With a small square
   C. By squaring the tool on the face of the workpiece
   D. With a thread gage

5. The number of threads per inch can be checked with a:
   A. Tool gage
   B. Metric rule by counting
   C. Ring gage
   D. Screw pitch gage

6. When threading, the carriage is moved along the ways by:
   A. A gear train on a rack
   B. The feed rod spline or keyway
   C. The lead screw thread
   D. The handwheel

7. The half-nuts should be engaged when threading odd numbered threads when the threading dial is positioned at:
   A. Any line
   B. Any numbered line
   C. Only one line
   D. Opposite lines only

8. For threading, the spindle should be turning:
   A. At about one-fourth normal turning speeds
   B. At the rpm given in standard charts for the type of metal you are working on
   C. At the slowest speed the lathe can be set
   D. None of the above

9. Left hand threads are cut by:
   A. Turning the tool upside down, reversing the rotation of the spindle, and moving the tool from left to right
   B. Using a standard tool, reversing the lead screw, and moving the tool from left to right
   C. Making a right hand thread and turning it end for end
   D. Using a left hand threading die; they cannot be made on an ordinary engine lathe

10. The thread is picked up when a threading tool is removed for grinding by:
   A. Replacing the tool in the holder and repositioning the tool by moving the compound and cross feed screws
   B. Replacing the tool in the holder and proceeding with threading
   C. Replacing the tool in the holder, engaging the half-nuts, and repositioning the tool with the compound and cross feed
   D. None of the above

Volume I, Section I Date ____________ Name ________________________________

UNIT 14. BASIC AND ADVANCED THREAD MEASUREMENT

POST TEST

Circle the letter preceding the correct answer.

1. The simplest way to check a thread is:
   A. With a pair of outside calipers
   B. To note when the threads come to a point
   C. To try the mating part
   D. None of the above

2. Internal threads may be quickly checked with a:
   A. Thread ring gage
   B. Thread plug gage
   C. Snap gage
   D. Thread comparator micrometer

3. The Go ring gage should enter the thread fully, but the No-Go ring gage should not engage the thread more turns than:
   A. 5
   B. 3
   C. 2½
   D. 1½

4. Snap gages, ring and plug gages, and trying the thread on the mating part depend on:
   A. The "feel" of the operator
   B. A snap of the gage
   C. Good eyesight
   D. Strong fingers

5. The thread comparator micrometer:
   A. Makes a comparison measurement that is checked with a plug gage
   B. Measures a thread directly on the pitch diameter
   C. Is the micrometer that is used with a three-wire set
   D. Shows a profile of the thread on a screen

6. What measuring instrument is used with the three-wire system?
   A. The optical comparator
   B. The thread comparator micrometer
   C. The screw thread micrometer
   D. An ordinary micrometer

7. The "best" wire size contacts the thread at the:
   A. Flanks at various positions
   B. Pitch diameter
   C. Outer edge
   D. Bottom

8. A screw thread micrometer:
   A. Is used to measure over wires
   B. Compares a thread to a known standard
   C. Measures the pitch diameter directly
   D. Measures the pitch directly

9. The optical comparator:
   A. Measures the thread angle, pitch, depth and truncation
   B. Makes a comparison measurement between a thread and a known standard such as a precision plug gage
   C. Measures the pitch diameter
   D. Can be used for measuring an internal thread

10. The purpose of using gages and measuring instruments to check threads is:
    A. To make sure that external and internal threads have acceptable finishes and major diameters
    B. To insure that a threaded part will fit with its mating part
    C. To insure the interchangeability of threaded parts
    D. They take less time than trying a nut or mating part

Volume I, Section I Date ____________ Name ______________________________

UNIT 15. CUTTING OF UNIFIED INTERNAL THREADS

POST TEST

Circle the letter preceding the correct answer.

1. Internal threads that are cut with a single point tool should have a bore size equal to:
   A. D = major D - 2 x basic thread height x percent of thread
   B. P x .541 inch
   C. The minor diameter of the internal thread
   D. The minor diameter of the external thread

2. The percent of thread of the internal thread is effected by:
   A. Varying the bore diameter
   B. Varying the major diameter
   C. Making taps with 60, 75 and 80 percent threads
   D. Making taps for certain classes of fits such as 1B, 2B and 3B

3. Tap drill charts are usually based on what percent of threads?
   A. 60
   B. 70
   C. 75
   D. 80

4. More precise tap drilled holes may be made by:
   A. Reaming
   B. Boring
   C. Drilling first with a slightly smaller drill
   D. All of the above

5. An 80 percent $\frac{3}{8}$ - 16 NC thread tap drill size is needed. Which of the following is correct?
   A. d = .375 - (.0625 x .541 x 2) = .307 inch diameter
   B. $\frac{1}{16}$ = .375 = P x .625 = .234 inch diameter
   C. $.375 - \left(\frac{.65}{16} \times 2 \times .8\right) = .310$ inch diameter
   D. $\left(\frac{.65}{16} \times 2 \times 8\right) - .375 = .285$ inch diameter

6. Large internal threads are often made on the lathe with single point tools because:
   A. It is faster than by tapping
   B. Cleaner, smoother threads are produced
   C. It is the only way the threads can be produced
   D. Various thread forms can be made and they are concentric to the axis of the work

7. For cutting internal right hand threads, the compound should be swiveled to:
   A. The right 29 degrees
   B. The left 29 degrees
   C. 90 degrees
   D. the right 60 degrees

8. Which of the following would be best suited for measuring the threads per inch of an internal thread?
   A. Rule
   B. Tap
   C. Screw pitch gage
   D. Screw plug gage

9. Deflection of the boring bar causes:
   A. A tapered thread
   B. An undersize, often bell mouth thread
   C. An oversize thread with taper
   D. None of the above

10. If d = D - (P x .541 x 2) is the formula for finding the minor diameter of a unified internal thread, the diameter bore you make for a 1½ - 6 UNC nut should be how many inches in diameter?
    A. 1.127
    B. 1.400
    C. 1.320
    D. 1.256

Volume I, Section I Date ____________ Name ______________________________

UNIT 16. TAPER TURNING, TAPER BORING AND FORMING

POST TEST

Circle the letter preceding the correct answer.

1. What other names are used for slight tapers and for steep tapers when they are used for machining parts?
   A. Self-holding tapers and quick release tapers
   B. Long tapers and short tapers
   C. Sticking tapers and releasing tapers
   D. Draw bolt tapers and Brown and Sharpe tapers

2. In what ways are tapers expressed?
   A. In millimeters per foot and in radians
   B. By included angles and by degrees and minutes
   C. By measuring the offset of the tailstock and by measuring the taper per inch or the taper per foot
   D. In degrees and minutes or by taper per inch or taper per foot

3. How can tapers be turned in a lathe?
   A. With the compound, taper attachment, offset tailstock and tool methods
   B. By the off hand method, the taper slide method, and the tapered tool method
   C. By the angular slide attachment, the offset center, and the single tool
   D. None of the above

4. A finished, tapered workpiece has an included angle of 70 degrees. If the taper is made with the compound, how many degrees should the setting be on the swivel base?
   A. 70
   B. 140
   C. 20
   D. 35

5. If the compound swivel base is set on 60 degrees at the lathe centerline index, how many degrees will the reading be at the cross slide index?
   A. 45
   B. 150
   C. 30
   D. 90

6. The formula for calculating the offset of the tailstock is: $\text{offset} = \frac{L \times (D - d)}{2 \times L_1}$,

   where L is the total length of the piece and L_1 is the length of the taper, D is the large diameter and d is the small diameter. If a shaft that is to be tapered on one end is eight inches long and the taper is to be three inches in length, the shaft diameter is $1\frac{1}{4}$ inches and the small end of the taper 1 inch, how many inches should the offset be?

   A. $\frac{1}{3}$ or .333
   B. $\frac{2}{3}$ or .666
   C. .100
   D. .250

7. How can the tailstock be measured for offset?
   A. With a micrometer caliper or an offset gage
   B. By using a rule to measure the distance between centers
   C. With a dial indicator, a rule, a toolholder and micrometer dial
   D. With a special gaging fixture

8. The two types of taper attachments are the:
   A. Ordinary and sliding
   B. Plain and telescoping
   C. Standard and interlocking
   D. Common and collapsing

9. Tapers may be measured when the work is in the lathe by using:
   A. A rule and micrometer caliper
   B. A taper micrometer
   C. A taper plug or ring gage
   D. All of the above

10. The end or edge of a tool may be set up with a protractor to cut a taper. What kinds of tapers may be made by this method?
   A. Long and slight
   B. Any angle and moderately long
   C. Very short at any angle
   D. Short and steep

Volume I, Section I Date ____________ Name ______________________________________

UNIT 17. USING STEADY AND FOLLOWER RESTS IN THE LATHE

POST TEST

Circle the letter preceding the correct answer.

1. A steady rest should be used to:
   A. Hold the tool steady so it won't chatter
   B. Support long shafts that are being threaded full length
   C. Support workpieces that extend three diameters from the chuck
   D. Support long shafts

2. The follower rest is used for:
   A. Supporting long, springy work by following the tool
   B. Supporting long, springy work and supporting long work for internal machining
   C. Resting the tool so it will not cause the work to chatter and for supporting the tool for extra heavy cuts
   D. Turning workpieces without a center and thus reducing friction; higher speeds can be used

3. When a shaft has centers, the steady rest is set up:
   A. By adjusting the lower jaws finger tight to the shaft while the dead center is in the shaft center, then adjust the top jaw
   B. By turning the shaft and checking for runout with a dial indicator; the jaws are set accordingly
   C. With the shaft between centers, the top jaw is brought down to touch the shaft, then adjust the other two jaws
   D. With the dead center in the shaft center, tighten up the lower two jaws with a wrench, then adjust the top jaw

4. You can prevent a finished shaft from being damaged by the steady rest jaws by:
   A. Keeping them good and tight and by using light oil
   B. Wrapping the shaft with abrasive cloth, abrasive side to the shaft, and by using high pressure lubricant
   C. Readjusting the top jaw when the shaft heats and expands and by using high pressure lubricant and protective material on the jaws
   D. Using hardened jaws, oil and adjust frequently

5. You can set up a steady rest when the shaft has no center by:
   A. Placing a punch mark in the center of the shaft and adjusting the steady rest jaws to align the punch mark to the dead center
   B. Placing a center punch mark in the center of the shaft and measuring to the steady rest frame with a steel rule; adjust the jaws to center the mark
   C. Using a dial indicator to show runout which can be adjusted out by moving the jaws
   D. Setting up a different diameter shaft that has a center and adjust the jaws to it, then place the shaft with no center in the lathe

6. The dial indicator is used to set up the:
   A. Steady rest
   B. Follower rest
   C. Workpiece in a four jaw chuck
   D. Workpiece in a three jaw chuck

7. What is the correct procedure for using the steady rest when the workpiece is rough?
   A. Turn the work slowly
   B. Use lots of oil
   C. Leave the jaws somewhat loose
   D. Turn a smooth bearing spot

8. A square shaft can be turned in a steady rest by:
   A. Bending a piece of extra heavy shim stock around it where the jaws are
   B. Using an external cat head
   C. Using an internal cat head
   D. Using a lathe dog

9. A long, slender shaft must be turned and threaded with an acme thread. It is too springy to machine without support. What can be used to back up the tool?
   A. Follower rest
   B. Steady rest
   C. Compound rest
   D. Tool rest

10. The follower rest jaws can be made to clear the dead center or tailstock spindle when the tool is returned to the start of the cut by:
    A. Readjusting the jaws outward and back in each pass
    B. Moving the jaws to the left of the tool
    C. Making the shaft two inches longer
    D. Making the shaft longer and undercutting the end

Volume I, Section I Date ____________ Name ______________________

UNIT 18. ADDITIONAL THREAD TURNING

POST TEST

Circle the letter preceding the correct answer.

1. When cutting a 1½ - 12 triple thread, the machinist should set the lathe to cut how many threads per inch?
   A. 4
   B. 3
   C. 1½
   D. 12

2. A two start nut turned on a two start bolt would in one revolution advance:
   A. Half the lead
   B. Half the pitch
   C. Twice the pitch
   D. Four times the pitch

3. The distance from a point on one thread to a corresponding point on the next thread on a four start threaded bolt is called the:
   A. Lead
   B. Thread form
   C. Start
   D. Pitch

4. Which one of the following thread starts exerts the most force for a given torque if all have the same pitch?
   A. Single
   B. Three
   C. Two
   D. Four

5. One method of indexing multiple threads is to:
   A. Engage the back gear
   B. Move the dog in the face plate
   C. Disconnect the back gear
   D. Disconnect the thread dial

6. One advantage of multiple lead threads is that they:
   A. Exert more force
   B. Are easier to make
   C. Are more common and are easier to obtain
   D. Provide rapid traverse

7. Multiple lead threads are:
   A. American National only
   B. Of any recognized thread form
   C. Acme and square threads only
   D. Unified, acme, square and buttress

8. You can tell the number of leads on a screw by:
   A. Counting the starting grooves at the end of the screw
   B. Counting the number of threads in one inch
   C. Using a screw pitch gage
   D. Viewing the thread in an optical comparator

9. You can help to avoid pitch error when cutting coarse, multiple lead threads by:
   A. Finishing one thread at a time
   B. Roughing all leads first, then finishing them
   C. Taking heavy cuts in all leads
   D. Roughing out a thread and finishing it before going to the next one

10. When using the compound slide method of indexing, lighter cuts should be taken than when using other methods because:
    A. It keeps the thread from tearing
    B. The compound at 90 degrees will move out of place more easily
    C. The cross feed reads on single depth and therefore makes twice the depth of cut
    D. It is difficult to fasten the toolholder securely enough in this position

Volume I, Section I Date ____________ Name ______________________________________

UNIT 19. ADDITIONAL THREAD FORMS

POST TEST

Circle the letter preceding the correct answer.

1. Five thread forms used on translating screws are:
   A. Acme, Buttress, Whitworth, square and modified square
   B. Square, stub Acme, Acme, Unified and Buttress
   C. Buttress, modified square, square, Acme and stub Acme
   D. Modified square, square, Acme, American National standard and stub Acme

2. Translating type screws are used:
   A. In translating machines
   B. For imparting motion to a mechanical part
   C. As a fastener to connect two dissimilar materials together
   D. Mostly for woodworking

3. The depth of thread in inches for a 1½ - 5 square thread is:
   A. .200
   B. .250
   C. .125
   D. .100

4. The depth of thread in inches for a 1½ - 5 General Purpose Acme thread is:
   A. .120
   B. .110
   C. .210
   D. .220

5. General Purpose Acme threads:
   A. Bear at the flanks
   B. Bear at the major diameter
   C. Have the same clearance at the root and the flank
   D. Generally have very poor finishes so fits are not important

6. How many degrees is the included angle of General Purpose Acme threads?
   A. 60
   B. 29
   C. 14½
   D. 10

7. Stub Acme threads are used:
   A. For short length screws
   B. Where more strength is required
   C. Where a shallow depth with coarse pitch is required
   D. On long screws for translating motion and power

8. How many degrees is the included angle of the modified square thread?
   A. 29
   B. 60
   C. 14½
   D. 10

9. Which is the most commonly used and easiest to machine of the translating type threads?
   A. Acme
   B. Modified square
   C. Square
   D. Buttress

10. Buttress threads are used:
    A. To translate motion
    B. For positioning mechanical parts
    C. To resist great forces that are exerted in one direction only
    D. On special bolts used for the construction of dams and large buildings

Volume I, Section I Date ____________ Name ______________________

UNIT 20. CUTTING ACME THREADS ON THE LATHE

POST TEST

Circle the letter preceding the correct answer.

1. The Acme threading tool forms an included angle of how many degrees?
   A. 30
   B. 55
   C. 29
   D. 60

2. Care should be exercised when grinding and measuring the following on the Acme threading tool. Which is correct?
   A. Back rake, thread angle, and relief angles
   B. End flat width, relief angle, and thread angle
   C. Side rake angle, thread angle, and relief angles
   D. Side rake, back rake, and relief angles

3. Before cutting coarse screw threads, the operator should lubricate:
   A. The leadscrew and gearbox
   B. The ways and cross slide
   C. The carriage and half-nuts
   D. All of the above

4. In what position is the compound normally set for cutting right hand external Acme threads?
   A. 14½ degrees to the right
   B. 14½ degrees to the left
   C. 29 degrees to the right
   D. Set at 90 degrees

5. The Acme tool is aligned to the work with:
   A. A square
   B. The eye
   C. An Acme tool gage
   D. A center gage

6. Which is the correct depth in inches for a 2½ - 3 general purpose external Acme thread?
   A. 1.510
   B. .1510
   C. .3533
   D. .1766

7. Which is the correct bore size in inches for an internal general purpose 2½ - 3 Acme thread?
   A. 2.3333
   B. 2.1667
   C. 1.9876
   D. 2.470

8. Very small internal Acme threads are made with:
   A. Acme tap sets
   B. Special boring bars
   C. Broaches
   D. None of the above

9. The fit is checked on internal Acme threads with:
   A. A screw pitch gage
   B. An Acme thread plug gage
   C. An Acme tool gage
   D. A bore gage

10. Good finishes are obtained when cutting Acme threads by using rigid setups and:
   A. Soluble oil, water based coolant
   B. High speeds and heavy cuts
   C. Low speeds, light cuts and cutting oil
   D. Tools with built up edges and low speeds with a good grade coolant

Volume I, Section I Date ____________ Name ________________________________

UNIT 21. CUTTING METRIC THREADS WITH ENGLISH MEASURE LATHES

POST TEST

Circle the letter preceding the correct answer.

1. English measure lathes can be made to cut metric threads by:
   A. Using a metric to English conversion micrometer collar on the cross slide handle
   B. Changing the gear ratio to 1:24.5 by inserting 129 and 50 tooth gears in the gear train
   C. Changing the numbers on the quick-change gearbox to threads per centimeter
   D. Changing the gear ratio to 1:2.54 by inserting 127 and 50 tooth gears in the gear train

2. Metric threads are expressed (measured) in:
   A. Threads per centimeter
   B. Pitches (in millimeters)
   C. Threads per 25.4 mm
   D. Threads per meter

3. When metric translating gears are in the gear train, the thread settings on the quick-change gearbox actually refer to:
   A. Threads per centimeter
   B. Threads per inch
   C. Metric pitches
   D. Inch measure pitches

4. Which two gears are used for adapting an English measure lathe to metric measure?
   A. 100 and 137
   B. 50 and 129
   C. 50 and 127
   D. 60 and 18

5. Which of the following is the ratio of these two gears?
   A. 1:2.54
   B. 1:24.5
   C. 1:127
   D. 1:39.37

6. When cutting metric threads on an English measure lathe, at the end of a threading pass the:
   A. Half-nuts should be disengaged, the tool backed out and returned to the starting position; use the same line on the threading dial for the next pass
   B. Procedure is exactly like that for cutting inch measure threads
   C. Lathe is reversed and the half-nuts remain engaged
   D. Half-nuts are left engaged, the tool is moved out, and the lathe is reversed

7. The quick-change gearbox should be set for how many threads for cutting an M12x1.25 thread?
   A. 12
   B. 24
   C. 8
   D. There is no whole number on the quick-change gearbox for this thread

8. What is the correct single depth of thread in millimeters for an M12x1.25 external thread if the formula is .613P?
   A. 7.35
   B. .77
   C. 9.19
   D. 1.78

9. The turned metric screw shank can be measured with:
   A. A metric micrometer
   B. An inch micrometer and conversion table or formula
   C. A metric vernier caliper
   D. All of the above

10. External metric screw threads may be checked for size with:
    A. A metric micrometer and best wire size, metric, 3-wires
    B. A metric micrometer and best wire size, inch, 3-wires
    C. Any metric nut having the same major diameter
    D. Any metric nut having the same pitch

Volume I, Section I Date ____________ Name ______________________________

UNIT 22. USING CARBIDES AND OTHER TOOL MATERIALS ON THE LATHE

POST TEST

Circle the letter preceding the correct answer.

1. What materials are used to make straight carbide inserts?
   A. Tungsten, cobalt and titanium
   B. Cobalt and tungsten carbide
   C. Tantalum carbide, tungsten carbide, titanium carbide and cobalt
   D. Titanium carbide and cobalt

2. Normal wear is seen on a carbide tool as:
   A. Cratering
   B. Breakage due to thermal shock
   C. Breakdown due to built up edge
   D. Edge or flank wear

3. What effect does increasing the cobalt content have on carbides?
   A. Tools become more wear resistant
   B. Tools become tougher
   C. Tools become harder
   D. No change

4. To improve the resistance of cemented carbides to cratering, the following change in composition is made:
   A. Increase the percentage of cobalt
   B. Increase the percentage of tungsten carbide
   C. Add titanium carbides
   D. Add tantalum carbide

5. To resist softening and deformation at high cutting speeds, the following cemented carbide would be best:
   A. Straight tungsten carbide
   B. One with titanium carbide added
   C. One with tantalum carbide added
   D. One with titanium carbide added and a high percentage of cobalt

6. Which insert shape is strongest and offers the greatest number of possible cutting edges?
   A. Round
   B. Triangular
   C. Square
   D. Diamond

7. Increasing the fpm by 50 percent over cutting speeds recommended for carbides will:
   A. Decrease tool life by over 80 percent
   B. Decrease tool life by over 60 percent
   C. Have less effect on tool life than increasing the recommended rate of feed by 50 percent
   D. Have no appreciable effect on carbide tool life

8. Which grades of the following CCPA number groups are used for machining steel?
   A. C-3, C-4
   B. C-7, C-8
   C. C-1 to C-8
   D. C-1 to C-4

9. The selection of nose radius must be based upon:
   A. Tool strength requirements only as determined by feed rate and depth of cut
   B. Surface finish requirements only as determined by part specifications and feed rate
   C. Tool strength and surface finish requirements
   D. The thickness of the insert, feed rate, and depth of cut

10. A Style A tool set at 90 degrees to the axis of the work with a .030 inch feed will produce a chip thickness of how many inches?
    A. .015
    B. .060
    C. .030
    D. .003

11. The term "clearance" refers to:
    A. Side relief on negative rake tools
    B. Tool shank clearance below the carbide tip
    C. End relief on the carbide part of a brazed tool
    D. Side relief on a positive rake tool

12. Ceramic tools are made of:
    A. Aluminum oxide
    B. Cemented iron oxide
    C. Porcelain
    D. Aluminum and carbon

13. Ceramic tools should be used:
    A. For interrupted cuts
    B. Low speeds only
    C. On any lathe setup
    D. Where excessive wear is evident on carbides

14. Diamond and polycrystalline diamond tools are used to:
    A. Replace carbide tools on most materials
    B. Machine hard, abrasive materials at high speed
    C. Make intermittent cuts at low speeds
    D. Take heavy cuts for high stock removal

15. Brazed carbide tools are ground on:
    A. Titanium oxide wheels
    B. Aluminum oxide wheels
    C. Tungsten carbide wheels
    D. Silicon carbide wheels

Volume II, Section A   Date ____________ Name ______________________________

UNIT 1. VERTICAL BAND MACHINE SAFETY

POST TEST

Circle the letter preceding the correct answer.

1. A primary safety consideration on the vertical band machine is:
   A. Ear protection
   B. Foot protection
   C. Eye protection
   D. Always clear chips with a rag and not your hands

2. You are using a two-idler wheel vertical band machine with a short blade running over only one-idler wheel. What is required when operating under this condition?
   A. A wheel brake must be applied to the unused idler wheel
   B. An additional guard on the left side of the blade wheel
   C. Band tension should be less
   D. Band tension should be more

3. Round stock cut on the vertical band machine:
   A. Is very common in the machine shop
   B. Both C and D
   C. Should be avoided if possible unless held in a vise or other suitable workholding fixture
   D. May turn and cause an injury as well as damage the blade

4. When changing a blade on the vertical band machine:
   A. All blade and wheel guards must be removed from the machine
   B. The speed selection must be set at the lowest speed setting
   C. It is preferable to shut off the electrical power to the machine tool
   D. It is preferable to shut off the electrical power to the machine shop

5. To keep fingers away from the blade:
   A. Use a pusher whenever possible
   B. Wear gloves whenever possible
   C. Push the workpiece with a rag used as a cushion
   D. Avoid sawing on the vertical band machine whenever possible

Volume II, Section A Date ____________ Name ______________________________________

UNIT 2. PREPARING TO USE THE VERTICAL BAND MACHINE

POST TEST

Circle the letter preceding the correct answer.

1. The process by which the band weld is softened to improve strength qualities is called:
   A. Softening
   B. Tempering
   C. Forging
   D. Annealing

2. Band tracking is adjusted by tilting or adjusting the:
   A. Worktable
   B. Idler wheels
   C. Tiltometer
   D. Tracometer

3. End grinding of the blade ends before welding should be done:
   A. On each end separately
   B. With the teeth on the same side
   C. With the teeth opposed
   D. On the pedestal grinder

4. When grinding the band weld:
   A. Be careful not to grind the teeth
   B. Grind on both sides of the band
   C. Check the thickness of the band in the grinding gage
   D. All of the above

5. The band guide setting gage should be used on:
   A. The same side on both upper and lower guides
   B. The opposite sides top and bottom
   C. The band guide adjustment only if the band is not available
   D. Narrow band guides only

6. After the blade has been welded:
   A. Any tooth spacing will be acceptable
   B. The teeth across the weld should be closer together for extra strength
   C. A small space should exist between the teeth across the weld
   D. Tooth spacing across the weld should be the same as the rest of the band

7. Band tension is accomplished by moving and adjusting the:
   A. Drive wheel
   B. Variable speed pulley
   C. Idler wheel
   D. Tensionmeter

8. Before operating the vertical band machine, you should:
   A. Check speed range transmission oil level
   B. Lubricate the variable speed pulley hub
   C. Check hydraulic oil level
   D. All of the above

9. The chip brush removes chips from the:
   A. Workpiece
   B. Band wheel
   C. Band guide
   D. Worktable

10. Properly end grind, weld, anneal and weld grind a scrap band sample or prepare a new band for the band machine in your shop. Submit the welded sample or band to your instructor for approval.

Volume II, Section A Date ___________ Name ___________________________________

UNIT 3. USING THE VERTICAL BAND MACHINE

POST TEST

Circle the letter preceding the correct answer.

1. You are sawing mild steel 6 inches thick. This will require a blade with what kind of pitch?
   A. Fine
   B. Coarse
   C. Raker
   D. Segmented pitch diamond blade

2. The variable speed pulley has the belt running near the outer edge. This will produce a band speed that is:
   A. Faster
   B. Slower
   C. High
   D. Low

3. The upper guide post should be adjusted so that:
   A. The blade guide just touches the workpiece
   B. One inch clearance exists between the band guide and the workpiece
   C. The band guide is as close to the work as possible
   D. None of the above

4. Recommended feed pressure should be determined by:
   A. Experimentation
   B. Using a longer pusher
   C. Counting the teeth in the band and multiplying by five
   D. Consulting the job selector

5. A fine pitch band should be used for material that is:
   A. Thin
   B. Thick
   C. Hard
   D. Soft

6. Scored bands can:
   A. Have reduced lives
   B. Become brittle and break
   C. Become less flexible
   D. All of the above

7. To insure that the band set is adequate for a specific contour cut, you should make a test cut on:
   A. A piece of wood
   B. Thin sheetmetal
   C. A scrap of the same material and thickness as the workpiece
   D. The workpiece

8. You are preparing to saw a very soft nonmetallic material that requires a smooth cut. You would probably use what type of band?
   A. Fine pitch
   B. Scalloped or wavy edge
   C. Low speed band
   D. Diamond edge

9. Shifting from high to low speed range:
   A. Must be done at the slowest band speed setting
   B. Can be done at any speed setting
   C. Must be done as quickly as possible so as not to grind transmission gears
   D. Should be avoided unless absolutely necessary

10. In order to cut a radius of $\frac{5}{8}$ inch, a saw width of ______ inch is required. (Consult the job selector on the band machine in your shop.)
   A. $\frac{1}{2}$
   B. $\frac{5}{16}$
   C. $\frac{1}{4}$
   D. $\frac{1}{16}$

Volume II, Section B Date ____________ Name ______________________________

UNIT 1. VERTICAL MILLING MACHINE SAFETY

POST TEST

Circle the letter preceding the correct answer.

1. Operating a milling machine is dangerous:
   A. Late in the evening
   B. When another person is watching
   C. When you are very tired or sick
   D. All of the above

2. A person is dressed safely for machine work when wearing:
   A. Short sleeve shirt
   B. No jewelry
   C. A cap over long hair
   D. All of the above

3. Eye protection in a shop:
   A. Should contain tinted lenses
   B. Should be worn
   C. Is not very important
   D. Can be sunglasses

4. Machine guards:
   A. Should be in place when a machine is operated
   B. Protect a machine from falling objects
   C. Should be removed when they interfere with the machine operation
   D. All of the above

5. Milling machine chips:
   A. Are very sharp
   B. Should not be removed with bare hands
   C. May be contaminated
   D. All of the above

6. A safe work area:
   A. Is a clean place
   B. Has only small parts laying on the floor
   C. Has a yearly safety inspection
   D. Is expensive to maintain

7. Heavy objects are:
   A. Lifted with a hoist
   B. Lifted by more than one person
   C. Lifted with the leg muscles and a straight back
   D. All of the above

8. Cutting tools are sharp and should be handled:
   A. With work gloves
   B. Very carefully
   C. With rags
   D. All of the above

9. The vertical milling machine head can be swivelled safely by:
   A. Loosening the clamping bolts completely
   B. Keeping a slight drag on the clamping bolts
   C. Alternately tightening and loosening the clamps
   D. All of the above

10. Measurements:
    A. Should be made only when the spindle is at a standstill
    B. Can be made while the spindle is slowly turning
    C. Can be made any time
    D. Have to be accurate

Volume II, Section B Date ___________ Name ___________________________

UNIT 2. THE VERTICAL SPINDLE MILLING MACHINE

POST TEST

Circle the letter preceding the correct answer.

1. A major component of the vertical milling machine is:
   A. The toolhead
   B. The gib adjustment
   C. The coolant pump
   D. All of the above

2. The quill can be moved by:
   A. The quill feed hand lever
   B. The quill feed hand wheel
   C. The quill power feed
   D. All of the above

3. The spindle speed range is changed from high to low with:
   A. The spindle motor running
   B. The spindle coasting
   C. The spindle stopped
   D. None of the above

4. The spindle brake is used:
   A. When changing tools
   B. To change the spindle speed range
   C. When engaging the power feed
   D. All of the above

5. The quill lock is used to:
   A. Change tools
   B. Provide rigidity when milling
   C. Take up backlash
   D. All of the above

6. Loose machine slides:
   A. Are tightened with gib adjustment screws
   B. Need to be lubricated
   C. Can be tightened with the table clamps
   D. All of the above

7. The ram:
   A. Can be moved
   B. Gives added machine capacity
   C. Holds the toolhead
   D. All of the above

8. On a variable speed spindle drive:
   A. The spindle is stopped for speed changes
   B. The spindle is revolved for speed changes
   C. The speed is changed automatically
   D. None of the above

9. The clamping devices of the machine slides:
   A. Should always be tight
   B. Should be loose
   C. Should be tightened except for the moving slide
   D. None of the above

10. The saddle supports:
    A. The knee
    B. The column
    C. The table
    D. None of the above

11. Match the part name with the letter identifying the same part in Figure 6.

    1. _____ Spindle brake
    2. _____ Column
    3. _____ Table clamp
    4. _____ Table traverse handle
    5. _____ Cross traverse handle
    6. _____ Table power feed
    7. _____ Variable speed control
    8. _____ Motor
    9. _____ Quill feed hand lever
    10. _____ Vertical traverse crank
    11. _____ Toolhead
    12. _____ Table
    13. _____ Spindle
    14. _____ Knee
    15. _____ Saddle
    16. _____ Forward-reverse motor switch
    17. _____ Table stop dog
    18. _____ Turret clamps
    19. _____ Knee clamp
    20. _____ Power feed change lever

Figure 6. Vertical milling machine. (Lane Community College)

Volume II, Section B   Date ____________ Name ______________________________

UNIT 3. VERTICAL MILLING MACHINE OPERATIONS

POST TEST

Circle the letter preceding the correct answer.

1. A precise square on the end of a shaft is best machined:
   A. With a vertical shaping attachment
   B. With a dividing head
   C. By accurately centering the cutter over the shaft
   D. All of the above

2. When milling a cavity:
   A. The cutting pressure should be against the cutter rotation
   B. The cutting pressure should be with the cutter rotation
   C. The backlash in the table feed mechanism should be ignored
   D. None of the above

3. Circular slots are best machined with:
   A. The aid of a rotary table
   B. Circular slot cutters
   C. The workpiece clamped to the table
   D. All of the above

4. When milling a keyway into a shaft:
   A. The cutter needs to be centered with the shaft
   B. The cutter has to be the correct size
   C. The cutter should be sharp
   D. All of the above

5. Angular cuts on workpieces can be made:
   A. With the peripheral teeth on an end mill
   B. By tilting the workpiece
   C. By tilting the work head
   D. All of the above

6. A vertical shaping attachment:
   A. Uses only small diameter end mills
   B. Is used to enlarge round holes
   C. Is used to machine irregular internal shapes
   D. All of the above

7. A right angle milling attachment:
   A. Makes possible the milling of internal slots
   B. Is used in hard to get to places on a workpiece
   C. Can be used to cut slots at different angles
   D. All of the above

8. Accurate round holes can be machined with the use of the:
   A. Offset boring head
   B. Rotary table
   C. Circular milling attachment
   D. Right angle milling attachment

9. Holes can be drilled on a vertical milling machine by:
   A. Using the quill power feed
   B. Using the sensitive quill feed
   C. Raising the knee of the machine
   D. All of the above

10. How many thousandths of an inch of material should be left for a finishing cut when roughing out a cavity?
   A. .010
   B. .030
   C. .060
   D. .080

Volume II, Section B Date ___________ Name ________________________________

UNIT 4. CUTTING TOOLS FOR THE VERTICAL MILLING MACHINE

POST TEST

Circle the letter preceding the correct answer.

1. End mills capable of making their own starting holes are termed:
   A. Starting hole
   B. Plunge cut
   C. Center cutting teeth
   D. Center drilled

2. Fast helix end mills are used to machine:
   A. Aluminum
   B. Brass
   C. Hard steel
   D. Cast iron

3. Carbide tipped end mills should be used to machine:
   A. Highly abrasive materials
   B. Very soft materials
   C. Deep grooves
   D. All of the above

4. To remove a considerable amount of material, you should use which kind of an end mill?
   A. Slow helix
   B. Regular helix
   C. Fast helix
   D. Roughing

5. Milling cutters with carbide inserts are used to:
   A. Avoid resharpening
   B. Machine most materials
   C. Remove material efficiently
   D. All of the above

6. Shell end mills are:
   A. Driven by shell end mill drivers
   B. Mounted on shell end mill arbors
   C. Always right hand cut
   D. None of the above

7. Dovetails are milled with:
   A. Single angle milling cutters
   B. Double angle milling cutters
   C. Dovetail cutters
   D. Tapered end mills

8. Ball end mills are used:
   A. To mill round bottom grooves
   B. To form fillets
   C. In tracer milling
   D. All of the above

9. The best method of holding and driving an end mill is:
   A. A jacobs chuck
   B. A split collet
   C. A solid collet
   D. An end mill driver

10. Frequently interchanged cutting tools should be held:
   A. In quick-change tool holders
   B. By the driving flats
   C. In a tool stand
   D. With setscrews

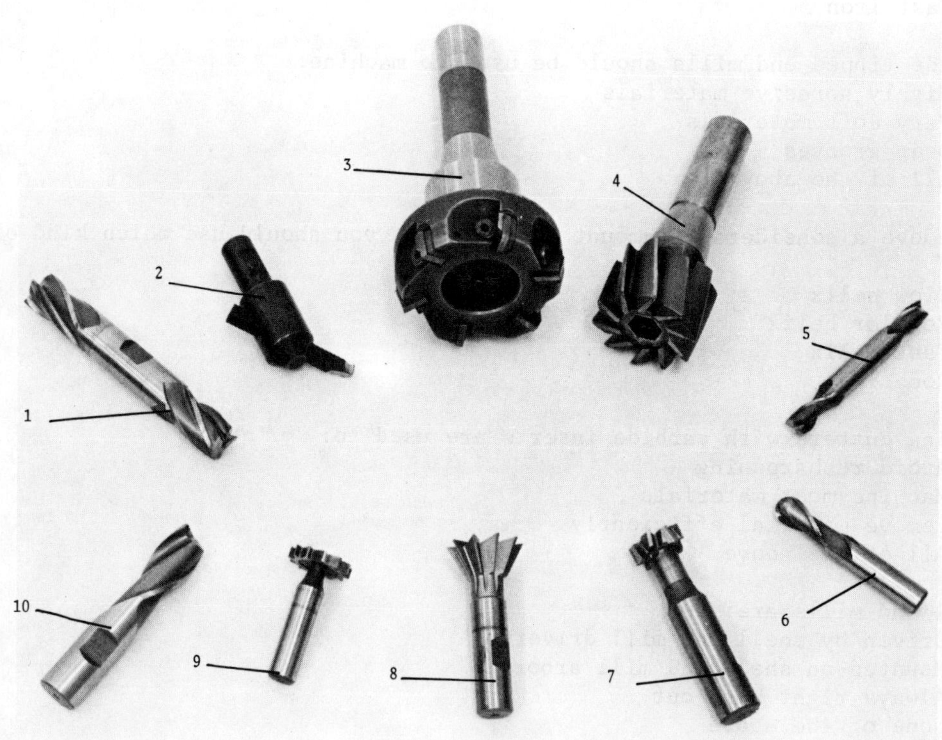

Figure 26.

11. Identify the milling cutters shown in Figure 26.

1.	6.
2.	7.
3.	8.
4.	9.
5.	10.

Volume II, Section B Date ____________ Name ______________________________

UNIT 5. SETUPS ON THE VERTICAL MILLING MACHINE

POST TEST

Circle the letter preceding the correct answer.

1. A workpiece which is to be clamped to the machine table can be aligned with the table axis by:
   A. Placing it against stops in the T-slots
   B. Measuring from the edge of the table to the side of the work
   C. Indicating the side of the workpiece
   D. All of the above

2. To align a vise on a machine table:
   A. Indicate the solid vise jaw
   B. Measure the vise jaw with a rule
   C. Place the vise against stops in the table T-slots
   D. Indicate the adjustable vise jaw

3. When is the tool head alignment checked with a dial indicator?
   A. Before any machining takes place
   B. Once every day
   C. Before any precise machining square to the table surface is performed
   D. When any tool changing takes place

4. Prior to indicating a tool head for squareness to the table, tighten:
   A. The knee clamping screws
   B. The saddle clamps
   C. The table clamps
   D. All of the above

5. To position the spindle axis precisely over a workpiece edge:
   A. Use a dial indicator and a precision parallel
   B. Use an edge finder
   C. Move the table while observing the micrometer dials
   D. All of the above

6. When an edge finder is used to align a spindle axis with a workpiece edge, the spindle RPM should be:
   A. 300
   B. 500
   C. 700
   D. 900

7. When the tip walks off sideways on a .200 inch diameter edge finder, the spindle axis is what part of an inch from the workpiece edge?
   A. .100
   B. .200
   C. .300
   D. .400

8. The center of an existing hole is aligned with the spindle axis with the aid of:
   A. An edge finder
   B. A dial indicator
   C. A precision rule
   D. All of the above

9. When aligning a work head, the indicator preload should be what part of an inch?
   A. .005
   B. .015
   C. .030
   D. .045

10. While aligning a work head, the head clamping bolts should be:
   A. Tight
   B. Loose
   C. Exerting a slight drag
   D. Removed

Volume II, Section B Date ____________ Name ________________________________

UNIT 6. USING END MILLS

POST TEST

Circle the letter preceding the correct answer.

1. Lower cutting speeds are used when machining:
   A. Hard materials
   B. Abrasive materials
   C. Tough materials
   D. All of the above

2. High cutting speeds are used with:
   A. Heavy cuts
   B. Light cuts
   C. Large diameter cutters
   D. All of the above

3. Cutting fluids should be used when machining:
   A. Cast iron
   B. Steel
   C. Brass
   D. All of the above

4. Cutting fluids:
   A. Prolong tool life
   B. Increase production
   C. Act as lubricants
   D. All of the above

5. On a setup that is not very rigid use a:
   A. Higher cutting speed
   B. Lower cutting speed
   C. Larger diameter cutter
   D. Heavy feed

6. Under normal cutting conditions, the depth of cut for an end mill should be no more than:
   A. ¼ the cutter diameter
   B. ½ the cutter diameter
   C. The diameter of the cutter
   D. 2 times the cutter diameter

7. The effects of a very small feed rate are:
   A. Very good surface finishes
   B. Long lasting cutting edges
   C. Rapid cutting edge failures
   D. Cutting edge chipping

8. The longest tool life can be obtained when using:
   A. The right cutting speed
   B. The correct coolant
   C. A feed rate that is not too low
   D. All of the above

9. What is the RPM for a ¼ inch diameter, four flute end mill at a cutting speed of 200 SFM?
   A. 1200
   B. 2200
   C. 3200
   D. 4200

10. What is the feed rate in IPM for a ½ inch diameter, two flute end mill with a cutting speed of 100SFM and a feed per tooth of .003 inch?
    A. 1.8
    B. 2.8
    C. 3.8
    D. 4.8

Volume II, Section B   Date ___________ Name ______________________________

UNIT 7. USING THE OFFSET BORING HEAD

POST TEST

Circle the letter preceding the correct answer.

1. An adjustable boring head is needed to make:
   A. Nonstandard size holes
   B. Holes in specific locations
   C. True cylindrical holes
   D. All of the above

2. The cutting edge of the boring tool:
   A. Must be at right angles to the axis of the tool slide
   B. Must be in line with the axis of the tool slide
   C. Can be at any angle to the axis of the tool slide
   D. None of the above

3. The hole size obtained by boring is affected by:
   A. The length of the boring tool
   B. The diameter of the boring tool
   C. The depth of cut
   D. All of the above

4. A bored hole can be tapered:
   A. If the tool slide is not locked
   B. Because of the deflection of the boring tool
   C. If the tool wears
   D. All of the above

5. Vibrations in a boring operation can be:
   A. Caused by a long boring tool
   B. Caused by an unbalanced cutting tool
   C. Stopped by increasing the feed rate
   D. All of the above

6. Rigidity in a boring operation is obtained by:
   A. Using a short, large diameter boring tool
   B. Increasing the cutting speed
   C. Decreasing the feed rate
   D. All of the above

7. When the depth of cut in a boring operation is increased, the:
   A. Tool deflection will increase also
   B. Tool deflection will not increase
   C. Tool will be deflected less
   D. Surface finish will improve

8. Hole size variations can be caused by:
   A. Tool wear
   B. Feed rate changes
   C. Changes in depth of cut
   D. All of the above

9. The cutting speed for a boring operation is affected by:
   A. The kind of work material machined
   B. The kind of tool material used
   C. The rigidity of the setup
   D. All of the above

10. Before a finishing cut is made:
   A. Determine the amount of hole size change for each graduation of the tool slide
   B. The feed rate should be increased
   C. The cutting speed is decreased
   D. All of the above

Volume II, Section C   Date ___________ Name ______________________________

UNIT 1. HORIZONTAL MILLING MACHINE SAFETY

POST TEST

Circle the letter preceding the correct answer.

1. Chips should be cleaned from the work area with:
   A. Your hands
   B. A rag
   C. An air hose
   D. A brush

2. While operating a milling machine, keep your hands away from the:
   A. Arbor support
   B. Moving table
   C. Revolving cutter
   D. Vise handle

3. It is dangerous to operate a milling machine when wearing:
   A. Loose clothing
   B. Loose, long hair
   C. Rings
   D. All of the above

4. Machine controls should be operated by:
   A. The machine operator
   B. The person nearest to them
   C. A highly skilled person
   D. The machinist's helper

5. Eye protection should be worn in a shop:
   A. When near a machine
   B. When operating a machine
   C. At all times
   D. When walking through the shop

6. Measurements should be made:
   A. After the spindle stands still
   B. During a finishing cut
   C. When needed
   D. Prior to the finishing cut

7. Heavy workpieces should be lifted with:
   A. A hoist
   B. Someone's help
   C. A straight back
   D. All of the above

8. A safe work area:
   A. Has no oil spills on the floor
   B. Is a clean area
   C. Is free of parts to stumble over
   D. All of the above

9. A safe machine operator:
   A. Is close to the machine controls
   B. Observes all other operators
   C. Talks with other operators
   D. Is carefree

10. Accidents can be prevented by:
   A. Thinking before doing
   B. Being careful and alert
   C. Learning and understanding safety rules
   D. All of the above

Volume II, Section C Date __________ Name ______________________________

UNIT 2. PLAIN AND UNIVERSAL HORIZONTAL MILLING MACHINES

POST TEST

Circle the letter preceding the correct answer.

1. The saddle moves when operating the:
   A. Vertical feed
   B. Cross feed
   C. Length feed
   D. None of the above

2. The front end of a milling machine spindle:
   A. Is the spindle nose
   B. Has a vertical fine adjustment
   C. Is the arbor support
   D. Is flexible

3. The difference between a plain milling machine and a universal milling machine is that the universal milling machine table:
   A. Is longer
   B. Is wider
   C. Swivels
   D. Has more travel

4. Milling machine table movements can be measured in inches as small as:
   A. .0005
   B. .001
   C. .005
   D. .010

5. Fast table movements are obtained by using the:
   A. Power feed
   B. Hand wheel
   C. Rapid traverse
   D. Instant locator

6. The spindle rotation is reversed:
   A. After the machine stops
   B. At slow spindle speeds
   C. At the end of each cut
   D. During light cuts

7. A universal milling machine is necessary to:
   A. Machine a part square
   B. Straddle mill
   C. Mill a helical gear
   D. None of the above

8. Spindle speeds are changed with the spindle motor running:
   A. On a variable speed drive
   B. On a geared head drive
   C. On a small milling machine
   D. To make shifting easier

9. The purpose of the overarm is:
   A. To hold the arbor support
   B. The extension of the spindle
   C. To hold large face mills
   D. Strengthen the column

10. Trip dogs:
    A. Engage power feeds
    B. Disengage power feeds
    C. Extend the table travel
    D. All of the above

11. With the use of the illustration (Figure 6), match the part letter with the number of the word describing it.

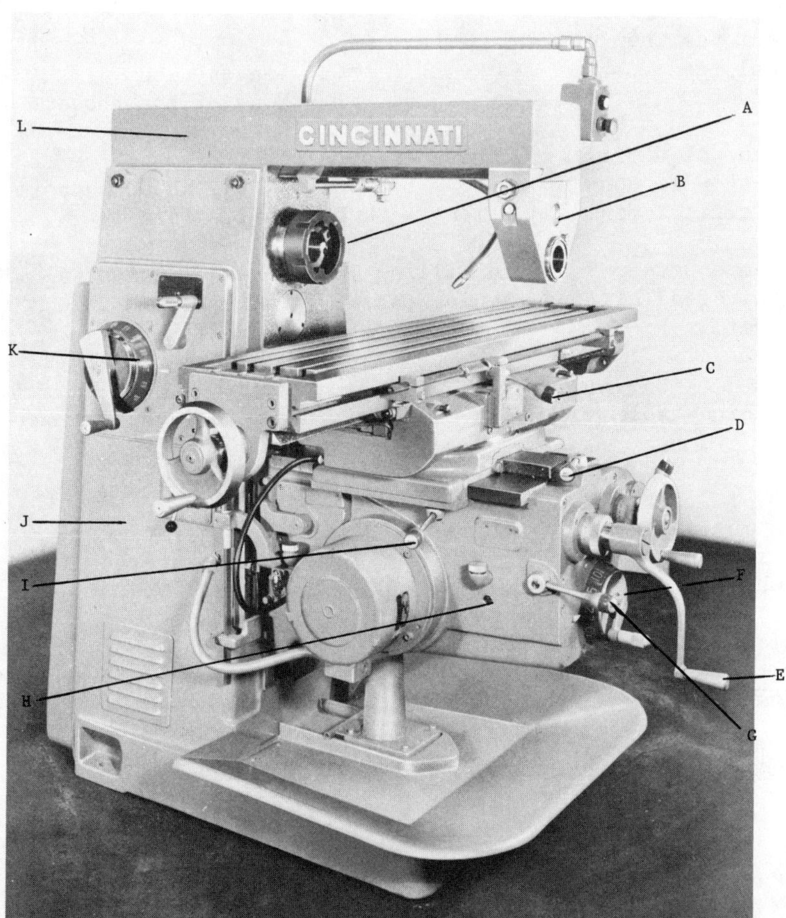

Figure 6. Horizontal milling machine. (Courtesy of Cincinnati Milacron.)

A. ____
B. ____
C. ____
D. ____
E. ____
F. ____
G. ____
H. ____
I. ____
J. ____

1. Overarm
2. Column
3. Speed change dial
4. Knee
5. Vertical feed crank
6. Arbor support
7. Spindle nose
8. Longitudinal feed lever
9. Feed change dial
10. Rapid traverse lever
11. Saddle clamp
12. Vertical power feed lever

Volume II, Section C Date __________ Name ________________________________

UNIT 3. TYPES OF SPINDLES, ARBORS AND ADAPTORS

POST TEST

Circle the letter preceding the correct answer.

1. A style C arbor is used to hold and drive:
   A. Shell end mills
   B. Large face mills
   C. Ball end mills
   D. All of the above

2. A small chip between the arbor shank and the spindle socket will make the:
   A. Arbor harder to drive
   B. Arbor longer
   C. Drive more positive
   D. Arbor run out

3. Arbors should be stored in an upright position because they:
   A. May bend laying on their sides
   B. Need to be stress relieved
   C. Need to be compressed slightly
   D. None of the above

4. The overarm support should be:
   A. As close to the cutter as possible
   B. As far from the cutter as possible
   C. Tight on the arbor
   D. Loose on the arbor

5. The national milling machine taper is how many inches per foot?
   A. $2\frac{1}{2}$
   B. 3
   C. $3\frac{1}{2}$
   D. 4

6. The arbor nut should be:
   A. Tightened after the arbor support is in place
   B. Tightened before the arbor support is in place
   C. Extra large for large cutters
   D. None of the above

7. When the arbor nut is tightened too much it will:
   A. Compress the cutter
   B. Compress the spacers
   C. Bend the arbor
   D. All of the above

8. The arbor is driven by:
   A. The friction between the tapers
   B. The keys in the spindle nose
   C. The pull of the draw-in bar
   D. All of the above

9. Milling machine adaptors are used to:
   A. Drive shank type milling cutters
   B. Increase the capabilities of the milling machine
   C. Increase the efficiency of the milling operation
   D. All of the above

10. Tapered shank end mills can be driven by:
   A. An end mill arbor
   B. Self-holding taper adaptors
   C. Spring chuck adaptors
   D. All of the above

Volume II, Section C Date __________ Name ________________________________

UNIT 4. ARBOR DRIVEN MILLING CUTTERS

POST TEST

Circle the letter preceding the correct answer.

1. Plain milling cutters are used to produce:
   A. Flat surfaces at right angles to the cutter axis
   B. Flat surfaces at any angle to the cutter axis
   C. Flat surfaces parallel to the cutter axis
   D. Surfaces with an irregular outline

2. Heavy duty plain milling cutters:
   A. Have many teeth
   B. Are used to machine heavy workpieces
   C. Chatter easily
   D. Have coarse teeth

3. Light duty plain milling cutters:
   A. Have many teeth
   B. Are used to machine light workpieces
   C. Have coarse teeth
   D. Are used to mill small steps

4. Contoured surfaces are machine with:
   A. Contour saws
   B. Stagger tooth cutters
   C. Form relieved cutters
   D. Helical plain milling cutters

5. Helical milling cutters:
   A. Have a smooth cutting action
   B. Chatter easily
   C. Leave rough surfaces
   D. Cannot be resharpened

6. When facing the spindle, a right hand cutter:
   A. Rotates counterclockwise
   B. Rotates clockwise
   C. Has form relieved teeth
   D. Has side cutting teeth

7. Straight tooth side cutting mills:
   A. Are used to mill deep grooves
   B. Are used to mill shallow grooves
   C. Are also called slab mills
   D. Have large chip spaces

8. Angular milling cutters are used:
   A. To mill dovetails
   B. To chamfer workpieces
   C. To mill V-notches
   D. All of the above

9. Metal slitting saws are used to:
   A. Mill flat surfaces
   B. Cut off materials
   C. Mill dovetails
   D. All of the above

10. Half side milling cutters are used to:
   A. Mill deep grooves
   B. Mill shallow grooves
   C. Straddle mill
   D. None of the above

11. Identify the milling cutters shown in Figure 18.

Figure 18. Arbor driven milling cutters. (Lane Community College)

1. ______________________ 6. ______________________

2. ______________________ 7. ______________________

3. ______________________ 8. ______________________

4. ______________________ 9. ______________________

5. ______________________ 10. ______________________

Volume II, Section C Date __________ Name ________________________________

UNIT 5. SETTING SPEEDS AND FEEDS ON THE HORIZONTAL MILLING MACHINE

POST TEST

Circle the letter preceding the correct answer.

1. Cutting speed is expressed as:
   A. Surface feet per second
   B. Surface feed per minute
   C. Inches per minute
   D. Surface feet per revolution

2. The cutting speed used to do a job depends on:
   A. The work material
   B. The condition of the machine
   C. The tool material
   D. All of the above

3. The cutting speed is:
   A. The same for soft or hard materials
   B. Lower for harder materials
   C. Lower for softer materials
   D. None of the above

4. When coolant is used, it will:
   A. Lengthen the life of the tool
   B. Increase the power requirement
   C. Shorten the life of the tool
   D. None of the above

5. What is the RPM for a 3½ inch diameter cutter with a CS of 150 SFM?
   A. 171
   B. 191
   C. 211
   D. 231

6. Feed rate on a milling machine is expresses in:
   A. Inches per second
   B. Inches per minute
   C. Feet per second
   D. Feet per minute

7. A feed rate that is too low will:
   A. Leave a very smooth finish
   B. Speed up the job
   C. Dull the cutter quickly
   D. All of the above

8. When starting a cut, it is best to:
   A. Decrease the feed at first
   B. Use the calculated feed rate
   C. Increase the feed at first
   D. None of the above

9. The feed is adjustable independently from the speed because:
   A. All cutters don't have the same number of teeth
   B. All cutters don't have the same diameter
   C. All materials don't machine in the same way
   D. All of the above

10. What is the feed rate in IPM for a 4 inch diameter cutter with 12 teeth, a feed per tooth of .010 inch and a CS of 100?
   A. 6
   B. 8
   C. 10
   D. 12

Volume II, Section C Date __________ Name ______________________________

UNIT 6. WORKHOLDING AND LOCATING DEVICES ON THE MILLING MACHINE

POST TEST

Circle the letter preceding the correct answer.

1. When a workpiece is fastened to the table with a clamp and bolt:
   A. The clamp should be as long as possible
   B. The bolt should be as close to the workpiece as possible
   C. The bolt should be as far from the workpiece as possible
   D. None of the above

2. A finished surface can be protected from clamping marks by:
   A. A thin piece of aluminum
   B. A strip of paper
   C. A piece of sheet metal
   D. All of the above

3. A stop block:
   A. Limits table travel
   B. Is used instead of a screw jack
   C. Is used to raise a workpiece
   D. Prevents work movement

4. A rough casting can be securely held for machining:
   A. By clamping it to the table
   B. In an all-steel vise
   C. In a fixture
   D. All of the above

5. A small gear is cut:
   A. In a dividing head
   B. On a rotary table
   C. In a small swivel vise
   D. In a gear cutting fixture

6. Work involving compound angles can be held in which type of vise?
   A. Compound
   B. Plain
   C. Universal
   D. Quick action

7. T-slots in a machine table:
   A. Are parallel to the table sides
   B. Can be used to align workpieces
   C. Are used to fasten attachments to the table
   D. All of the above

8. Before placing rough castings on a machine table:
   A. Place a shim on the table
   B. Mount the cutter in the machine
   C. Align the screw jacks on the table
   D. All of the above

9. Clamping a workpiece on an unsupported section:
   A. May bend the workpiece
   B. May break the workpiece
   C. May distort the workpiece
   D. All of the above

10. A workpiece should be secured in a vise by:
    A. Striking the crank with a lead hammer
    B. Striking the crank with a machinists hammer
    C. Tightening the crank by hand
    D. Tightening the screw jack

Volume II, Section C Date __________ Name ______________________________

UNIT 7. PLAIN MILLING ON THE HORIZONTAL MILLING MACHINE

POST TEST

Circle the letter preceding the correct answer.

1. The cutting pressure from a milling cutter:
   A. Holds the vise on the table
   B. Should be against the solid jaw
   C. Should be against the movable jaw
   D. None of the above

2. Which is the more accurate tool for aligning a vise?
   A. Precision square
   B. Precision aligning tool
   C. Dial indicator
   D. None of the above

3. The table of a universal milling machine:
   A. Should be aligned before the vise is squared
   B. Should be aligned after the vise is squared
   C. Cannot be accurately aligned
   D. Is longer than that of a plain milling machine

4. A vise can be aligned by indicating the:
   A. Solid jaw
   B. Movable jaw
   C. Table
   D. Vise base

5. After the depth of cut is set:
   A. Tighten the knee locking clamps
   B. Take a trial cut
   C. Increase it by .010 inch to reduce the overcut
   D. None of the above

6. The depth of cut for a finish cut should be approximately what part of an inch?
   A. .005
   B. .020
   C. .060
   D. .080

7. A milling machine setup should be examined for:
   A. Clearance between the vise and cutter
   B. Clearance between the vise and overarm
   C. Clearance between the table and spindle nose
   D. All of the above

8. The smallest diameter cutter that will do the job should be used because it:
   A. Travels the shortest distance
   B. Makes the smallest chips
   C. Takes less time to set up
   D. All of the above

9. When climb milling, the force of the cutter:
   A. Holds the workpiece down
   B. Pushes the workpiece away from the cutter
   C. Is greater than in conventional milling
   D. All of the above

10. The cutter is stopped from rotating during the return movement of the table because:
   A. It would mark the workpiece
   B. It saves power
   C. It is quicker
   D. All of the above

Volume II, Section C   Date __________ Name ______________________________

UNIT 8. USING SIDE MILLING CUTTERS ON THE HORIZONTAL MILLING MACHINE

POST TEST

Circle the letter preceding the correct answer.

1. Half side milling cutters are:
   A. Used to cut shallow grooves
   B. Used to straddle mill
   C. Used to cut deep grooves
   D. All of the above

2. The most efficient side milling cutter:
   A. Is the smallest diameter cutter that can be used
   B. Is the largest diameter cutter that can be used
   C. Has teeth on one side only
   D. Has teeth only on the periphery

3. Workpieces should be measured:
   A. While they are warm
   B. After removing them from the vise
   C. Before removing them from the vise
   D. With a steel rule

4. To machine grooves with an accurate width, use:
   A. A grooving saw
   B. A half side milling cutter
   C. A plain grooving mill
   D. An interlocking side milling cutter

5. In gang milling, the depth of the individual steps is controlled by:
   A. The depth of the cutters
   B. The diameter of the cutters
   C. The width of the cutters
   D. All of the above

6. In straddle milling, the width of the workpiece is controlled by the:
   A. Diameter of the half side milling cutters
   B. Width of the interlocking side mills
   C. Depth of cut
   D. Width of the spacers

7. The width of a groove made by a cutter:
   A. Is wider than the cutter
   B. Is slightly narrower than the cutter
   C. Depends on the diameter of the cutter
   D. Is always the same

8. Layout lines on a workpiece:
   A. Identify where machining is to take place
   B. Should be accurate
   C. Help in preventing machining errors
   D. All of the above

9. Accurate cutter positioning on a workpiece is accomplished by:
   A. Locating the cutter with an accurate steel rule
   B. Holding the workpiece in a vise
   C. Using a precision square
   D. Using the machine dials

10. In gang milling, the RPM of the spindle is calculated for cutters with the:
   A. Largest diameter
   B. Smallest diameter
   C. Greatest width
   D. Narrowest width

Volume II, Section C Date __________ Name ______________________________

UNIT 9. USING FACE MILLING CUTTERS ON THE HORIZONTAL MILLING MACHINE

POST TEST

Circle the letter preceding the correct answer.

1. Heavy duty face mills:
   A. Have few teeth
   B. Have many teeth
   C. Are used for finish cuts
   D. None of the above

2. Light duty face mills:
   A. Have few teeth
   B. Have many teeth
   C. Are used for roughing cuts
   D. None of the above

3. Positive rake angle face mills as compared with negative rake mills:
   A. Use less power
   B. Generate less heat
   C. Create lower cutting pressures
   D. All of the above

4. A large lead angle on the cutting tool:
   A. Makes a chip thinner than the feed per tooth
   B. Makes a chip thicker than the feed per tooth
   C. Permits the cutting of square shoulder steps
   D. None of the above

5. Face mills:
   A. Generate surfaces square to the cutter axis
   B. Are mounted on the spindle nose
   C. Are driven by keys
   D. All of the above

6. Cutting fluids:
   A. Are used with high speed steel cutters
   B. Are coolant and lubricant
   C. Can be applied as a mist
   D. All of the above

7. Effective face milling requires:
   A. A sharp cutting tool
   B. A rigid setup
   C. The right cutting speed
   D. All of the above

8. Face mills can generate:
   A. Concave surfaces
   B. Irregular surfaces
   C. Surfaces parallel to the cutter axis
   D. All of the above

9. The width of a face milling cut should be:
   A. Less than the diameter of the cutter
   B. Equal to the diameter of the cutter
   C. In direct proportion to the depth of cut
   D. As wide as the available spindle horsepower allows

10. Shell end mills:
   A. Are small diameter face mills
   B. Are arbor driven face mills
   C. Cut surfaces square to the cutter axis
   D. All of the above

Volume II, Section D   Date ________ Name ________________________

UNIT 1. INDEXING DEVICES

POST TEST

Fill in the number in Figure 7 next to the name identifying the part.

Figure 7. Indexing components of a dividing head (Lane Community College).

A. _____ Indexing plate stop
B. _____ Index pin
C. _____ Sector arms
D. _____ Spindle nose
E. _____ Direct indexing holes
F. _____ Index plate
G. _____ Spindle lock
H. _____ Index crank
I. _____ Direct indexing pin
J. _____ Plunger

Volume II, Section D Date __________ Name ______________________________

UNIT 2. DIRECT AND SIMPLE INDEXING

POST TEST

Circle the letter preceding the correct answer.

1. Direct indexing is performed:
   A. On the side index plate
   B. With the worm engaged
   C. On the spindle nose
   D. Through a gear train

2. Simple indexing:
   A. Uses the side index plate
   B. Uses the spindle nose index holes
   C. Is performed with the work disengaged
   D. Is not very accurate

3. All hole circles in the answers to this question can be used. Which is the best one?
   A. 24
   B. 32
   C. 40
   D. 56

4. A direct index plate with 24 holes is available. Which of the divisions can not be performed?
   A. 3
   B. 6
   C. 8
   D. 9

5. The sector arms are used:
   A. When direct indexing
   B. On the side index plate
   C. To divide a circle evenly
   D. All of the above

For the following problems, hole circles with 24, 25, 28, 30, 42, 46, 51, 57, and 66 holes are available.

6. Show the calculations to index for 8 spaces.

7. Show the calculations to index for 12 spaces.

8. Show the calculations to index for 11 spaces.

9. Show the calculations to index for 14 spaces.

10. Show the calculations to index for 57 spaces.

Volume II, Section D Date _________ Name ______________________________

UNIT 3. ANGULAR INDEXING

POST TEST

Circle the letter preceding the correct answer.

1. On a 24 hole direct indexing plate, how many degrees is the angular distance between holes?
   A. 15
   B. 25
   C. 35
   D. 45

2. To drill 2 holes 105 degrees apart using direct indexing and the 24 hole circle, the number os spaces to move is:
   A. 5
   B. 7
   C. 9
   D. 11

3. On a dividing head with a 40:1 ratio, one turn of the index crank revolves the spindle how many degrees?
   A. 9
   B. 15
   C. 27
   D. 54

4. On the dividing head in question 3, which hole circle can be used to divide in whole degrees?
   A. 19
   B. 28
   C. 47
   D. 54

5. How many turns of the index crank are required to index 63 degrees?
   A. 9
   B. 4
   C. 7
   D. 12

6. How many turns of the index crank are required to index 540 minutes?
   A. 1
   B. 3
   C. 5
   D. 7

7. How many hole positions do you turn the index crank to index 3 degrees 30 minutes, using a 54 hole circle?
   A. 21
   B. 22
   C. 23
   D. 24

8. How many turns of the index crank are needed to index 19 degrees?

A. $1\frac{1}{8}$

B. $2\frac{1}{9}$

C. $3\frac{1}{10}$

D. $4\frac{1}{9}$

9. How many turns and holes are needed in the 54 hole circle to index 11 degrees 20 minutes?

A. $\frac{31}{54}$

B. $1\frac{12}{54}$

C. $1\frac{14}{54}$

D. $1\frac{16}{54}$

10. How many turns and holes are needed in the 54 hole circle to index 9 degrees 10 minutes?

A. $1\frac{1}{54}$

B. $1\frac{10}{54}$

C. $2\frac{1}{54}$

D. $2\frac{10}{54}$

Volume II, Section E Date __________ Name ____________________________________

UNIT 1. INTRODUCTION TO GEARS

POST TEST

Circle the letter preceding the correct answer.

1. Gears connecting parallel shafts are:
   A. Spur gears
   B. Herringbone gears
   C. Helical gears
   D. All of the above

2. The gear ratio in a worm gear set with a 100 tooth gear and a four start worm is:
   A. 25:1
   B. 50:1
   C. 75:1
   D. 100:1

3. What gear material gives best results in a gear set that is under shock loads?
   A. Cast iron
   B. Steel
   C. Brass
   D. All of the above

4. Two intersecting shafts at 90 degrees to each other may use which kind of gears?
   A. Helical
   B. Spur
   C. Worm
   D. Miter

5. Thrust bearings to counteract axial thrust are needed with which kind of gear?
   A. Spur
   B. Helical
   C. Herringbone
   D. All of the above

6. Cast iron gears equal in size to a steel gear have a load bearing capacity of what percent?
   A. 25
   B. 50
   C. 75
   D. 100

7. Nylon gears are sensitive to:
   A. Temperature changes
   B. Moisture
   C. High speeds
   D. All of the above

8. A differentail in hardness between a pinion and a gear:
   A. Makes the cheaper gear wear out faster
   B. Makes a more quiet running gear train
   C. Makes both gears wear more evenly
   D. Eliminates axial thrust

9. Which of the gear ratios uses a "hunting tooth" principle?
   A. 13:39
   B. 17:51
   C. 21:42
   D. 25:76

10. Cast iron is used for gears because:
    A. It machines easily
    B. It makes quiet running gears
    C. It has good wear resistance
    D. All of the above

Volume II, Section E Date __________ Name ______________________________

UNIT 2. SPUR GEAR TERMS AND CALCULATIONS

POST TEST

Circle the letter preceding the correct answer.

1. The strongest gear tooth is made with a pressure angle of how many degrees?
   A. 14½
   B. 19
   C. 22
   D. 25

2. What is the center distance in inches between 2 gears with pitch diameters of 1.600 and 2.400 inches?
   A. 1.800
   B. 2.000
   C. 2.200
   D. 2.400

3. What is the center distance in inches of 2 gears with 24 teeth and 48 teeth and a diametral pitch of 12?
   A. 2.400
   B. 2.600
   C. 2.800
   D. 3.000

4. What is the outside diameter in inches for a 48 tooth gear, 10 diametral pitch?
   A. 5.000
   B. 5.200
   C. 5.400
   D. 5.600

5. What part of an inch is the whole depth of tooth on a 36 tooth, 8 diametral pitch, 20 degrees pressure angle gear?
   A. .241
   B. .261
   C. .281
   D. .301

6. A gear has a pitch diameter of 3.800 inches and a diametral pitch of 10. How many teeth are in the gear?
   A. 32
   B. 34
   C. 36
   D. 38

7. What part of an inch is the tooth thickness for a 50 tooth gear, 6 diametral pitch?
   A. .241
   B. .262
   C. .283
   D. .304

8. What part of an inch is the pitch diameter of a gear with 48 teeth, 6 diametral pitch?
   A. 8
   B. 12
   C. 15
   D. 18

9. The working depth of a tooth on a 40 tooth gear, 10 diametral pitch is what part of an inch?
   A. .200
   B. .250
   C. .300
   D. .400

10. Fill in the number in Figure 4 next to the gear tooth term describing it.

    A. _____ Addendum

    B. _____ Dedendum

    C. _____ Whole depth

    D. _____ Pitch diameter

    E. _____ Tooth thickness

    F. _____ Outside diameter

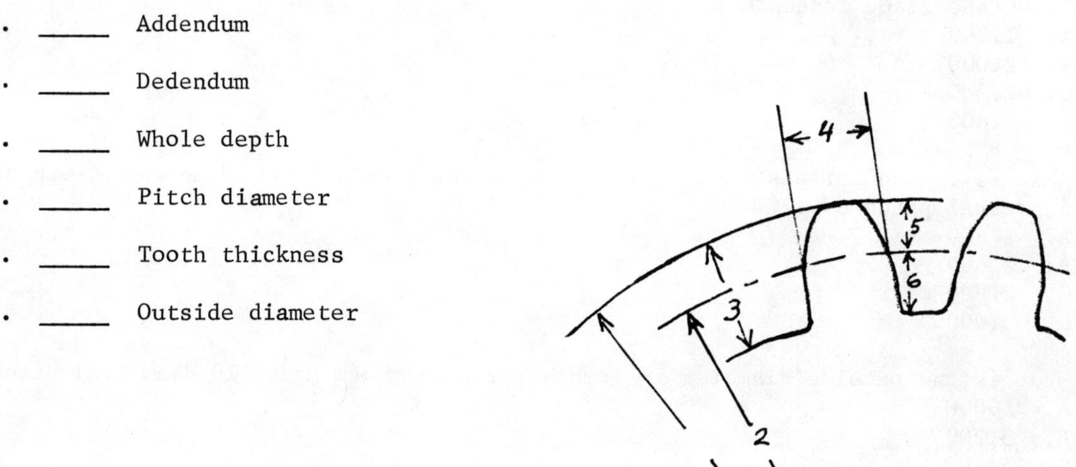

Figure 4.

Volume II, Section E   Date __________ Name ________________________________

UNIT 3. CUTTING A SPUR GEAR

POST TEST

Circle the letter preceding the correct answer.

1. Spur gears machined in a milling machine are:
   A. Very accurate
   B. Expensive
   C. Limited in their accuracy
   D. Not usable

2. A standard set of gear cutters consists of how many cutters?
   A. 6
   B. 8
   C. 10
   D. 12

3. If the tailstock center is higher than the dividing head center, what will be the effect on the gear being cut?
   A. Teeth will be deeper on the side nearest the tailstock
   B. Gear will not be affected
   C. Gear will not mesh with another one
   D. Gear blank will come off the mandrel

4. A gear cutter number 4 cuts from 26 to 34 teeth. The cutter makes the correct tooth shape on a gear with how many teeth?
   A. 26
   B. 28
   C. 30
   D. 34

5. Information on the side of a gear tooth cutter includes the:
   A. Outside diameter of the gear
   B. Pitch diameter of the gear
   C. Working depth of the gear teeth
   D. Whole depth of the gear teeth

6. The cutting forces created by the gear cutter should be:
   A. Directed toward the foot stock
   B. Directed toward the small diameter of the mandrel
   C. Directed toward the dividing head
   D. Reduced by decreasing the cutting speed

7. The work and the cutter should be located as close to the column as possible:
   A. For a rigid setup
   B. To reduce the chance of chatter
   C. To obtain a good surface finish
   D. All of the above

8. To cut a gear with 50 teeth, the fraction of a turn that the index crank has to be rotated is:
   A. $\frac{4}{5}$
   B. $\frac{5}{4}$
   C. $\frac{7}{9}$
   D. $\frac{5}{8}$

9. The number of holes included between the sector arms to move 8 holes in the 40 hole circle are:
   A. 8
   B. 9
   C. 10
   D. 40

10. The cutting speed used, when gear cutting, is determined by the:
    A. Diameter of the gear cutter
    B. Diameter of the gear being cut
    C. Number of teeth on the gear cutter
    D. Size of the gear teeth being cut

Volume II, Section E Date __________ Name ______________________________

UNIT 4. GEAR INSPECTION AND MEASUREMENT

POST TEST

Circle the letter preceding the correct answer.

1. Gear tooth dimensions can be measured with:
   A. A gear tooth vernier caliper
   B. An optical comparator
   C. A micrometer and 2 pins
   D. All of the above

2. A gear tooth vernier caliper measures:
   A. Diametral pitch
   B. Chordal addendum
   C. Chordal tooth thickness
   D. All of the above

3. One scale of the gear tooth vernier caliper is set to the:
   A. Chordal addendum
   B. Chordal dedendum
   C. Whole depth
   D. Circular tooth thickness

4. The dimension obtained from a handbook for measuring a gear with a micrometer and two pins is for how much backlash?
   A. Zero
   B. .001 inch
   C. .005 inch
   D. .010 inch

5. A gear tooth vernier caliper measures the tooth thickness at the:
   A. Outside diameter
   B. Pitch diameter
   C. Rooth diameter
   D. Base circle

6. When measurements are made with a gear tooth vernier caliper, it is important that:
   A. The gear is cooled off
   B. All burrs are removed from the gear
   C. The gear teeth are lightly lubricated
   D. All of the above

7. The gears that can be measured with a micrometer and 2 pins are:
   A. Spur gears
   B. Even numbered teeth gears
   C. Internal spur gears
   D. All of the above

8. The optical comparator measures:
   A. Tooth profile
   B. Tooth thickness
   C. Tooth height
   D. All of the above

9. The dimension given in a handbook for gear measurements over pins:
   A. Is usually for a diametral pitch of one
   B. Needs to be divided for diametral pitches other than one
   C. Is calculated for a specific pin diameter
   D. All of the above

10. For a gear to have .002 inch backlash:
   A. Machine the whole depth deeper by .002 inch
   B. Obtain this dimension from handbook tables
   C. Reduce the outside diameter by .002 inch
   D. All of the above

Volume II, Section F Date __________ Name ______________________________

UNIT 1. FEATURES AND TOOLING ON THE HORIZONTAL SHAPER

POST TEST

Circle the letter preceding the correct answer.

1. Name the shaper features indicated in Figure 37.

   A. ______________________

   B. ______________________

   C. ______________________

   D. ______________________

   E. ______________________

   F. ______________________

   G. ______________________

   H. ______________________

   I. ______________________

   J. ______________________

Figure 37. (Courtesy of Cincinnati Incorporated)

2. The clapper box on the shaper:
   A. Provides the feeding motion on the toolhead
   B. Provides the feeding motion on the toolhead
   C. Permits the cutting tool to tilt up on the return stroke
   D. Is locked down when carbide tools are used

3. The hydraulic shaper:
   A. Has a cutting to return ratio of 3:2
   B. Has a table feeding device driven by an eccentric and a ratchet mechanism
   C. Uses a rocker arm to connect the piston and ram
   D. Usually has independent control of cutting and return speed

4. Rapid traverse on the shaper is a:
   A. Device to position the ram during set up
   B. Device to obtain rapid table movements
   C. Device to feed the toolhead across the work
   D. Power device to move the pivot on the crank gear of the shaper to set stroke length

5. A 12-inch shaper could be expected to:
   A. Hold and work on a cubic workpiece 12 inches on a side
   B. Hold a workpiece 12 inches in width and length, but about 6 inches high
   C. Hold a workpiece 12 inches high, but have a stroke of about twice the height of the workpiece
   D. Have a working width of 12 inches, but not 12 inches in the other working relations

6. A toe dog is a:
   A. Special type of strap clamp
   B. Holddown piece for the work
   C. Fitting that goes into a T-slot
   D. Device for setting the stroke length on a hydraulic shaper

7. What type of shaper vise is best used for holding workpieces that are not parallel?
   A. Fixed base vise
   B. Single screw swivel base vise
   C. Serrated jaw single screw vise
   D. Serrated jaw multiple screw vise

8. A shaper fixture:
   A. Locates the cutting tool in relation to the workpiece
   B. Is attached to the machine with straps and stops
   C. Is a workholding device for rapid location and workholding
   D. Is serrated on the clamping surface to prevent slippage of the part under the load of cutting

9. Shaper tools prepared for cast iron usually have:
   A. Less side and end clearance than tools prepared for steel
   B. Greater side and end clearance than steel tools
   C. Less side and back rake than tools for steel
   D. More side and back rake than tools prepared for steel

10. You are deciding which side of the toolholder you are going to use for mounting your cutting tool for shaping. What factors will you use in your choice?
    A. Depth of cut and feed rate
    B. Expected tool deflection and cutting speed
    C. Visibility and expected tool deflection
    D. Expected tool deflection and feeding rate

Volume II, Section F Date __________ Name ______________________________

UNIT 2. CUTTING FACTORS ON SHAPERS AND PLANERS

POST TEST

Circle the letter preceding the correct answer.

1. On high speed planers, cemented carbide tools can be used effectively. What is the most commonly used carbide for planing on steel workpieces?
   A. C-2
   B. C-4
   C. C-6
   D. C-8

2. What is the most basic source of machining recommendations for planing?
   A. American Machinist
   B. Machinery's Handbook
   C. New American Machinist's Handbook
   D. Machining Data Handbook

3. Finishing speeds on planers or shapers are usually:
   A. Much higher than shallow roughing speeds
   B. Lower than deep roughing speeds
   C. About one-third less than shallow roughing speeds
   D. Much higher than deep roughing speeds

4. Cutting speeds for planing and shaping for deep roughing cuts on low, medium, and high carbon steels are similar. What change is usually made to compensate for differences in the machinability of the higher carbon materials?
   A. Feed rate is reduced
   B. Depth of cut is reduced
   C. Feed rate is increased
   D. Depth of cut in increased

5. What limitations to depth of cut and feed rate is there in planing and shaping?
   A. Workholding
   B. Machine power and rigidity
   C. Workpiece configuration and strength
   D. All of the above

6. Why is it important to maintain the maximum depth of cut relative to other machining factors?
   A. The work of cutting is spread out over more cutting edge
   B. It reduces to overall machine loading relative to increased feed
   C. It concentrates the heat of the cut better into the workpiece resulting in cooler cutting
   D. The statement is false; maximum feed rate is more important

7. The cutting stroke of a shaper uses about 220 degrees of crankshaft rotation. As compared to the average velocity, does this mean the ram is:
A. Faster on the cutting stroke by about 11 percent
B. Slower on the return stroke by $\frac{2}{5}$
C. Slower on the cutting stroke by about 11 percent
D. Faster on the return stroke by a factor of 2

8. You have a 13 inch long workpiece of 304 stainless steel with a rated shallow roughing speed of 35 sfpm to be machined on a heavy duty crank shaper. Which of the following listed strokes per minute would be the best match for this job?
A. 8
B. 16
C. 32
D. 64

9. You are rough machining a well-fastened, heavy steel plate on an adequately powerful planer. Your depth of cut will be .625 inch. Which of the following rates of feed in inches would be considered par for this combination?
A. .016
B. .032
C. .064
D. .090

10. You are to make a shallow (.006 inch) finishing cut on free machining steel with a planer. You have a square nose finishing tool $\frac{3}{4}$ inch wide. Which of the following feed rates in inches would you attempt to set in use for this job?
A. .056
B. .132
C. .320
D. .560

Volume II, Section F   Date ________ Name ______________________________

UNIT 3. SHAPER SAFETY AND USING THE SHAPER

POST TEST

Circle the letter preceding the correct answer.

1. Why should a shaper be placed where there is at least 18 inches between the longest movement of the ram and any solid surface?
   A. If the link inside the shaper should fail, the ram would stop in that distance
   B. That is about the maximum width of a person, so it is a matter of safety
   C. The largest horizontal shapers have a stroke about 36 inches in length, which is 2 by 18 inches
   D. The distance leaves room to get the shaper stopped if the clutch is engaged with long ram travel and high stroke rate

2. A chip screen is:
   A. A safety device to control flying chips
   B. A device for removing cutting oil from chips before they are salvaged
   C. A device to separate chips for salvage by size
   D. None of the above

3. Why must stroke length and stroke rate be set at a minimum when securing the shaper?
   A. It provides a safe starting situation for the next operator
   B. It prevents the possiblilty of having the machine accidentally "self-destruct" by an unaware operator
   C. It adds a measure of safety to others in the shop
   D. All of the above

4. Workholding procedures on the shaper are given an extra measure of care because:
   A. The T-slots run the length of the table and the part could slide
   B. You are usually working toward an open end of the vise
   C. The work is subjected to impact on each cutting stroke
   D. Slippage of the workpiece could break the cutting tool

5. When "indicating in" a shaper equipped with a universal table:
   A. The procedures are the same as used with the plain table shaper
   B. The table must be checked for parallel in the corss feed direction
   C. Both table and tilt plate angles must be neutralized
   D. The tilt plate angle must be checked

6. Using a piece of round bar stock in workholding in a shaper vise:
   A. Is unnecessary if the vise is very accurately made
   B. Forces a reference surface on the part into full contact with the vise reference surface
   C. Prevents the part from lifting when the vise is tightened
   D. B and C above

7. If work is being squared from the end of a shaper vise:
   A. The squareness of the part is completely dependent on the squareness of the vise
   B. The squareness of the part is not as dependent on the squareness of the vise as in the case of squaring with vertical workholding
   C. There is excessive tendency for the vise to be knocked out of squareness
   D. It must be checked for square in two directions

8. You have a 17 inch long workpiece of gray cast iron in annealed condition that you are to machine on a 28 inch heavy duty hydraulic shaper. Your anticipated depth of cut is ½ inch with a feed rate of .050 inch. The rated deep roughing speed for this condition is 60 SFPM. What cutting speed will you set on the ram speed control?
   A. 18
   B. 23
   C. 50
   D. 60

9. You have a light duty 7 inch bench shaper on which you are setting up to machine a 5 inch cube of low carbon leaded steel with rated shallow roughing speed of 95 SFPM and as much feed as the machine can take. What is the calculated number of strokes per minute?
   A. 35
   B. 65
   C. 95
   D. 110

10. When finish cutting a symmetrical V in a workpiece on a shaper, the
    A. Toolhead should be repositioned for the second side of the cut
    B. Table should be repositioned after the finishing cuts for the second side
    C. Tool should be repositioned for the second side, but the toolhead shoud remain in its original position
    D. Table should remain in place and the workpiece reversed for the second side

Volume II, Section F Date __________ Name ______________________________

UNIT 4. FEATURES AND TOOLING OF THE PLANER

POST TEST

Circle the letter preceding the correct answer.

1. Name the following components and control features of the planer shown in Figure 13.

   A. ____________________________

   B. ____________________________

   C. ____________________________

   D. ____________________________

   E. ____________________________

   F. ____________________________

   G. ____________________________

   H. ____________________________

   I. ____________________________

   J. ____________________________

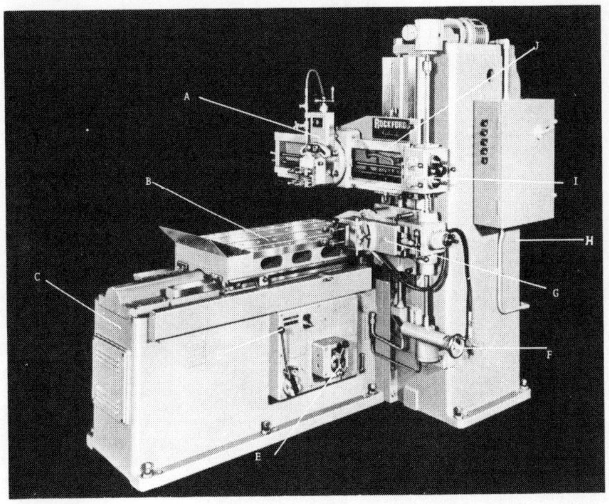

Figure 13. Components and controls (Courtesy of Rockford Machine Tool Company)

2. Where a planer is equipped with two railheads:
   A. Only one may be used at a time
   B. The two heads must be operated together
   C. The heads must be operated independently
   D. They may be operated either independently or together

3. Planer drives:
   A. Are usually either hydraulic or rack and pinion
   B. Are usually either hydraulic or pneumatic
   C. Require direct current motors
   D. Are usually capable of high planing speeds

4. The planer table:
   A. Rides on film of pressurized oil
   B. Has both T-slots and holes for poppets and stops
   C. Is sometimes doubled on very large planers
   D. All of the above

5. Thin work on the planer:
   A. Is difficult to do
   B. Is usually held in a fixture
   C. May be done by using a stop, poppets, and toe dogs
   D. Is limited to thicknesses over one inch

Volume II, Section F Date __________ Name ______________________________

UNIT 5. PLANER SAFETY AND USING THE PLANER

POST TEST

Circle the letter preceding the correct answer.

1. The most compelling safety problems that arise out of planer use are:
   A. Heavy workpieces and operator entrapment
   B. Operator entrapment and tripping hazards
   C. Heavy workpieces and runaway tables
   D. Unattached fastening devices and heavy workpieces

2. How is a planer table protected from rough edges on a workpiece?
   A. The workpiece is filed flat before being placed on the table
   B. Compressible material is used for protection
   C. The table is hard and needs no special protection
   D. A special spray is used that forms a protective surface

3. If the eye of a cable sling is not free to swivel, it:
   A. Upsets the center of gravity of the workpiece
   B. Causes the sling to effectively shorten on one side
   C. Can exert leverage that can twist off the clamp
   D. Creates no additional problems

4. A poppet and planer pin:
   A. Can be used to hold down a heavy part
   B. Are part of the feed mechanism of a planer
   C. Can be used to prevent table "runaways"
   D. Are often used to force a workpiece to a stop

5. If the planer is equipped with a tool lifter:
   A. The rail head is raised on each return stroke
   B. The clapper box apron need not be angled to relieve the tool
   C. A carbide type lathe toolholder can be used where otherwise it would be a problem
   D. It becomes very difficult to maintain a full supply of cutting tools

6. The table stop must be set on the starting side of the cut to allow for:
   A. The tool head to drop before the next cut
   B. The clapper box apron to return to center
   C. The feeding action to be completed
   D. All of the above

7. Finishing tools for planers:
   A. Are usually operated at relatively high cutting speeds
   B. Are used with a very fine feed rate to achieve the best possible surface finish
   C. Generally have substantial side rake for a shearing cut
   D. Are generally used with a coarse feed rate and a shallow depth of cut

8. On a workpiece that is out of balance, what critical step is necessary before the crane can be released?
   A. The poppet and stops must be secure
   B. All of the clamping must be completed
   C. A clamp must be installed to prevent the part from tumbling
   D. The part must have the jacks in place and be completely adjusted

9. Planer jacks are used:
   A. To oppose the cutting forces on parts that are not fully supported
   B. To raise workpieces to insert protective material between the workpiece and the machine table
   C. In conjunction with hardened rollers to move workpieces when a crane is not available
   D. To raise and position the cross rail on older type planers

10. The height gage and indicator are:
    A. Used to set the tool height on a planer
    B. Used for checking the level of a workpiece
    C. Used to establish the height of a workpiece
    D. B and C above

Volume II, Section G Date ________ Name ____________________

UNIT 1. MECHANICAL AND PHYSICAL PROPERTIES OF METALS

POST TEST

Circle the letter preceding the correct answer.

1. Which of the following are the three categories of hardness?
   A. Ductile, malleable, and plastic
   B. Tensile, compressive, and shear
   C. Resistance to penetration, elastic, and abrasion resistant
   D. Resistance to penetration, fatigue, and creep

2. A property of metals that enables them to permanently deform under a compressive load is called:
   A. Malleability
   B. Ductility
   C. Plasticity
   D. Creep

3. When a ductile metal is cooled below its transition temperature, it becomes:
   A. Tougher
   B. Plastic
   C. Softer
   D. Brittle

4. Creep occurs in the:
   A. Elastic range
   B. Plastic range
   C. Transition zone
   D. Temperature range between room temperature and a 200° F rise

5. The three basic stresses are:
   A. Elastic, resistance to penetration, and abrasion
   B. Tensile, compressive, and shear
   C. Elasticity, plasticity, and ductility
   D. Expansion, conductivity, and creep

6. Elimination of stress raisers such as tool marks or undercuts can improve:
   A. The modulus of elasticity
   B. The creep strength
   C. Fatigue strength
   D. Conductivity

7. A metal that is a good conductor of electricity is:
   A. Usually a very tough metal
   B. Also a good conductor of heat
   C. Usually a poor conductor of heat
   D. Generally alloyed with another good conductor to increase its electrical conductance

8. Which of the following coefficients of thermal expansion would have the highest rate of expansion per degree F. per unit length in inches?
   A. .0000063
   B. .000017
   C. .000011
   D. .0000024

9. What is the unit stress in pounds of a 3 inch square bar with a load of 81,000 pounds?
   A. 9,000
   B. 10,000
   C. .111
   D. 90

10. Hardness, strength, and modulus of elasticity increase:
    A. With an increase in temperature
    B. With a decrease in temperature
    C. When metals are annealed
    D. None of the above

Volume II, Section G Date __________ Name ______________________________

UNIT 2. THE CRYSTAL STRUCTURE OF METALS

POST TEST

Circle the letter preceding the correct answer.

1. Which of the following are parts of an atom?
   A. Molecule, bond
   B. Proton, shell
   C. Dendrite, lattice
   D. Electron cloud, grain

2. The metallic bond:
   A. Is rigid and directional
   B. Depends upon positive and negative ions
   C. Is an electron cloud of valence electrons
   D. Has little or nothing to do with the mechanical properties of metal

3. Which of the following are crystalline structures of metals?
   A. BBC, PCP, CFC
   B. CPH, FCC, BCC
   C. XYZ, XXX, LXX
   D. FCT, BCB, CPC

4. The growth from a nucleus that forms a grain in solidifying metal is called a:
   A. Dendrite
   B. Grain boundary
   C. Molecule
   D. Metallic bond

5. Grain boundaries are:
   A. Continuations of the regular lattice structure from grain to grain
   B. Weaker at normal temperatures than the rest of the grain
   C. In a misfit pattern and are stronger at normal temperatures than the rest of the grain
   D. Only important at high temperatures

6. Body-centered tetragonal structures are formed from quenched austenitized carbon steel because:
   A. The carbon atoms have no room in the interstices of BCC at low temperatures and the crystal is distorted
   B. The carbon tries to come out of solution and it stretches the lattice in doing so
   C. The differential in cooling rate of internal lattices to external lattices caused this distortion in the crystals
   D. A new phase is formed for a different allotropic structure

7. Allotropic means it:
   A. Is a material that expands upon solidification
   B. Was originally discovered in the tropics
   C. Takes an excessive amount of heat to melt it
   D. Can exist in different phases or crystal structures under various conditions

8. Fine grained steel is:
   A. Not as useful as coarse grained steel
   B. Preferred for most applications
   C. Preferred for carburizing since it has increased hardenability
   D. Weaker than coarse grain steels

9. Metals dissolve other metals when molten:
   A. Always completely
   B. Almost never
   C. Either completely or in varying degrees of solubility
   D. In varying degrees of solubility, and in some cases not at all

10. Solid solutions can be:
   A. Substitutional or interstitial
   B. Mixtures and insoluble
   C. Intermittent
   D. Approximate

Volume II, Section G Date _________ Name ______________________

UNIT 3. PHASE DIAGRAMS FOR STEELS

POST TEST

Circle the letter preceding the correct answer.

1. Match the correct numbers on the phase diagram (Figure 16) with the following:

A. _____ Solidus line

B. _____ Liquidus line

C. _____ Area of liquid and solid

D. _____ Area of 100% solubility

E. _____ Eutectic point

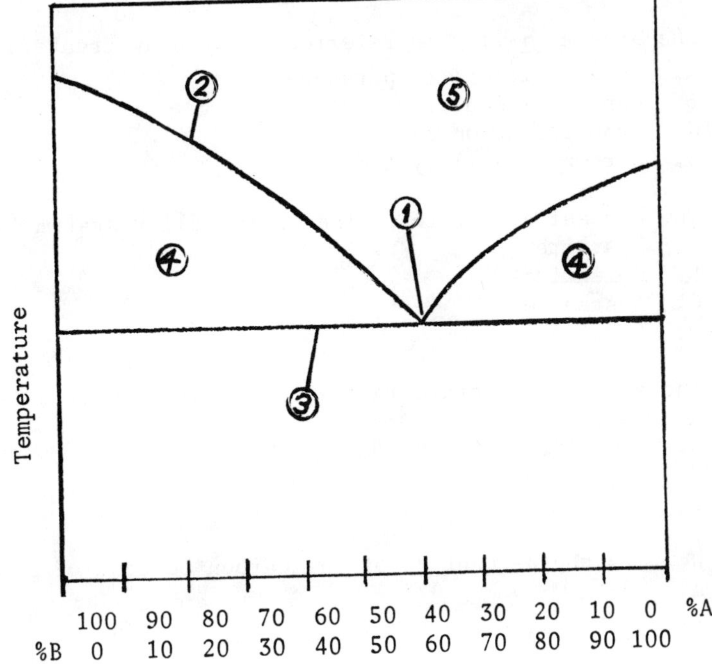

Figure 16.

2. The austenite phase:
   A. Can dissolve .08 percent carbon interstitially
   B. Can dissolve 2 percent carbon interstitially
   C. Can exist only at room temperature
   D. Has a body-centered cubic crystalline structure

3. At what line do low carbon steels begin to form ferrite when cooled from the austenite phase?
   A. A_{cm}
   B. A_1
   C. $A_{3,1}$
   D. A_3

4. When a phase change occurs on cooling, heat is released. How is this shown on a cooling curve graph?
   A. By a short horizontal line
   B. A sloping line
   C. A dip in the line
   D. A dotted line

5. Eutectic means lowest melting temperature. What does eutectoid mean?
   A. Lowest soluble point
   B. Lowest cementite temperature
   C. 50-50 percentage of any alloy
   D. Lowest transition temperature

6. The A_1 - $A_{3,1}$ line is referred to by heat treaters as the:
   A. Lower critical temperature
   B. Upper critical temperature
   C. Transformation range
   D. Carbon solubility line

7. The hardest structure in the carbon alloy system is:
   A. Pearlite
   B. Cementite
   C. Austenite
   D. Ferrite

8. The softest structure in the carbon alloy system is:
   A. Pearlite
   B. Cementite
   C. Austenite
   D. Ferrite

9. What is the percentage of the carbon content of eutectoid carbon steel?
   A. .95
   B. .20
   C. .83
   D. 2

10. What affect do alloying elements have on the eutectoid composition?
    A. Move it to the right
    B. Move it to the left
    C. No affect
    D. Eliminates the eutectoid

Volume II, Section G   Date ________ Name ______________________________

UNIT 4. I-T DIAGRAMS AND COOLING CURVES

POST TEST

Circle the letter preceding the correct answer.

1. The austenitizing temperature for a carbon steel is:
   A. The eutectoid temperature
   B. 100° F (38° C) above the upper critical limit
   C. 50° F (10° C) above the A_3 or $A_{3,1}$ lines
   D. At the A_3 or A_{cm} lines

2. Martensite is produced in carbon steel by:
   A. Slowly cooling from the upper critical temperature
   B. Rapid quenching from the austenitizing temperature
   C. Quenching to below the Ms temperature from just under the lower critical limit
   D. Normalizing heat treatment

3. Ms and Mf mean:
   A. The starting of formation of martensite and the point of 100 percent complete formation
   B. The starting point of melting through the mushy area to the finishing point of melting
   C. The metallic structure and metallic ferrite
   D. Metal solubility and face-centered cubic metals

4. The critical cooling rate is the time necessary to undercool austenite to below:
   A. The A_3, $A_{3,1}$ line
   B. Or through the S-curve
   C. The isothermal temperature that forms coarse pearlite
   D. The M temperature

5. The microstructure of a .8 percent carbon steel in which the cooling curve cuts partly through the nose of the S-curve would be:
   A. Ferrite and martensite
   B. Fine pearlite and martensite
   C. Coarse pearlite and martensite
   D. Coarse pearlite

6. Carbon and alloying elements tend to move the S-curve:
   A. To the right
   B. To the left
   C. Up
   D. Down

7. The two steps normally used for hardening steels for useful articles are:
   A. Tempering and annealing
   B. Austenitizing and drawing
   C. Hardening and tempering
   D. Normalizing and tempering

8. Quench cracks are basically caused by:
   A. The stresses caused by the difference between internal and external cooling rates
   B. Water getting into the pores of the metal and turning to steam
   C. Defects in the metal that are opened up further by heating and the quench
   D. Using the wrong tool steel

9. How does the I-T diagram for .06 percent carbon steel show that no martensite can be produced by quenching from the austenitizing temperature?
   A. It shows the nose of the S-curve far to the right of the diagram
   B. It shows the nose of the S-curve far into the zero time line
   C. The Ms temperature is freezing temperature for water
   D. There cannot be even a part of an S-curve with such low carbon content

10. The I-T diagram of a steel with deep hardening characteristics would have:
   A. An S-curve far to the left
   B. High Ms and Mf temperatures
   C. An S-curve far to the right
   D. A double "nose" on the diagram

Volume II, Section G Date __________ Name ______________________________

UNIT 5. HARDENABILITY OF STEELS AND TEMPERED MARTENSITE

POST TEST

Circle the letter preceding the correct answer.

1. Hardenability can be measured by the:
   A. McQuaid-Ehn test
   B. Metcalf experiment
   C. Jominy end-quench
   D. Rockwell Hardness test

2. How do the cooling rates near the quenched end differ from those further from the end? The cooling rates near the quenched end are:
   A. Slower
   B. Faster
   C. The same until they get to the Ms temperature
   D. Start out fast near the end and become slow as the temperature drops

3. The microstructure of a eutectoid steel with a rapid cooling curve that passes to the left of the S-curve nose should be:
   A. Martensite
   B. Ferrite and pearlite
   C. Pearlite and bainite
   D. Bainite

4. Circulation or agitation of the quench tends to:
   A. Decrease hardenability
   B. Keep it cleaner
   C. Cool the part more slowly, thus keeping the internal stresses down and yet maintaining full hardness
   D. Increase hardenability

5. SAE 1095 carbon steel will harden to approximately a maximum of:
   A. RC 93
   B. RC 67
   C. RC 60
   D. RC 38

6. When eutectoid steel is furnace annealed, its microstructure should be:
   A. Fine pearlite
   B. Fine grained ferrite
   C. Coarse pearlite
   D. Martensite

7. Austempering is:
   A. A method of tempering martensite in a lead or salt bath
   B. A method of quenching and tempering to produce a better product
   C. A method of tempering austenite at 1200° F (649° C)
   D. None of the above

8. Tempering should be done:
   A. After the part has been tested for hardness
   B. After grinding off the decarburization
   C. The next day; it needs to age overnight
   D. Right after quenching while the part is still warm

9. Tempering range that shows a reduction of notch bar toughness in steels is called the:
   A. 1000° F (538° C) to 1250° F (679° C) range
   B. Blue brittle
   C. Light straw
   D. Cherry red

10. Hardness, when tempering, can be predicted by consulting a:
    A. Phase diagram
    B. Cooling curve on an I-T diagram
    C. Mechanical properties chart
    D. Stress-strain diagram

Volume II, Section G Date __________ Name ____________________________________

UNIT 6. HEAT TREATING STEELS

POST TEST

Circle the letter preceding the correct answer.

1. Furnaces used for heat treating steels are:
   A. Open hearth, Bessemer
   B. Blast, Bessemer
   C. Electric, gas
   D. Puddling, soaking pit

2. Carbon steel when heated to high temperatures in the presence of air:
   A. Carburizes
   B. Decarburizes
   C. Rusts
   D. Will harden only the surface

3. A soaking period at high temperatures is needed to:
   A. Complete the dispersion of carbon atams and equalize internal and external temperatures
   B. Insure a complete mixture of austenite before quenching
   C. Completely carburize the surface of the metal so it will fully harden when quenched
   D. Convert a shallow hardening steel into a deeper hardening steel

4. Agitating the part in the quenching medium:
   A. Causes the steel to harden to only $\frac{1}{8}$ inch depth
   B. To break down the vapor barrier for more rapid quenching
   C. Is not usually necessary
   D. Causes warping and bending

5. The heat treater maintains better control of the product by tempering:
   A. By the color method
   B. After the part has been hardened for 24 hours
   C. Before the part gets completely down to the Mf temperature
   D. In the furnace for a specified time

6. Quench cracks:
   A. Appear blackened and run toward the center of the part
   B. Appear as a "chicken wire" network
   C. Cause the piece to crumble into small granules
   D. None of the above

7. Quench cracks may be caused by:
   A. Overheating
   B. Time delay between quench and tempering
   C. Wrong selection of steel
   D. All of the above

8. Decarburization can be avoided in a furnace by:
   A. Having an oxidizing atmosphere
   B. Wrapping the piece in stainless steel foil
   C. Using an electric furnace
   D. Laying the part on top of cast iron chips

9. When grinding hardened steel, two kinds of surface failures are:
   A. Decarburization and pitting
   B. Porosity and discoloration from the quench medium
   C. Changes in hardness on the surface and internal stresses
   D. None of the above

10. When distortion must be kept to a minimum, which steel type should be used for hardening?
    A. Air hardening
    B. Oil hardening
    C. Water hardening
    D. Low carbon

Volume II, Section H Date __________ Name ____________________

UNIT 1. SELECTION AND IDENTIFICATION OF GRINDING WHEELS

POST TEST

Circle the letter preceding the correct answer.

1. For grinding most steels, the preferred abrasive is:
   A. Diamond
   B. Silicon carbide
   C. Cubic boron nitride
   D. Aluminum oxide

2. Grade in a grinding wheel specification refers to the:
   A. Strength with which the bond holds the grain
   B. Relative hardness of the abrasive grain in the wheel
   C. Dollar value of the abrasive grain
   D. Relative hardness of the bond in the wheel

3. The bond in most machine shop grinding wheels is:
   A. Shellac
   B. Rubber
   C. Vitrified
   D. Resinoid

4. In relation to the area of grinding contact, the grade of the wheel:
   A. Should be harder as the contact area increases
   B. Should be harder as the contact area decreases
   C. Remains about the same regardless of change
   D. Should be hardest for grinding large flat surfaces

5. The finest grit size of the ranges listed below is:
   A. 8 to 36
   B. 36 to 100
   C. 150 to 240
   D. 280 to 500

6. Most machine shop grinding wheel grades fall in the range of:
   A. A to F
   B. G to L
   C. M to R
   D. S to Z

7. Grinding on the periphery of an abrasive wheel:
   A. Requires a somewhat softer wheel than for side grinding
   B. Requires a definitely softer wheel than for side grinding
   C. Requires a harder wheel than for side grinding
   D. Has no effect on wheel grade

8. Grit sizes for most machine shop grinding wheels fall in the range of:
   A. 8 to 36
   B. 36 to 120
   C. 120 to 240
   D. 280 and finer

9. If the grinding face of a wheel becomes shiny and smooth, this condition is called glazing. This shows that the wheel:
   A. Grade is too hard
   B. Has the wrong abrasive
   C. Grit size is too coarse
   D. Structure is too open

10. If the grinding face of a wheel picks up and holds bits of the work material, this is called loading. This shows that the wheel:
   A. Grade is too soft
   B. Has the wrong abrasive
   C. Grit size is too coarse
   D. Structure is too dense

Volume II, Section H Date ___________ Name _________________________________

UNIT 2. GRINDING WHEEL SAFETY

POST TEST

Circle the letter preceding the correct answer.

1. For grinding wheel safety, you should:
   A. Make sure it is the proper specification for the job
   B. Dress it to be sharp and free cutting
   C. Run it at or below the recommended speed
   D. Make sure there is plenty of coolant

2. Which of the following bonded wheels has the lowest maximum safe grinding speed?
   A. Vitrified
   B. Resinoid
   C. Shellac
   D. Rubber

3. A 10 inch diameter vitrified wheel is being operated on a surface grinder at 2250 RPM. In relation to its safe speed, this speed is:
   A. Well above
   B. A little above
   C. Well below
   D. A little below

4. For a given spindle speed (RPM), grinding wheel speed in surface feet per minute (SFPM):
   A. Decreases with an increase in diameter
   B. Increases with an increase in diameter
   C. Is not affected by an increase in diameter
   D. Is probably a safe speed

5. As the operator, you need to give a ring test only when:
   A. A wheel is received from the supplier
   B. The wheel is first mounted
   C. You suspect a wheel is cracked
   D. A wheel is mounted or remounted

6. The ring test is done on the wheel to determine the:
   A. Bond
   B. Grade
   C. Abrasive size
   D. Soundness

7. Since grinding wheels can cut hard, tough materials, they:
   A. Can easily be cracked
   B. Need only minimum care in handling
   C. Require extraordinary care in handling
   D. Need no particular protection

8. After starting a cylindrical grinder, you are sufficiently safe if you stand:
   A. In normal operating position
   B. A little to one side of the wheel
   C. Well away from the wheel
   D. Leaning over the wheel to check coolant flow

9. The most important thing an operator should wear while operating a grinder is:
   A. Gloves
   B. A long sleeved shirt
   C. Safety glasses
   D. An air filter over his nose and mouth

10. When you finish grinding with coolant, you should:
    A. Turn off the coolant at the same time you turn off the grinder
    B. Let the wheel run a few minutes, and then turn off the coolant
    C. Have turned off the coolant before you stopped grinding
    D. Leave the coolant flowing until the end of the work period

Volume II, Section H Date ___________ Name ______________________________

UNIT 3. CARE OF ABRASIVE WHEELS: TRUING, DRESSING, AND BALANCING

POST TEST

Circle the letter preceding the correct answer.

1. Grinding wheel dressing and truing are:
   A. Basically the same operation
   B. Done with the same equipment
   C. Two different terms for the same operation
   D. Only for form grinding

2. Since all grinding wheels are balanced at the factory, they:
   A. Do not need to be balanced in the shop
   B. Need to be balanced only when first mounted
   C. Should be balanced each time they are dressed
   D. Should be balanced each time they are mounted

3. When comparing crush dressing and plated diamond roll or block dressing, which of the following is correct?
   A. Crush dressing provides a faster cut but not as good finish
   B. A diamond plated dresser is preferred if there are only a few parts
   C. The diamond plated dresser is more flexible and has wider use
   D. Crush dressing can be used only on a surface grinder

4. On a grinding wheel rotating clockwise, the correct position for the single point diamond in a dresser is:
   A. Pointing in the direction of rotation 15 degrees past the center line
   B. Pointing in the direction of rotation 15 degrees ahead of the center line
   C. At a 15 degree angle directly on the vertical center line
   D Vertical and directly on the center line

5. In truing a grinding wheel, it is essential to start:
   A. Wherever the wheel happens to be when you set the diamond at an approximate position for dressing
   B. At the low (closest to the spindle) point on the wheel
   C. At the highest point on the wheel
   D. At a point about midway between high and low

6. The depth of infeed (or downfeed) per pass in dressing should be no more than what part of an inch?
   A. .01
   B. .001
   C. .0001
   D. .00001

7. In dressing a wheel for rough cuts, you should use:
   A. Lighter passes (about .0005 in.) and slow traverse
   B. Heavier cuts (about .001 in.) and slow traverse
   C. Heavier cuts and fast traverse
   D. Lighter cuts and fast traverse

8. Single point diamond form dressing:
   A. Can produce a wide variety of forms
   B. Is most useful in production grinding
   C. Requires less operator skill than other form dressing
   D. Is often done freehand

9. Of the following statements, the one that is most critical in using single point diamond dressing tools is:
   A. Position the diamond at the correct angle
   B. Discard a diamond as soon as it shows wear
   C. Use fast traverse to prevent overheating
   D. Turn the diamond frequently in its holder

10. Single point diamond dressing should preferably be done:
   A. Dry
   B. Wet
   C. Either way, depending on the machine equipment
   D. At somewhat less than operating speed

Volume II, Section H Date ___________ Name ___________________________________

UNIT 4. GRINDING FLUIDS

POST TEST

Circle the letter preceding the correct answer.

1. There are so many grinding fluids because:
   A. There are so many companies making them
   B. Of the many varieties of wheels and bonds
   C. Different qualities in the fluids are required by different users
   D. There are so many varying requirements for grinding fluids

2. If there is a lot of fluid flowing over the workpiece, it:
   A. Will keep the workpiece cool
   B. May be doing no good whatsoever
   C. Is a sign of a good installation
   D. Will keep the workpiece lubricated

3. The primary mark of a well designed fluid nozzle is that it:
   A. Is large enough to transmit lots of fluid
   B. Keeps air away from the cutting area
   C. Is directed at the wheel-work interface
   D. Is small in order to raise fluid pressure

4. The reason that most grinding is done wet is that it:
   A. Increases production
   B. Keeps the work cooler
   C. Causes fewer problems
   D. Requires simpler design

5. For maximum efficiency, the coolant should be applied:
   A. With a straight nozzle
   B. With a "wrap around" nozzle
   C. In large quantities
   D. Through the wheel

6. For maximum lubricating benefit, the fluid should be:
   A. Straight oil
   B. Stick lubricant
   C. Water-based chemical coolant
   D. Water-based soluble oil

7. The temperature of the wheel-workpiece interface is:
   A. About 500° F (260° C)
   B. About 1000° F (538° C)
   C. About 2000° F (1093° C)
   D. Over 3000° F (1649° C)

8. For maximum cooling ability, you should use:
   A. Straight oil
   B. Tap water
   C. Stick lubricant
   D. Water-based coolant

9. If the work in the shop requires the removal of extremely fine particles from the grinding fluid, you should probably have a:
   A. Filtering system
   B. Settling system
   C. Centrifugal system
   D. All of the above

10. The major responsibility of the grinder operator is to see that:
   A. The coolant tank is full
   B. The solution is of the proper richness or leanness
   C. There is no "tramp" swarf recirculating in the coolant
   D. All of the above

Volume II, Section H Date __________ Name ______________________

UNIT 5. HORIZONTAL SPINDLE, RECIPROCATING TABLE SURFACE GRINDERS

POST TEST

Circle the letter preceding the correct answer.

1. A surface grinder is one for grinding:
   A. Any kind of surface
   B. Mostly cylindrical surfaces
   C. Mostly flat surface
   D. Mostly formed surfaces

2. The workpiece theoretically might make contact with the wheel as a result of the movement of:
   A. The wheel
   B. The workpiece, left and right
   C. The workpiece, forward and back
   D. All of the above

3. Besides rotating, the grinding wheel:
   A. Moves forward and back
   B. Moves up or down
   C. Moves from left to right and back
   D. Does not move

4. In grinding a surface on this type of grinder, the chuck usually travels farthest in:
   A. Cross feeding
   B. Rotating
   C. Traversing
   D. Down feeding

5. An electromagnetic chuck is used on a surface grinder because it:
   A. Is easy to maintain
   B. Will hold any workpiece
   C. Makes every surface of a workpiece available for grinding
   D. Is the fastest way to set up most work

6. The surface to be ground must typically be:
   A. Parallel to the edges of the chuck
   B. At right angles to the chuck
   C. Parallel to the top surface of the chuck
   D. Centered on the chuck

7. The most precise handwheel control on the grinder is the:
   A. Down feed
   B. Cross feed
   C. Traverse
   D. Chuck

8. The zeroing slip ring is used because:
   A. It is an inexpensive option
   B. Most operators prefer it
   C. It usually comes with the grinder
   D. It reduces the chance for error

9. Attachments or accessories are used because they:
   A. Make it easier to do quality work
   B. Increase the variety of work that can be ground
   C. Are relatively inexpensive
   D. Increase the productivity of the grinder

10. Of the following, the one that is never considered an accessory is the:
   A. Wheel safety guard
   B. Centerless grinder attachment
   C. Wheel dresser
   D. Magnetic sine chuck

Volume II, Section H Date ___________ Name ____

UNIT 6. WORKHOLDING ON THE SURFACE GRINDER

POST TEST

Circle the letter preceding the correct answer.

1. On a reciprocating table surface grinder, the electromagnetic chuck is made of:
   A. Solid steel
   B. Alternating rings of steel and nonmagnetic metal
   C. Alternating strips of steel and nonmagnetic metal
   D. Cast iron

2. The main purpose of the special electrical switch on the chuck is that it:
   A. Determines the amount of power going to the chuck
   B. Must be heavy enough for the current used
   C. Is required for direct current
   D. Demagnetizes the workpiece

3. Before you mount a workpiece on the chuck, you must:
   A. Clean off the top of the chuck
   B. Check the coolant level
   C. Turn on the electric current
   D. Check the amount of stock to be removed

4. One of these four characteristics of the workpiece is <u>not</u> a factor in workholding. It is the:
   A. Weight
   B. Area of the chucking end
   C. Shape
   D. Area to be ground

5. A chuck should be reground when it is out of flat by more than what part of an inch?
   A. .010
   B. .0010
   C. .00010
   D. .000010

6. A way to chuck aluminum, brass, and other nonferrous metals is to use:
   A. A vacuum chuck
   B. Steel blocking with magnetically operated clamps
   C. Double-faced tape
   D. All of the above

7. The principal precaution in chucking thin work is to use:
   A. The least amount of power that will hold the work safely
   B. One-third to one-half of the power available
   C. At least half the available power
   D. Double-faced tape

8. The basic accessory in grinding work square is:
   A. An angle plate
   B. A magnetic sine chuck
   C. A V-block
   D. A clamp

9. For grinding the reference surface on a part to be ground square, you would probably chuck the workpiece on:
   A. A sine chuck
   B. Magnetic parallels
   C. The electromagnetic chuck
   D. A vacuum chuck

10. On a reciprocating surface grinder, the surface to be ground always travels:
    A. At right angles to the chuck
    B. Parallel to the chuck
    C. Diagonally with the chuck
    D. In a circle with the chuck

Volume II, Section H Date __________ Name ______________________________

UNIT 8. USING THE SURFACE GRINDER

POST TEST

Circle the letter preceding the correct answer.

1. In comparison with other aluminum oxide abrasives, white aluminum oxide is:
   A. Tougher than the others
   B. Above average toughness
   C. Below average in brittleness or friability
   D. More brittle or friable than other aluminum oxides

2. For general purpose surface grinding, the probable grit size range of the abrasive grain is:
   A. 36 and coarser
   B. 46 to 60
   C. 80 to 120
   D. 150 and finer

3. The probable range of grades or hardness for general purpose surface grinding wheels is:
   A. G and softer
   B. H through K
   C. L through P
   D. R and finer

4. In mounting the wheel, the machine condition that need <u>not</u> be checked is:
   A. Supply of coolant
   B. Diameter of flanges
   C. Cleanliness of the spindle
   D. Fit of the wheel on the spindle

5. The best way to check a magnetic chuck for nicks and burrs is to:
   A. Rub it with a squeegee or soft cloth
   B. Flood it with coolant
   C. Rub your hand lightly over it
   D. Check it closely by eye using a strong light

6. Paper is used to protect the chuck and the work:
   A. Only during the roughing passes
   B. During roughing or finishing, as chosen by the operator
   C. Only during finishing
   D. During both roughing and finishing

7. Down feed per pass during roughing is what part of an inch?
   A. .01 to .02
   B. .001 to .002
   C. .0001 to .0002
   D. .00001 to .00002

8. Down feed per pass during finishing is what part of an inch?
   A. .01 to .02
   B. .001 to .002
   C. .0001 to .0002
   D. .00001 to .00002

9. To square the end of a workpiece with a ground side, the surface clamped to the angle plate must be:
   A. The ground side
   B. The side opposite the ground side
   C. Either of the other two sides
   D. The opposite end

10. To correct small errors in squareness, the workpiece can best be shimmed by:
   A. Very thin strips of steel
   B. Tissue paper
   C. Newspaper
   D. Heavy wrapping paper

Volume II, Section H Date ___________ Name ________________________________

UNIT 9. PROBLEMS AND SOLUTIONS IN SURFACE GRINDING

POST TEST

Circle the letter preceding the correct answer.

1. Of the following, which would most definitely be regarded as your responsibility as an operator?
   A. Aligning the chuck
   B. Checking and replacing wheel bearings
   C. Lubricating the machine
   D. Regrinding the chuck

2. The first thing to check for if you see chatter marks is:
   A. Vibration
   B. Wheel dressing (the condition of the wheel's grinding face)
   C. Wheel grade or hardness
   D. Abrasive grit size

3. If you see random scratches or "fishtails" on the work, you would probably check the:
   A. Coolant level
   B. Coolant filters
   C. Wheel safety guard
   D. All of the above

4. Too much grinding heat can cause:
   A. Chatter marks
   B. Discoloration or burning
   C. "Fishtails"
   D. Work to be out of parallel

5. The objection to a burnished surface is that it:
   A. Has a poor appearance
   B. Is different from the required pattern
   C. Does not wear well
   D. Is discolored

6. Correct wheel dressing is important because it:
   A. Prevents many grinding problems
   B. Makes the wheel cut well and fast
   C. Produces a satisfactory finish
   D. Prevents wheel loading

7. If work is not flat, the first place to check is:
   A. Wheel grade or hardness
   B. Wheel bearings
   C. Chuck alignment
   D. Length of grinding stroke

8. If work is not parallel, the first thing to check is:
   A. Tightness of the nuts holding the wheel flanges
   B. Chuck alignment
   C. Chuck flatness
   D. Coolant level

9. Probably the hardest work to grind flat is:
   A. Soft, nonferrous metal
   B. Irregularly shaped work
   C. Thick work
   D. Thin work

10. If thin work is out of flat, the first step in correcting the condition is to:
    A. Chuck the workpiece with the bulge up
    B. Chuck the work with the bulge down and the ends shimmed
    C. Redress the wheel
    D. Check the coolant level

Volume II, Section H Date ___________ Name ______________________________

UNIT 10. CYLINDRICAL GRINDING MACHINES

POST TEST

Circle the letter preceding the correct answer.

1. Among cutting tool machines, the cylindrical grinder most resembles a:
   A. Planer
   B. Shaper
   C. Milling machine
   D. Lathe

2. Among cylindrical grinding machines, the greatest variety of work can be done on a:
   A. Universal grinder
   B. Plunge grinder
   C. Traverse grinder
   D. Angle head grinder

3. The amount of stock removed by a cylindrical grinder from the diameter of a shaft in relation to the wheel infeed, is approximately:
   A. Half the infeed
   B. Equal to the infeed
   C. Twice the infeed
   D. All of the above, depending on the grit size

4. On a cylindrical grinder, the workpiece surface moves in relation to the direction of travel of a wheel surface:
   A. In the same direction
   B. In the opposite direction
   C. Alternately, in the same and opposite directions
   D. In a direction determined by machine design

5. Traverse grinding on a cylindrical grinder is most often done by:
   A. Moving the rotating wheel back and forth across the workpiece
   B. Moving the rotating workpiece back and forth across the face of the wheel
   C. Angling the wheelhead to 45 degrees
   D. Swiveling the table to the desired angle

6. The work center on the headstock:
   A. May be live or dead, depending on the work
   B. Is always live
   C. Is always dead
   D. Drives the workpiece

7. The work center in the footstock:
   A. May be live or dead, depending on the work
   B. Is always live
   C. Is always dead
   D. Drives the workpiece

8. Even with accessories, which of the following types of grinding cannot be done on a universal cylindrical grinder?
   A. Rotary surface grinding
   B. Traverse grinding
   C. Internal grinding
   D. Reciprocating surface grinding

9. Grinding an OD and an adjoining shoulder is best done with a wheel dressed:
   A. Straight with the face parallel to the axis of the workpiece
   B. With a crush-form dresser with the face parallel to the work axis
   C. With a diamond plated form dresser with the face at right angles to the work axis
   D. To 45 degrees on either side of the wheel axis and mounted at a 45 degree angle

10. Cylindrical grinding is:
   A. Almost always done with a coolant
   B. Done with a coolant or without, depending on the design of the machine
   C. Done with a coolant or without, depending on the workpiece material
   D. Almost always done dry

Volume II, Section H Date __________ Name ________________________________

UNIT 11. USING THE CYLINDRICAL GRINDER

POST TEST

Circle the letter preceding the correct answer.

1. Cylindrical grinding is mostly done with which kind of wheel?
   A. Straight
   B. Cylinder
   C. Straight cup
   D. Flaring cup

2. The major difference between wheels for cylindrical grinding and wheels for surface grinding is in the:
   A. Abrasive type
   B. Grit size
   C. Grade or hardness
   D. Bond type

3. In cylindrical grinding the diameter reduction per revolution of the workpiece is approximately what amount of infeed of the wheel?
   A. Half
   B. Equal to
   C. Twice
   D. Three times

4. If a part has a taper of .010 in./ft, the difference between two dial indicator readings 12 inches apart would be what part of an inch?
   A. .001
   B. .0025
   C. .010
   D. .005

5. In center-type cylindrical grinding:
   A. Both ends of the workpiece must always be lubricated
   B. The footstock end of the workpiece must always be lubricated
   C. The headstock end of the workpiece must always be lubricated
   D. Sometimes neither end needs to be lubricated

6. Recommended wheel overrun at each end of the workpiece is:
   A. At least an inch
   B. Two-thirds of the wheel diameter
   C. One-half of the wheel diameter
   D. One-third of the wheel diameter

7. Wheel speed in center-type cylindrical grinding is in the range of 5500 to 6500 SFPM, usually the higher speed. Work speed for most parts will probably be in the range of what SFPM?
   A. 10 to 50
   B. 50 to 100
   C. 100 to 150
   D. 150 to 200

8. On most center-type cylindrical grinders:
   A. Work speed is variable, wheel speed (RPM) is constant
   B. Work speed is constant, wheel speed (RPM) is variable
   C. Both work speed and wheel speed are variable
   D. Both work speed and wheel speed are constant

9. In finish cylindrical grinding, the traverse rate should be how many inches per workpiece revolution?
   A. One
   B. Three-fourths
   C. One-half
   D. One-fourth

10. To compensate for significant wheel wear (two inches or more reduction in diameter) you should:
    A. Reduce work speed accordingly
    B. Increase work speed accordingly
    C. Leave work speed unchanged
    D. Adjust work speed according to material hardness

Volume II, Section H Date __________ Name ______________________________

UNIT 12. CYLINDRICAL GRINDING PROBLEMS AND SOLUTIONS

POST TEST

Circle the letter preceding the correct answer.

1. As a general rule, if you suspected that chatter marks in cylindrical grinding was a problem, you would most likely start by checking:
   A. Wheel bond
   B. Cleanliness of the coolant
   C. Vibration in the grinder
   D. Vibration away from the grinder

2. Burning or surface discoloration is a problem of:
   A. Both cylindrical and surface grinding
   B. Cylindrical grinding only
   C. Surface grinding only
   D. Wet grinding only

3. Increasing work rotation speed has the effect of:
   A. Increasing wheel wear
   B. Decreasing wheel wear
   C. Making the wheel act harder
   D. Making the wheel act softer

4. Which of the following could be a factor in causing chatter marks or wave marks?
   A. Wheel grade
   B. Wheel balance
   C. Machine vibration
   D. All of the above

5. "Burlap finish" is almost always an indication of:
   A. A wheel that is too hard
   B. Looseness in the dresser
   C. A wheel that is too soft
   D. Misalignment of the work centers

6. Truing lines are usually caused by:
   A. Dressing with a diamond cluster dresser
   B. A diamond that is too dull
   C. A diamond that is too sharp
   D. A diamond that is too large

7. Feed lines usually indicate:
   A. Too fast traverse speed
   B. Dirty coolant
   C. Misalignment of work centers
   D. Loose work centers

8. In case of poor quality work, you first move should be to check carefully the:
   A. Defects in the work
   B. Condition of the machine
   C. Coolant filters
   D. Grit size of the wheel

9. Most shops tend to use grinding wheels that are too:
   A. Soft
   B. Hard
   C. Coarse
   D. Fine

10. Which of the following would probably be the most difficult fault to remedy?
    A. Chatter marks
    B. Burning
    C. Combination of faults
    D. Feed lines

Volume II, Section H Date __________ Name ____

UNIT 13. CUTTER AND TOOL GRINDING FEATURES AND COMPONENTS

POST TEST

1. Match the features and components of the cutter and tool grinder to the letters marked on Figure 17.

_____ Tilting wheelhead

_____ Front cross slide handwheel

_____ Front table hand control

_____ Swivel table

_____ Sliding table

_____ Table swivel scale

_____ Workhead

_____ Wheelhead vertical control handwheel

_____ Tailstock

_____ Table dogs

Figure 17. Cutter and tool grinder (Courtesy of Cincinnati Milacron).

Circle the letter preceding the correct answer.

2. The cylindrical grinding attachment is used for:
   A. End mills
   B. Plain milling cutters
   C. Formed milling cutters
   D. External and internal cylindrical grinding

3. Grinding arbors are used for sharpening:
   A. End mills
   B. Plain and formed mill cutters
   C. Reamers
   D. Single point tools

4. The micrometer type tooth rest support:
   A. Permits measurement of the finished tool diameter
   B. Allows for tool helix
   C. Allows for tooth offset
   D. Permits adjustment

5. The offset tooth rest:
   A. Provides support for helical tooth milling cutters
   B. Provides support for sharpening reamer chamfers
   C. Is usef for grinding taps
   D. Is not used with the cutter and tool grinder

6. Which of the following operations is <u>not</u> usual with the cutter and tool grinder?
   A. Surface grinding
   B. Offhand grinding of single point tools
   C. Internal and external cylindrical grinding
   D. Sharpening of rotary type cutting tools

Volume II, Section H Date ____________ Name ______________________________

UNIT 14. CUTTER AND TOOL GRINDER SAFETY AND GENERAL SETUP PROCEDURES

POST TEST

Circle the letter preceding the correct answer.

1. The adaptation of grinding wheel guards for operator protection is:
   A. Easier on cutter and tool grinders than on other types of grinding machines
   B. Unnecessary because the wheels are typically so small
   C. Difficult because of the variety of wheel sizes and applications
   D. Not required because wheels are ring tested before use

2. Flaring cup wheels and dish wheels are used frequently on cutter and tool grinders because they:
   A. Have more available abrasive grain
   B. Are stronger and can withstand higher speeds
   C. Are easier to use with wheel guards
   D. Withstand side grinding stresses

3. For the first minute of wheel operation, you should:
   A. Not grind because the spindle bearings are not warmed up
   B. Not dress the wheel or it will chatter
   C. Stand aside you won't get sprayed with loose abrasive grit
   D. Stay out of line to avoid danger from wheel breakage

4. Swivel table alignment is critically important because it:
   A. Affects the clearance angles of the tools
   B. Is difficult to mill flat surfaces with conical cutters
   C. Affects the mounting of the centers
   D. Affects arbor runout

5. Runout on grinding arbors:
   A. Is not of great importance
   B. Causes taper in workpieces machined with an irregular cutter
   C. Causes variations in tooth height, resulting in rough cutter operation
   D. Puts stress on the grinding centers and results in poor finish on the tool being ground

6. If the sharpened cutter has excessive clearance, it will:
   A. Tend to lift workpieces out of the milling vise
   B. Tend to generate excess heat during the milling process
   C. Be inefficient as a cutting tool
   D. Tend to result in cutter tooth breakage

7. The cutter clearance gage:
   A. Can be used to check both primary relief and secondary clearance
   B. Can be used to adjust the tooth rest blade
   C. Consists of two dial indicators and centers
   D. Can be used to check taper on cutters

8. You are preparing to grind a six degree (sine of 6° = .10453) primary relief with a flaring cup wheel that does not tilt with the tooth rest attached to the grinding head. The cutter is 2½ inches in diameter and the grinding wheel is 5 inches in diameter. What direction will you move the grinding head, and what distance in inches?
   A. Up .261
   B. Up .118
   C. Down .261
   D. Down .118

9. You are preparing to grind a primary relief of 6 degrees with a straight (type 1) wheel of 6 inch diameter on a 3 inch diameter plain milling cutter with the tooth rest attached to the table. What direction will you move the wheelhead, and what distance in inches?
   A. Up .314
   B. Down .314
   C. Up .157
   D. Down .157

10. When using a straight (type 1) grinding wheel for producing relief and clearances with the tooth support attached to the wheelhead, the combination of calculation and of wheelhead movement is:
   A. Sine of the angle X cutter diameter, and raise
   B. Sine of the angle X wheel diameter, and raise
   C. Sine of the angle X cutter diameter, and lower
   D. Sine of the angle X wheel diameter, and lower

Volume II, Section H Date __________ Name ______________________________

UNIT 20. MISCELLANEOUS CUTTER AND TOOL GRINDING OPERATIONS

POST TEST

Circle the letter preceding the correct answer.

1. A cutting off wheel is reinforced to:
   A. Allow side grinding
   B. Prevent shattering under cutting off stresses
   C. Have greater stiffness to make a straighter cut
   D. Hold the abrasive more firmly for longer wear

2. Reshaping of the end of a cut-off end mill with a cutting off wheel:
   A. Saves grinding time by removing material in chunks
   B. Can only be done on two-fluted end mills
   C. Is a dangerous practice because of potential wheel failure
   D. Is a routine that can be as easily done by conventional straight wheel grinding

3. Finish gashing of end mills after sharpening:
   A. Is a simple operation that is easily done
   B. Can be done readily with a cut off wheel
   C. Is a highly skilled and demanding operation
   D. Is unnecessary except in extreme cases

4. Adjustable hand reamers:
   A. Are simpler to sharpen than fixed size hand reamers
   B. Are accurate, simple to use tools
   C. Produce a better finish than machine reamers of the same size
   D. Do not often produce accurate holes

5. On the starting taper of a hand reamer:
   A. Secondary clearance is sometimes necessary
   B. No clearance is needed because of the taper
   C. Secondary clearance is usual
   D. Secondary clearance <u>only</u> is applicable

6. In sharpening adjustable hand reamers, the tooth rest is usually attached to the wheelhead because the:
   A. Diameter of the reamer is more important than the grinding wheel diameter
   B. Blades of the reamer are uniformly straight
   C. Diameter of the grinding wheel is more important than the reamer diameter
   D. Blades are sometimes not accurately straight

7. The sharpening of hand reamers for use in differing materials:
   A. Should be substantially different in clearance and margins
   B. Should be only slightly different in clearance and margins
   C. Need not be different in clearance and may be used effectively in most materials
   D. Is identical to preparing machine reamers for the same use

8. An eccentric step drill:
   A. Produces oversized holes
   B. Causes no special difficulties
   C. Is used to generate holes like a fly cutter
   D. Must have accurate step lengths

9. Sharpening a large tap:
   A. Can usually be done by flute grinding alone
   B. Can often be done offhand on a pedestal grinder
   C. Usually requires the use of a form relief attachment
   D. Is usually uneconomical

10. For grinding of carbide tipped lathe and planer tools on a cutter and tool grinding machine:
   A. Silicon carbide grinding wheels are preferred
   B. Aluminum oxide grinding wheels are preferred
   C. Diamond wheels are more economical than other wheels
   D. A magnetic chuck is used to hold the tool for grinding

POST TEST ANSWERS

Volume I, Section A

Unit 1

1. B
2. A
3. D
4. C
5. A
6. ~~B~~ C
7. B
8. C
9. A
10. A
11. A
12. B
13. D
14. C
15. A
16. C
17. A
18. C
19. A
20. C

Unit 3

1. C
2. B
3. D
4. A -
5. B
6. C
7. A
8. D
9. A
10. B

Unit 4

1. A
2. D
3. B
4. C
5. A
6. D
7. C
8. B
9. A
10. C

Unit 5

1. B
2. B
3. D
4. B
5. A
6. D
7. C
8. B
9. A
10. A

Unit 6

1. A
2. C
3. A
4. D
5. B
6. A
7. C
8. D
9. A
10. B

Unit 8

1. A
2. D
3. B
4. C
5. A
6. D
7. B
8. C
9. B
10. C

Volume I, Section B

Unit 2

1. A
2. C
3. D
4. A
5. A
6. C
7. B
8. D
9. A
10. D

Unit 3

1. B
2. A
3. C
4. C
5. A
6. D
7. B
8. C
9. D
10. D

Unit 4

1. C
2. D
3. B
4. C
5. A
6. A
7. D
8. B
9. B
10. C

Unit 5

1. D
2. B
3. C
4. B
5. A
6. D
7. D
8. A
9. B
10. C

Volume I, Section C

Unit 1.	Unit 5.	Unit 7.	Unit 8.
1. B	1. C	1. C	1. C
2. C	2. B	2. B	2. D
3. C	3. D	3. A	3. D
4. A	4. C	4. D	4. C
5. B	5. A	5. A	5. A
6. D	6. D	6. D	6. B
7. C	7. B	7. C	7. A
8. B	8. C	8. B	8. .1007, .144, .150, 3.000
9. D	9. B	9. C	9. .1007, .144, .050, 3.000, .100 (two .050 inch wear blocks)
10. A	10. D	10. D	10. D

Volume I, Section D

Unit 1.	Unit 2.	Unit 3.	Unit 4.	Unit 5.	Unit 6.
1. B	1. B	1. B	1. B	1. C	1. B
2. A	2. C	2. B	2. A	2. B	2. A
3. D	3. A	3. A	3. D	3. D	3. D
4. C	4. C	4. C	4. C	4. A	4. B
5. B	5. B	5. B	5. A	5. C	5. C
6. D	6. B	6. A	6. D	6. B	6. A
7. C	7. A	7. D	7. B	7. D	7. D
8. A	8. B	8. B	8. C	8. B	8. B
9. B	9. B	9. A	9. D	9. A	9. C
10. D	10. C	10. C	10. B	10. C	10. C

Unit 7.	Unit 8.	Unit 9.	Unit 10.	Unit 11.	Unit 12.
1. C	1. B	1. C	1. C	1. D	1. B
2. A	2. D	2. C	2. B	2. C	2. A
3. C	3. A	3. D	3. C	3. A	3. B
4. B	4. C	4. A	4. A	4. B	4. D
5. D	5. B	5. B	5. C	5. D	5. A
6. A	6. A	6. C	6. B	6. A	6. D
7. B	7. C	7. A	7. D	7. B	7. B
8. C	8. B	8. B	8. D	8. C	8. A
9. B	9. C	9. C	9. B	9. A	9. C
10. C	10. B	10. A	10. C	10. D	10. B

Volume I, Section E

Unit 1.

1. B
2. D
3. B
4. C
5. A

Unit 2.

1. A
2. D
3. C
4. B
5. A
6. B
7. B
8. C
9. A
10. C

Volume I, Section F

Unit 2.

1. A
2. C
3. B
4. D
5. B
6. A
7. D
8. B
9. A
10. C

Volume I, Section G

Unit 1.

1. A
2. D
3. C
4. A
5. B
6. B
7. D
8. A
9. C
10. D

Unit 2.

1\. M Guard
D Variable speed control
F Base
N Head
E Column
I Quill return spring
J Motor
H Table lock
B Depth stop
G Quill lock handle
K Table lift crank
C Power feed
O Table
L Switch
A Spindle

2\. A Spindle
B Column
E Drill head
C Radial arm
D Base

Unit 3.

D Drill point angle
O Body
B Chisel edge angle
Y Axis of drill
U Margin
K Flute
G Land
I Helix angle
T Web
P Cutting lip
E Lip relief angle
J Body clearance
N Shank length
W Straight shank
C Tang
X Taper shank

Unit 6.

1. C
2. B
3. A
4. C
5. D
6. A
7. C
8. B
9. A
10. C

Unit 7.

1. B
2. C
3. A
4. B
5. D
6. A
7. B
8. C
9. B
10. B

Unit 8.

1. C
2. C
3. B
4. A
5. C
6. A
7. B
8. D
9. A
10. D

Unit 9.

1. B
2. B
3. C
4. C
5. D
6. D
7. D
8. A
9. D

Volume I, Section H

Unit 1.	Unit 2.	Unit 3.	Unit 4.
1. D	1. D	1. C	1. B
2. B	2. A	2. B	2. C
3. C	3. A	3. B	3. A
4. A	4. B	4. D	4. B
5. C	5. A	5. B	5. D
6. A	6. C	6. D	6. D
7. D	7. D	7. D	7. C
8. B	8. B	8. D	8. A
9. C	9. A	9. A	9. B
	10. D	10. D	10. D

Volume I, Section I

Unit 1.	Unit 2.			
1. A	1. 1. C	11. O	21. D	2. 1. G
2. C	2. P	12. I	22. W	2. J
3. B	3. U	13. Z	23. J	3. I
4. A	4. A	14. B	24. G	4. F
5. C	5. Q	15. CC	25. T	5. D
6. D	6. DD	16. R	26. F	6. E
7. B	7. S	17. K	27. V	7. C
8. C	8. H	18. AA	28. E	8. B
9. B	9. EE	19. BB		9. A
10. B	10. X	20. Y		10. H

Unit 3.	Unit 4.	Unit 5.	Unit 6.	Unit 7.	Unit 8.
1. C	1. C	1. B	1. B	1. B	1. C
2. A	2. B	2. C	2. C	2. D	2. B
3. C	3. A	3. A	3. A	3. C	3. A
4. B	4. D	4. D	4. B	4. B	4. D
5. D	5. C	5. D	5. C	5. A	5. A
6. A	6. A	6. A	6. D	6. B	6. C
7. B	7. B	7. D	7. C	7. C	7. B
8. C	8. D	8. A	8. A	8. D	8. D
9. D	9. C	9. B	9. B	9. A	9. A
10. A	10. D	10. C	10. C	10. B	10. C

Volume I, Section I

Unit 9.	Unit 11.	Unit 12.	Unit 13.	Unit 14.	Unit 15.
1. C	1. C	1. B	1. A	1. C	1. C
2. B	2. A	2. C	2. B	2. B	2. A
3. A	3. B	3. D	3. B	3. D	3. C
4. D	4. C	4. A	4. A	4. A	4. D
5. B	5. A	5. A	5. D	5. A	5. C
6. A	6. D	6. C	6. C	6. D	6. D
7. C	7. B	7. A	7. B	7. B	7. A
8. C	8. C	8. B	8. A	8. C	8. C
9. A	9. B	9. D	9. B	9. A	9. B
10. B	10. B	10. A	10. C	10. C	10. C

Unit 16.	Unit 17.	Unit 18.	Unit 19.	Unit 20.	Unit 21.
1. A	1. D	1. A	1. C	1. C	1. D
2. D	2. B	2. C	2. B	2. B	2. B
3. A	3. A	3. D	3. D	3. D	3. A
4. D	4. C	4. A	4. B	4. A	4. C
5. C	5. A	5. B	5. A	5. C	5. A
6. A	6. C	6. D	6. B	6. D	6. D
7. C	7. D	7. B	7. C	7. B	7. C
8. B	8. B	8. A	8. D	8. A	8. B
9. D	9. A	9. B	9. A	9. B	9. D
10. C	10. D	10. A	10. C	10. C	10. A

Unit 22.

1. B	11. B
2. C	12. A
3. B	13. D
4. C	14. B
5. C	15. D
6. A	
7. A	
8. B	
9. C	
10. C	

Volume II, Section A

Unit 1.	Unit 2.	Unit 3.
1. C	1. D	1. B
2. B	2. B	2. A
3. B	3. C	3. C
4. C	4. D	4. D
5. A	5. A	5. A
	6. D	6. D
	7. C	7. C
	8. D	8. B
	9. B	9. A
	10. Student should submit a properly welded band.	10. C

Volume II, Section B

Unit 1.	Unit 2.			Unit 3.
1. C	1. A	11. 1. F	11. I	1. B
2. D	2. D	2. N	12. D	2. A
3. B	3. C	3. Q	13. S	3. A
4. A	4. A	4. T	14. M	4. D
5. D	5. B	5. B	15. C	5. D
6. A	6. A	6. J	16. H	6. C
7. D	7. D	7. E	17. R	7. D
8. D	8. B	8. L	18. O	8. A
9. B	9. C	9. P	19. G	9. D
10. A	10. C	10. A	20 K	10. B

Unit 4.

1. C	11. 1. Four flute, double end, end mill
2. A	2. Fly cutter
3. A	3. Shell mill with carbide inserts
4. D	4. Shell end mill on arbor
5. D	5. Two flute, double end, end mill
6. B	6. Two flute, single end, ball end mill
7. A	7. T-slot cutter
8. D	8. Single angle milling cutter
9. D	9. Woodruff keyslot milling cutter
10. A	10. Two flute, single end, end mill

Volume II, Section B

Unit 5.	Unit 6.	Unit 7.
1. D	1. D	1. D
2. A	2. B	2. B
3. C	3. B	3. D
4. A	4. D	4. D
5. D	5. A	5. D
6. C	6. B	6. A
7. A	7. C	7. A
8. B	8. D	8. D
9. B	9. C	9. D
10. C	10. D	10. A

Volume II, Section C

Unit 1.	Unit 2.		Unit 3.
1. D	1. B	11. A. 7	1. A
2. C	2. A	B. 6	2. D
3. D	3. C	C. 8	3. A
4. A	4. B	D. 10	4. A
5. C	5. C	E. 5	5. C
6. A	6. A	F. 9	6. A
7. D	7. C	G. 12	7. C
8. D	8. A	H. 4	8. B
9. A	9. A	I. 11	9. D
10. D	10. B	J. 2	10. B

Unit 4.

1. C	11. 1. Helical plain milling cutter
2. D	2. Light duty plain milling cutter
3. A	3. Staggered tooth milling cutter
4. C	4. Staggered tooth metal slitting saw
5. A	5. Side milling cutter
6. A	6. Concave milling cutter
7. B	7. Plain metal slitting saw
8. D	8. Double angle milling cutter
9. B	9. Convex milling cutter
10. C	10. Involute gear cutter

Volume II, Section C

Unit 5.	Unit 6.	Unit 7.	Unit 8.	Unit 9.
1. B	1. B	1. B	1. B	1. A
2. D	2. D	2. C	2. A	2. B
3. B	3. D	3. A	3. C	3. D
4. A	4. D	4. A	4. D	4. A
5. A	5. A	5. A	5. B	5. D
6. B	6. C	6. B	6. D	6. D
7. C	7. D	7. D	7. A	7. D
8. A	8. A	8. A	8. D	8. A
9. A	9. D	9. A	9. D	9. A
10. D	10. A	10. A	10. A	10. D

Volume II, Section D

Unit 1.

A. 6
B. 4
C. 7
D. 2
E. 9
F. 5
G. 3
H. 8
I. 10
J. 1

Unit 2.

1. C
2. A
3. D
4. D
5. B
6. $\frac{40}{8}$ = 5 complete turns of the index crank.
7. $\frac{40}{12} = \frac{10}{3} = 3\frac{1}{3}$ turns. Use 66 hole circle.
   $\frac{1}{3} \times \frac{22}{22} = \frac{22}{66}$ and go 22 holes
8. $\frac{40}{11} = 3\frac{7}{11}$. Use 66 hole. $\frac{7}{11} \times \frac{6}{6} = \frac{42}{66}$. 3 turns and 42 holes in the 66 hole circle.
9. $\frac{40}{14} = 2\frac{12}{14} = 2\frac{6}{7}$ turns. Use 42 hole circle $\frac{6}{7} \times \frac{6}{6} = \frac{36}{42}$.
   2 turns and 36 holes in the 42 hole circle.
10. $\frac{40}{57}$ = 40 holes in the 57 hole circle.

Unit 3.

1. A
2. B
3. A
4. D
5. C
6. A
7. A
8. B
9. C
10. A

Volume II, Section E

Unit 1.

1. D
2. A
3. B
4. D
5. B
6. C
7. A
8. C
9. D
10. D

Unit 2.

1. D
2. B
3. D
4. A
5. C
6. D
7. B
8. A
9. A
10. A. 5
    B. 6
    C. 3
    D. 2
    E. 4
    F. 1

Unit 3.

1. C
2. B
3. A
4. A
5. D
6. C
7. D
8. A
9. B
10. A

Unit 4.

1. D
2. C
3. A
4. A
5. B
6. B
7. D
8. D
9. D
10. B

Volume II, Section F

Unit 1.

1. A. Tilt table
   B. Apron
   C. Cross rail
   D. Cross feed engagement lever
   E. Rail elevating crank
   F. Stroke adjusting shaft
   G. Ram
   H. Ram adjusting shaft
   I. Tool (swivel) head
   J. Tool lifter
2. C
3. D
4. B
5. A
6. B
7. D
8. C
9. C
10. C

Unit 2.

1. C
2. D
3. C
4. A
5. D
6. A
7. C
8. B
9. C
10. D

Unit 3.

1. B
2. A
3. D
4. C
5. C
6. D
7. A
8. D
9. D
10. D

Unit 4.

1. A. Rail head
   B. Table (platen)
   C. Bed
   D. Table start-stop control
   E. Cutting speed control
   F. Feed control
   G. Sidehead
   H. Housing (column)
   I. Feedbox
   J. Rail
2. D
3. A
4. D
5. C

Unit 5.

1. A
2. B
3. C
4. D
5. B
6. C
7. D
8. C
9. A
10. D

Volume II, Section G

Unit 1.	Unit 2.	Unit 3.	
1. C	1. B	1. A. 3	
2. A	2. C	B. 2	2. B
3. D	3. B	C. 4	3. D
4. A	4. A	D. 5	4. A
5. B	5. C	E. 1	5. D
6. C	6. A		6. A
7. B	7. D		7. B
8. C	8. B		8. D
9. A	9. D		9. C
10. B	10. A		10. B

Unit 4.	Unit 5.	Unit 6.
1. C	1. C	1. C
2. B	2. B	2. B
3. A	3. A	3. A
4. D	4. D	4. B
5. B	5. B	5. D
6. A	6. C	6. A
7. C	7. B	7. D
8. A	8. D	8. B
9. B	9. B	9. C
10. C	10. C	10. A

Volume II, Section H

Unit 1.	Unit 2.	Unit 3.	Unit 4.	Unit 5.	Unit 6.
1. D	1. C	1. B	1. D	1. C	1. C
2. A	2. A	2. B	2. B	2. D	2. D
3. C	3. D	3. A	3. C	3. B	3. A
4. B	4. B	4. A	4. B	4. C	4. D
5. D	5. D	5. C	5. D	5. D	5. C
6. B	6. D	6. B	6. A	6. C	6. D
7. C	7. A	7. C	7. C	7. A	7. A
8. B	8. B	8. A	8. D	8. D	8. A
9. A	9. C	9. A	9. A	9. B	9. C
10. D	10. B	10. B	10. A	10. A	10. B

Volume II, Section H

Unit 8.	Unit 9.	Unit 10.	Unit 11.	Unit 12.
1. D	1. D	1. D	1. A	1. D
2. B	2. A	2. A	2. C	2. A
3. B	3. D	3. C	3. C	3. D
4. A	4. B	4. B	4. D	4. D
5. C	5. C	5. B	5. B	5. B
6. A	6. A	6. A	6. D	6. C
7. B	7. A	7. C	7. B	7. C
8. C	8. B	8. D	8. A	8. A
9. A	9. C	9. D	9. C	9. B
10. B	10. A	10. A	10. A	10. C

Unit 13.

1. G Tilting wheelhead
   A Front Cross slide handwheel
   C Front table hand control
   E Swivel table
   I Sliding table
   J Table swivel scale
   F Workhead
   B Wheelhead vertical control handwheel
   H Tailstock
   D Table dogs

2. D
3. B
4. D
5. A
6. B

Unit 14.	Unit 20.
1. C	1. B
2. D	2. A
3. D	3. C
4. B	4. D
5. C	5. A
6. D	6. D
7. A	7. A
8. D	8. A
9. A	9. C
10. C	10. C

AUDIOVISUAL RESOURCES

Support materials in the form of visual aids, such as motion pictures, film strips, television recordings, and overhead projector transparencies are useful adjuncts to machine shop programs. While it has been our intent to make Machine Tools and Machining Practices as visually intensive as possible, the motion picture can often add an additional dimension to the teaching task. In one school, DeAnza College, more than 140 motion picture and film strip titles in machine shop and related practices are available for students to sign out and use at any moment. The cost of this extensive film library and projectors was about the same as a No. 2 horizontal milling machine. The films can be viewed by individuals or small groups in special study-projection carrels or, of course, by conventionally structured classes.

Another method, used by Lane Community College, is a phone access system in which films are requested by phone and transmitted by cable to a monitor located in a student study area. This approach centralizes the film handling, but does not have the resolution of direct viewing.

One of the real difficulties, besides the cost of acquiring an extensive film library, is the process of determining what is available on the market, and making evaluations of these materials in relation to your program. The Westinghouse Learning Directory, published in 1970-71, was an aid to determining the full spectrum of available materials in both printed and not printed forms. This was a set of seven books, each about the size of a telephone directory for a medium sized city. In 1972-73 an additional volume was added, and the project was terminated. This source provided the acquisition information for a substantial majority of instructional media up to that time. Another source, which also provides a synopsis of film content, is the Catalog of United States Government Produced Audiovisual Materials. The catalogs are issued at intervals and the current edition is about the size of a small city telephone directory.

As a background to the source of most of the government films listed that cover machine shop practices, the majority were made during World War II. At that time it was necessary to train machine tool workers on specific machines very quickly. In response to this requirement, the United States Office of Education, in cooperation with American industry, schools, and motion picture production companies, produced some 125 motion pictures covering a wide variety of machine shop functions. In addition to these motion pictures, booklets were prepared for the instructor's guidance in administering the films, and a film strip with overlays of questions covering the main points of the motion pictures were available for review and reinforcement. The instructor's booklets are out of print, but on occasion collections of the booklets can sometimes be found in the libraries of universities emphasizing technical programs. These institutions are sometimes willing to lend the booklets for local copying. The follow-up film strips were available for sale until 1974, but are no longer cataloged. These films may be purchased at a very reasonable price from

National Audiovisual Center
National Archives and Records Service
General Services Administration
Washington, D. C. 20409

Another excellent source for motion picture listing is a 40 page, 1976 publication, "Motion Pictures Available from Members of the National Machine Tool Builders Association." This booklet can be obtained from

The National Machine Tool Builders Association
7901 Westpark Drive
McLean, Virginia 22101

The Association also has a film of their own, "One Hoe for Kalabo," that shows the place of machine tools in present day industrial civilization as compared with a primitive civilization in a part of Rhodesia. The film is suited for a broad spectrum of audiences, and puts machining practices in perspective for students considering a career in the machine tools field. This film can be requested free of rental charges from any of the 30 nation wide libraries of

Modern Talking Pictures Service, Inc.
International Building
45 Rockefeller Plaza
New York, New York 10021

The NMTBA publication also lists, for sale or rental, safety films produced by the American National Standards B-11 Committee. These safety films are specific to the classes of machines covered in the various safety standards. Most of the films listed are available without charge to schools, colleges, and technical societies. The publication provides detailed information on how to request these films, a synopsis of content, and other details necessary to the user.

Most machine shop instructors are vitally interested in recruiting capable students that are motivated toward making a career in some aspect of machine tool manufacturing processes. One way to this end is to get, and keep, the attention of career counselors who work with students in the stages of developing career awareness. An excellent motion picture, "Is a Career in Machining for You," is available from

AIMS Instructional Media Services, Inc.
Hollywood, California 90028

It is a film that shows a broad spectrum of machinist functions and levels, and is most suitable for use by counselors. It is a useful plan for machine shop instructors to budget for the purchase of a film like this, and either place it in the hands of appropriate counselors, or to make arrangements to personally take the film for showing to interested groups of students considering the possibility of becoming machinists. The personal approach has the added advantage of providing question and answer interaction after the film is shown.